RESEARCH FOR MARKETING

Other books by Michael J. Baker include

MARKETING: THEORY AND PRACTICE
MARKETING STRATEGY AND MANAGEMENT
MARKETING: AN INTRODUCTORY TEXT

RESEARCH FOR MARKETING

Michael J. Baker

MACMILLAN

First published 1991 by
MACMILLAN PRESS LTD
Houndmills, Basingstoke, Hampshire RG21 2XS
and London
Companies and representatives
throughout the world

ISBN 0–333–47020–6 hardcover
ISBN 0–333–47021–4 paperback

A catalogue record for this book is available
from the British Library.

10   9   8   7   6   5   4   3   2
03   02   01   00   99   98   97   96   95

Printed in Hong Kong

Contents

List of figures

List of tables

Preface

During the 1980s there emerged a broadly based consensus that success in an increasingly competitive global market-place depends significantly upon organisations being marketing-orientated and customer-driven. Starting with Peters and Waterman's *In Search of Excellence* in 1980 through to Michael Porter's *The Competitive Advantage of Nations* in 1990 there has been a continuous stream of managerial best-sellers concerned with the nature and sources of competitive success as a basis for prescribing strategies and courses of action to enable firms to succeed in a climate of accelerating technological and economic change. In content and approach these books have ranged from the rigorously scientific to the managerially anecdotal. But, despite this variation, there is universal agreement that competitive success depends fundamentally upon a clear understanding of the markets in which one wishes to compete and of the customers and competitors that comprise these markets. By contrast, there is also universal agreement that the primary source of failure is an inadequate knowledge and understanding of the market-place.

In light of this universal agreement one might anticipate that the development of a marketing information system (MIS) and extensive investment in marketing research would be a priority. All the evidence indicates the opposite. For example, in *Marketing and Competitive Success* (1989) Susan Hart and I report the findings of a rigorous survey in which we found that only 42 per cent of the sample firms had an in-house marketing research function and that only 58 per cent ever made use of any marketing research from external agencies. We also found that there was a significant and positive association between the use of marketing research and competitive success. Many similar surveys in the UK, Europe and North America report the same findings. Clearly, there is a need for much more attention to be given to the role of research in developing marketing and corporate strategy.

Research for Marketing is an attempt to cater for the anticipated growth in demand for information an the subject as students and managers recognise its importance as an essential and first element in the formulation of strategy and management of the marketing mix. Now, there are already many excellent textbooks available on the subject of marketing research, so why write another one? Quite simply because the majority of available books are concerned with the *practice* of marketing research and are written from the perspective of the expert who is actually going to carry out the marketing research function. This book is written for those who want an overview of what marketing research is and what it can and cannot do. More particularly, it is written from the perspective of those who may want to commission research and are looking for guidance on how to define their problem and information needs and how to communicate these to a practitioner; how to assess the suitability of alternative research strategies and the precise methods and instruments to be used; how to place a value on the work agreed upon and how to evaluate the quality of the findings. In other words, this book is written for the *user* of marketing research rather than the *doer*. Together with *Marketing* (5th edition, forthcoming) and *Marketing Strategy and Management* it is intended to provide a basic library for the market manager

University of Strathclyde   MICHAEL J. BAKER

Dedication

This book is dedicated to the many research assistants who, over the years, have played such an important role in my own research for marketing.

> Stephen T. Parkinson
> Jennifer L. Drayton
> Anita M. Kennedy
> Margaret Potts (née Dickie)
> Caroline Black
> Susan Hart
> Gordon Peaston
> Linda Service
> Clare Cameron
> Jennifer Skene

Acknowledgements

The author and publishers wish to thank the following for permission to reproduce copyright material:

Advertising Research Foundation, Inc., New York, for material from *Guidelines for the Public Use of Market and Opinion Research*, copyright 1981 Advertising Research Foundation, Inc.

Harvard Business School Publishing Division for the illustration 'Mead Johnson's Marketing Intelligence System', from Lee Adler (1967) 'Systems Approach to Marketing', *Harvard Business Review*, 45(3), May–June, pp. 105–18.

Prentice-Hall, Inc., Englewood Cliffs, New Jersey, for a table from David J. Luck and Ronald S. Rubin, *Marketing Research*, 7th edn, copyright 1987, p. 119. Reprinted by permission of Prentice-Hall, Inc. Englewood Cliffs, New Jersey.

Richard D. Irwin, Inc., Homewood, Illinois, for material from P. L. Alreck and R. B. Settle, *The Survey Research Handbook*, 1985.

Sage Publications, Inc., California, for the table 'How to Get Started When Searching Published Sources of Secondary Data' from David Stewart (ed.), *Secondary Research: Information, Sources and Methods*, copyright 1984 by Sage Publications, Inc., reprinted by permission of Sage Publications, Inc.

Every effort has been made to contact all the copyright-holders, but if any have been inadvertently overlooked the publishers will make the necessary arrangements at the earliest opportunity.

CHAPTER 1

'Look before you leap'

Introduction

In recent years it has become increasingly fashionable to talk of accelerating technological change, increased international competition and environmental turbulence. Taken together these trends are seen as calling for a radically different approach to business and management than that which has prevailed for the better part of this century. In response to this call for a radical change in business attitudes and practices 'marketing' has emerged as both a philosophy of business and a business discipline best suited to survival and success as we move into the twenty-first century.

While the focus of this book is concerned primarily with only one aspect of marketing – research – it will be helpful to establish first what marketing is, or might be, what factors have led to its current eminence, and what are the prospects that it will continue to fulfil the expectations promised for it in the years to come. Given this overview it will then be possible to address the more concrete issues as to the nature, scope and practice of marketing research from the perspective of the user. This qualification is particularly important for there are many excellent books concerned with technical and professional aspects of marketing research which go far beyond the needs of the manager who is concerned to establish the contribution which research may be able to offer in helping him to solve practical marketing problems. Thus the purpose of this book is not to replicate such texts but to help the manager (student) understand the scope, process and techniques of marketing research to the point where they will be able to engage in a meaningful dialogue with marketing research professionals and exercise informed judgement of the proposals and findings offered by such professionals.

The title of this chapter expresses in a nutshell the desirability of seeking to evaluate outcomes before committing oneself to a possibly irreversible course of action. Few, if any, would quarrel with the good sense and logic of such advice. In the real world, however, perfect information is hard to come by and, even if it were available, the time and cost required to secure it might make it both irrelevant and unnecessary. In everyday life we are accustomed to taking decisions based upon our experience and best judgement about the likely consequences of our actions and, in a Darwinian sense, there is a natural self-selection of those who are better at making decisions/judgements than others. It was Napoleon who expressed a wish for 'lucky Generals'. In reality he wanted generals who had succeeded in the past albeit that it was difficult, if not impossible, to define just what it was that had enabled them to succeed in a highly competitive confrontation with, presumably, equally qualified generals on the other side. This quality is precisely that looked for in the successful manager – an ability to make good (correct) decisions on the majority of occasions on which called upon to do so.

The justification for this book is a belief in two basic propositions:

1. Decision making can be learned.
2. No decision should be taken until one has carefully evaluated the nature of the problem to be solved and reviewed all of the information relevant to the problem that can be obtained within the prevailing time and cost constraints.

This is not to say that some individuals will not make better decision-makers than others, as clearly they will, but to assert that the overall quality of decision making can be improved significantly by following a structured approach and taking full advantage of the tools and techniques available to assist decision-makers. Given the trends referred to in the opening sentence of this introduction, the need for a professional and structured approach to decision making becomes more acute with every passing day.

Environmental turbulence

As noted earlier it has become increasingly fashionable in recent years to speak of environmental turbulence as if it were a new phenomenon discovered by later twentieth-century man. Given that the origins of the word are to be found in the Latin *turba* meaning 'confusion or uproar', from which 'disturb' is also derived, this is a typical case of modern arrogance. That said, the increased incidence of flying has made many of us aware of the uncomfortable unease engendered by physical turbulence in our environment and endowed the term with an immediacy and impact which it may previously have lacked.

Fortunately most turbulence is predictable in that it originates with a discontinuity such as those between pressure systems in the atmosphere or when approaching the sound 'barrier'. Normally we can measure and plot these discontinuities and, while we are occasionally taken by surprise by clear air turbulence, in the majority of cases we can take actions to minimise or avoid interruptions to a smooth progression from where we are to where we want to be. It follows that environmental forecasting is as important to the corporate strategist and marketer as meteorological forecasting is to the airline pilot. Unfortunately, and to pursue the analogy, the further in advance that we try to predict specific events the less accurate our specific predictions become and the less willing many people become to make the effort. A major consequence of this managerial myopia has been the emphasis upon short-term financial milking and paper entrepreneurialism which dulled the competitive edge of the UK and USA and allowed the Japanese, West Germans and others with a long-term vision of the future to penetrate our domestic markets and steal our foreign markets.

Despite the fact that the history — and progress — of man is one of continuous change, people prefer to act and behave as if the future will be like the present and so ignore, avoid or resist change. But, not only is change continuous — it is accelerating. It follows that if management is to fulfil its primary roles of analysis, anticipation, planning and control then it must give particular attention to the nature and direction of change. In doing so, it is clear that change as a process exhibits distinct regularities or patterns 'with dimensions of direction, magnitude, pace and duration that can be seen and measured'.

Failure to recognise and use change leads to three common errors:

1. Believing yesterday's solutions will solve today's problems.
2. Assuming present trends will continue.
3. Neglecting the opportunities of future change.

The American automobile industry is an example of Error 1 in that it is still pursuing Alfred Sloan's manufacturing and marketing strategy enunciated in the early 1920s. Basically this strategy is founded on the concept of trading-up or 'upsizing' and is facilitated by trade-ins and instalment buying. The economies of scale for a full line of cars exist in using many of the sub-assemblies and components of cheaper models in the more expensive models enabling, in Sloan's words, 'the mass production of automobiles to be reconciled with variety of product' (Sloan 1963). But, the strategy does not work in reverse so that when the market wants small, high quality, low cost cars 'down sizing' is not a feasible route to continued profitability. As a result foreign competitors, who had anticipated the change, were able to penetrate the US market and establish a foothold from which it has proved extremely difficult to dislodge them.

'A variant of this error' is the so-called 'sailing ship phenomenon' whereby the introduction of steam-ships stimulated conventional shipbuilders to build better sailing ships rather than switch to the new technology. Numerous examples of the phenomenon are to be found, not only in product development but also in systems and procedures, especially as a result of recent advances in information technology.

Error 2 assumes present trends will continue – an assumption of linearity totally belied by the cyclical behaviour of most phenomena. Thus, while one may be able to project a theoretical trend or smooth past oscillations to represent past change as a continuous process, the reality is that attempts at achieving equilibrium invariably result in over correction around the central trend and give rise to bursts of acceleration and deceleration, of stop and go clearly apparent in the business and related economic cycles.

The energy crises of the 1970s provide clear evidence of the impracticality of the inevitable logic of extrapolation *if one assumes no reaction to restore equilibrium*. If one assumes that consumption of any finite resource will continue to grow in accordance with past trends then, inevitably, the finite resource will become exhausted. But, such projections precipitate actions which themselves initiate counter-reactions.

Thus projections of future oil scarcity encourage supply restriction and price rises; but price rises encourage the exploitation of previously marginal resources (which increases supply) conservation and energy saving practices (which decreases demand) and innovation to find alternative energy sources (which may make the previously scarce resource obsolete). Thus oil demand declined by over 15 per cent between 1979 and 1984, prices plummeted and the oil producers, both countries and companies, moved from growth to recession.

Error 3 is the neglect of the opportunities offered by change and is usually illustrated by reference to the small number of radical innovations which have subsequently revolutionised an industry/market. In reality such examples are the exception rather than the rule and, while they will always enjoy the attention given to exceptions, the managerial requirement to plan and control require that innovation and change should be managed in such a way as to try and dampen the violent oscillations which discontinuous or radical change can precipitate. Clearly, the need is to recognise that change is inevitable and so welcome it as an opportunity rather than regarding it as a threat to the comfortable familiarity of the status quo.

Once we accept that change is inevitable then clearly we will be more prepared to meet and even modify it. It is for this reason that in successful companies so much effort has been devoted to environmental analysis in an attempt to define broad underlying trends and assess their implications in terms of future scenarios. Thus a survey of top European Chief Executive Officers (CEOs) in the early 1980s identified eight factors which characterise the environment facing top management, namely:

1. A demand for quality and advice.
2. A move towards a service culture.

3. An emphasis upon the specialist.
4. Shortening strategic time horizons.
5. Scenario planning is replacing forecasting.
6. A reduction in head office functions.
7. A wider international outlook.
8. Tighter legislation.

These trends correspond closely to those identified by Naisbitt in his best-selling book *Megatrends*. According to Naisbitt (1984) we are changing from an industrial to an information society, from a national to a world economy in which decentralisation and diversity are replacing centralisation and homogeneity, and in which participation and self-help are replacing representative democracy and institutional help. This shift from an industrial society founded on high mass consumption to a post-industrial information era reflects a change in emphasis from quantity to quality, from standardisation to customisation, from centralisation to decentralisation, from dependence to self-help, from autocracy to participation, from hierarchy to network, from transportation to communication and from information scarcity to information overload.

Clearly these are massive changes and call for equally massive changes in the way we think about, and do business. In fact the conditions which precipitated, what I have always referred to as the *rediscovery* of the marketing concept.

The rediscovery of marketing

As we all know there are almost as many definitions of marketing as there are persons willing to formulate one. Despite this variety most contain the common elements that start with and concentrate upon the consumer as the catalyst for an exchange relationship which gives satisfaction to both buyer and seller. In recent times, and in my own opinion, there has been a tendency to over-emphasise the interests of the consumer and my own preferred definition of marketing is that it is concerned with *mutually* satisfying exchange relationships. If this is the case then, it is ironic that marketing, as both a philosophy of business and business function, should be perceived as new. In reality marketing came into existence with the first exchange of goods and services, and has been the catalyst for economic growth through its encouragement of task specialisation and the division of labour which, in turn, have led to the emphasis upon the pursuit of comparative advantage and involvement in international trade.

Given the existence of unsatisfied basic needs it is unsurprising that society perceives its main priority as increasing the volume of output of such basic goods. The pursuit of efficiency in the application of technology to production, results in it becoming concentrated and requires the creation of channels of distribution to enable mass production to be converted into mass consumption. The consequence of this, of course, is that the producer loses direct contact with his customer and tends to perceive demand as the homogeneous entity beloved of economists rather than representing the differentiated needs of a heterogeneous collection of individuals who comprise the 'market'.

It is unsurprising, therefore, that as our ability to increase supply accelerates and the natural growth of markets decelerates through a slowing down of population growth, there begins to develop a mismatch between the producer's perception of consumer needs and the reality. One consequence of this misperception which became apparent in the 1950s and early 1960s was the rise of consumerism and environmentalism. Many marketing scholars claim that consumerism is the shame of marketing. My own view is that it is exactly the opposite – consumerism is in fact a protest against the absence of marketing.

The origins of the consumerist movement were prompted by the scholarly writings of persons like John Kenneth Galbraith (1956, 1958), who pointed to the excesses of materialism, and the populist works of people like Vance Packard in books such as *The Wastemakers* (1960) and the *Hidden Persuaders* (1957). In turn, particular focus was given by Ralph Nader's indictment of the quality of American motor-cars in his '*Unsafe at any Speed*' (1966). Sued unsuccessfully by General Motors, Nader became the giantkiller and numerous others sprang to his cause. While this groundswell of complaint against the lack of perceived quality and value for money in many goods and services was undoubtedly justified, one must remember that this was and is a relative perception that requires a high level of material well-being before it is likely to find expression. Beggars can't be choosers and, as Maslow's (1970) well-known need hierarchy reminds us, we progress upwards from satisfying basic physiological needs through higher order needs for safety, love and esteem before we arrive at the point where we have a sufficient level of material satisfaction that we can become concerned with the more abstract and spiritual 'better' things of life. Elsewhere I have suggested that Maslow's esteem stage corresponds to Walt Rostow's (1962) age of high mass consumption in his model of economic growth. In Rostow's model the final stage of economic development was originally but unoriginally labelled the 'age beyond high mass consumption'. In a revised version which reflected the changes in American society during the 1950s and 1960s Rostow relabelled the ultimate stage of economic development as 'the search for quality'. Clearly, a search for quality implies that the individual will want to define quality more precisely in terms of their own particular needs and wants. It follows that if producers are to succeed then they, too, must spend more time and energy in defining individual needs and aggregating them into worthwhile market segments.

In essence, then, marketing is a very simple philosophy which requires producers to start with the identification and specification of consumer needs, and then mobilise their companies' assets and resources to achieve a mutually satisfying exchange relationship from which both parties derive the benefits they are seeking. While this is a simple and appealing proposition there is no doubt that producers have been very slow to change. Levitt articulated the need in 1960 in his seminal article entitled 'Marketing Myopia' but despite his emphasis upon the inevitability of change in the ways in which basic human needs like transportation and entertainment may be satisfied comparatively few managers and companies fully appreciated the implications. As is so often the case it took a crisis to precipitate a change, but in the process there were many casualties. Thus, the energy crises of 1974 and 1978 and the recessions which followed in their wake, have resulted in a widescale reappraisal by producers as to the changes in organisation and activity which are called for by the new environment in which they find themselves.

What now?

The past decade has witnessed a flood of managerial bestsellers purporting to contain the secrets of competitive success. Few would argue that something called a marketing orientation has a major part to play in achieving this goal. The problem rests in converting managers to a true belief in consumer sovereignty, which constitutes the substance of marketing, rather than allowing them to drift into the acquisition of the trappings of a marketing function. Such a change will require a fundamental shift in attitude of a kind which may only be accomplished by effective education and communication.

Given that human beings exercise control over the other factors of production, it seems reasonable to claim that output or performance is a function of the interaction between the knowledge, skills and attitudes of those people. The reason why people speak of knowledge, skills and attitude in that sequence is because it reflects the sequence of personal development.

Knowledge is distilled experience of the way things are and the way in which they work. Equipped with knowledge we can attempt particular tasks and acquire skills in the practice and application of that knowledge. In the process we will develop attitudes which will tend to reinforce the importance of the knowledge and skills acquired. It is unsurprising, therefore, that people will resist change which challenges their knowledge base or seeks to make obsolete the skills they have acquired. To accomplish change one must first change attitudes, for only if this is accomplished will people be willing to acquire new knowledge and skills.

As indicated, the changes in the balance between demand and supply have been apparent for decades and, with the benefit of hindsight, it is not difficult to understand the social and economic turbulence which exist at the interface between a society concerned with increasing quantity to one which is able to pursue an enhanced quality of life.

Attitudes have changed, and it seems inevitable that quality will now take precedence over quantity and that, ultimately, this will depend upon the quality of management and implementation. Thus, as we move towards the millennium, we have rediscovered the importance of defining quality from the consumer's point of view and have recognised that its achievement depends upon the supplier's understanding of that need and his skill in matching it.

Clearly, the changes referred to in the preceding pages indicate that an ability to monitor, evaluate and even anticipate such change will be critical to successful decision making in the future. To collect, analyse and interpret the relevant information is the purpose of research and there seems little doubt that marketing research – once the Cinderella of marketing – is now coming into its own.

In this chapter we will review the function of marketing research and its definition, scope, classification and contribution to a marketing information system to provide a foundation for the remainder of the book.

The function of marketing research

The authors of one of the best known and most widely used texts on marketing research (Tull and Hawkins, 1987) are unequivocal when they state that the function of marketing research is to provide information that will assist marketing managers in recognising and reacting to marketing opportunities and problems. In essence, marketing research exists to help marketing managers make better decisions. It is a service function. It exists to provide information to help the marketing manager identify and react to marketing problems and opportunities. Given an increasingly competitive environment and the continuing growth and improvement in information technology, the ability to use information requires a thorough understanding of the types of information available and how this information is created. In the field of marketing and, indeed, business as a whole, it is the role of marketing research to provide information so that well founded decision may be taken. According to Parasuraman (1986) these decisions fall into three main categories – setting marketing goals, developing and implementing marketing plans, and evaluating the effectiveness of marketing plans.

Setting goals is a logical starting point for any decision-making process. In the area of marketing decision making, managers set, or should set, goals relating to various aspects of marketing their products for at least two very good reasons. First, they are critical for developing marketing plans as goals serve as the criteria for determining what should or should not be included in these marketing plans. Second, marketing goals serve as standards, or yardsticks, against which the ultimate results of marketing plans can be judged and so aid evaluation of the effectiveness of the plans and their implementation.

While it is perfectly feasible for decision-makers to set goals which they wish to achieve purely on the basis of their subjective judgement and wishes, there is no way of ensuring that such goals will be potentially useful. To be useful in developing plans and evaluating the results of those plans, goals must be realistic. In a marketing context what is realistically achievable would depend on the opportunities and constraints in the market-place. Thus, if a marketer wants to establish goals that are realistic he or she should have good information from the market-place. Marketing research can be valuable here, both by uncovering marketing opportunities as well as identifying constraints which may limit particular courses of action.

As more and more firms embrace the marketing concept and seek to become marketing orientated, so this increases the need to determine and measure customer needs as the basis for formulating marketing plans. Once one has developed a clear understanding of the market-place, then one's success will depend very much upon developing and implementing an effective marketing plan. While there may be a relatively small number of elements in the marketing mix the numbers of permutations and combinations of these elements is almost infinite. Clearly, the better the marketer understands the specific needs of his potential market, the better able he will be to focus on those elements which offer the best likelihood of success in that market. Similarly, once the plan has been implemented one will have a basis for measuring performance against intended results and determining how effective the implementation is and has been. To do so Parasuraman (1986) suggests that we need to answer control-related questions such as: what is the market share of our product? is this increasing, decreasing or staying the same? who are the users? are the nature of the users and the volume of their purchases consistent with our expectations (goals)? if not, why not? Thus, continuous marketing research of performance against plan is a vital element in the control of the marketing function and provides the basis for revising and improving both the plan and its implementation.

As Tull and Hawkins (1987) point out:

> the decision-making process in marketing is essentially the same as it is in any area of human affairs ... it is necessary for those involved in making decisions to (i) establish objectives, (ii) measure performance/potential, (iii) select the problem/ opportunity to pursue; (iv) develop alternatives; (v) choose the best alternative; and (vi) implement the alternative.

It is suggested that problems are identified when one has articulated an objective and measurement of performance indicates that this is not being met.

Similarly, opportunities occur when the potential exists to exceed the original objective through the adoption of a new strategy or approach. As noted earlier, while one may set an objective on the basis of subjective judgement, how is one to know whether this is a realistic target without some under-standing of the area to which the objective relates? For example, if one is considering entering a particular market it would seem essential that one have a clear understanding of the size and composition of that market. Such data as the number of customers, percentage of customers who are 'heavy users', the criteria used in arriving at purchase decisions, the existence of definable segments, the number of competitors and their marketing expenditures, the basis of competition in terms of the product service offering, and so on, would all appear to be necessary if one is to determine whether or not to enter such a market. As will become clear later in this book, marketing research can provide all these types of data and more. Research will also be useful in helping the decision-maker rank order problems and opportunities and so set priorities in the terms of the sequence in which issues are to be addressed and the effort to be applied to them.

The marketing decision

Green and Tull (1966) point out that decisions are made to solve problems. A problem may be said to exist when the following conditions are faced:

1. There are one or more objectives to be met.
2. There are two or more alternative courses of action that could be taken.
3. There is uncertainty as to which course of action will maximise the attainment of the objectives.

Implicit in these objectives are two additional ones:

4. The problem exists in an environment that effects the objectives, the admittable alternative courses of action, and the degree of uncertainty concerning the outcome of each course of action.
5. There are one or more decision-makers.

Green and Tull then go on to suggest that there are six types of management decisions that may be usefully distinguished:

1. Deciding what the problems are that need to be solved – recognising and defining the problems currently faced by the organisation.
2. Selecting the immediate problem for solution – determining priorities by importance of the problems and the timing of their solution.

3. Solving the problem selected – finding alternative solutions, evaluating the consequences of each, and selecting the most favourable one.
4. Implementing the solution – making the decisions necessary to carry out the solution decided upon.
5. Modifying the original solution based upon observation of results – making decisions as to whether, when, and how original solutions should be modified after experiencing results.
6. Establishing policy – deciding which of the problems occur often enough and are sufficiently similar to warrant a policy decision; making the policy decision.

The primary characteristic of marketing management, therefore, is the making of these types of decisions concerning marketing problems. Piercy and Evans (1983) propose that marketing decisions can be divided into those relating to strategy and those involving operations. Marketing strategy decisions include such issues as: (i) Defining what business the firm is in – the mission; (ii) choosing the product/markets; (iii) choosing methods of growth; (iv) designing a configuration of marketing variables for each mission.

Marketing operations decisions relate to the deployment of the marketing mix and include the following:

1. Product policy
   ● launches, modifications, withdrawals, packaging, branding.
2. Pricing policy
   ● levels, discounts, production, export levels.
3. Communication
   ● salesforce: budget activities, goals.
   ● advertising: budget, media, messages, goals.
   ● promotion: budget, methods, goals.
4. Distribution
   ● channel: recruit, motivate, control distributors.
   ● logistics: stock levels, transport and storage as customer services.

As a working generalisation, it is fair to say that the more and better the information available, the more likely it is that the decision-maker will make a good decision. That said, hard information is much more difficult to come by in the marketing arena than it is, say, in the experimental or physical sciences. As noted earlier, while there is only a limited number of elements in the marketing mix, one can use an almost infinite number of combinations of these elements which makes it exceedingly difficult to determine the precise contribution of any one of them. Further, marketing mixes are addressed at customers who are liable to change over time, if for no other reason that they learn how to respond to different marketing mixes in particular ways. If one then recognises that the decision to purchase a particular product or service is only one of hundreds of possible purchase decisions the customer is called upon to make, it is obvious that good hard information will always be at a premium. The primary function of marketing research is to seek to supply such information.

Having explored the functions of marketing research it will now be helpful to attempt some definitions of the activity.

Definitions

' "Research" connotes a systematic, objective and thorough investigation of a subject or a problem in order to discover relevant information or principles' (Green and Tull, 1966) and, therefore, the term marketing research 'is a set of techniques and principles for systematically collecting, recording, analysing, and interpreting data that can aid decision-makers who are involved with marketing goods, services, and ideas' (Parasuraman, 1986). This is distinctly different from the term 'market research' which is concerned with 'the process of making investigations into the characteristics of given markets, namely, location, size, growth potential, observed attitudes' (Glossary of Marketing Terms, 1977), 'which would obviously deprive management of vital contributions which can be made by researchers studying the marketing problems of an organisation as a whole' (Chisnall, 1986).

The *Macmillan Dictionary of Marketing and Advertising* (Baker, 1984) defines marketing research as a branch of social science which uses scientific methods to select information about all those factors which impinge upon the marketing of goods and services, and so includes the measurement and analysis of markets, the study of advertising and effectiveness, distributive channels, competitive products and marketing policies, and the whole field of consumer behaviour. In his *Principles of Management*, (1953), E. F. L. Brech defines the objectives of undertaking research as 'to reduce the areas of uncertainty surrounding business decision'. The British Institute of Management (1970) defines marketing research as 'the objective gathering, recording and analysing of all facts about problems relating to the transfer and sale of goods and services from producer to consumer or user'. The last word in this definition emphasises that marketing research is equally concerned with industrial goods, a point which is frequently overlooked in definitions which refer solely to consumers.

Alternative definitions include:

'Marketing research is the systematic and objective search for and analysis of information relevant to the identification and solution to any problem in the field of marketing' (Green and Tull, 1966).

'The systematic gathering, recording and analysing of data about problems relating to the marketing of goods and services' (American Marketing Association, 1961).

'Marketing Research is a formalised means of obtaining information to be used in making marketing decisions' (Tull and Hawkins, 1987).

'Marketing Research is the systematic and objective approach to the development and provision of information for the marketing management decision-making process' (Kinnear and Taylor, 1987).

'Marketing Research is the systematic design, collection, analysis and reporting of data and findings relevant to a specific marketing situation facing the company' (Kotler, 1983).

The scope of marketing research

In *Marketing* (4th edition, 1985) it was indicated that marketing research comprises a number of distinct sub-areas identified as: market research; sales research; product research; advertising research; business economics research; export marketing research; and motivational research. To this listing we should also add pricing research and distribution research. The kinds of issues and questions to be addressed within each of these specific sub-areas may be summarised as follows.

Market research

The size and nature of the market in terms of the age, sex, income, occupation and social status of consumers.
The geographical location of potential consumers.
The market shares of major competitors, i.e. brand share analysis.
The structure, composition and organisation of distributive channels serving the market.
The nature of economic and other environmental trends affecting the structure of the market.
What your customers want to buy and how much they are willing to spend.
How much of the available money you are getting.
How much you should be getting and could be getting with better techniques.

What is the behaviour of your market share?
What is your future potential in this market?
What is the credit worthiness of customers?
What is the address and telephone number of customers?

Sales research

Determination of territorial variations in sales yield.
The establishment and revision of sales territories.
Sales call planning.
Measurement of the effectiveness of salesmen.
Evaluation of sales methods and incentives.
Cost–benefit analysis of physical distribution systems.
Retail audits.
Details of suppliers.
Reorder time.

Product research

Analysis of the competitive strengths and weaknesses of existing products, i.e.
    both one's own and one's competitors.
Investigation of new uses for existing products.
Product concept testing.
Product testing.
Packaging research.
Variety reduction.
How effective are existing products in meeting customer needs.
The sales potential of a new product.
Helps identify problems with presentation, e.g. packaging.
Helps identify obsolete lines in the product range.

Advertising research

Copy research.
Media research.
Measurement of advertising effectiveness to ensure advertising objectives are
    being met, achieved or maintained.

Business economics

Business economics research can uncover the economic climate of the industry the company is working in and the economic condition of the company itself, thereby identifying the constraints it has to work within. Economic shocks in the environment will be carefully monitored together with the financial condition of the company, in order to prevent major financial difficulties from damaging the company. Such research might include, *inter alia*, input–output analysis; short- and long-range forecasting, i.e. based on trend analysis; price and profit analysis.

Export marketing research

The export marketer has to be aware of the major differences between countries when he is selling the product. Export marketing requires an understanding of the target market environment and the application of all the tools of marketing: the use of market research and the identification of market potential; and the product design decision, pricing decisions, distribution and channel decisions and advertising and promotion decisions (Keegan, 1984).

In other words export marketing research includes any or all of the elements of domestic marketing research applied to the specific foreign market concerned.

Motivation research

This is a branch of research concerned with establishing the real reason or motives that condition consumers' or users' responses to marketing offerings. Many of the techniques have been developed from those used in clinical psychology and frequently give rise to qualitative data rather than quantitative data.

Competition

What competition exists?
Who your competitors are, where they are and what they are doing.
What constitutes the competition: (a) traders with similar merchandise; (b) other types of competition.

Where is the competition?
How your competitors' share of the market is behaving relative to your own.
Are there any changes? New shops, shopping centre, new items or services available.
What products are on the market and who manufactures and sells them?
What are the branding and advertising policies used by competitors?
Have competitors introduced new products?

Classification of marketing research

According to Kinnear and Taylor (1987) marketing research can be classified as (i) exploratory research; (ii) conclusive research and (iii) performance-monitoring (routine feedback) research. The stage in the decision-making process for which the research information is needed determines the type of research required. They proceed to define these classes of research as follows.

Exploratory research

Exploratory research is appropriate for the early stages of the decision-making process. This research is usually designed to obtain a preliminary investigation of the situation with a minimum expenditure of cost and time. The research design is characterised by flexibility in order to be sensitive to the unexpected and to discover insights not previously recognised. Wide ranging and versatile approaches are employed. These include secondary data sources, observation, interviews with experts, group interviews with knowledgeable persons, and case histories. Exploratory research is appropriate in situations where management is searching for potential problems: seeking new insights, ideas or hypotheses regarding the situation; or desires a more precise formulation of the problem and the identification of the relevant variables in the decision situation. Once these issues have been adequately investigated and the decision situation thoroughly defined, exploratory research can be useful in identifying alternative courses of action. Here the manager seeks clues to innovative marketing approaches. The objective is to broaden the domain of alternatives identified, with the hope of including the 'best' alternative in the set of alternatives to be evaluated.

Conclusive research

Conclusive research provides information which helps the manager evaluate and select a course of action. The research design is characterised by formal research procedures. This involves clearly defined research objectives and information needs. Often a detailed questionnaire is drawn up, along with a formal sampling plan. It should be clear how the information to be collected relates to the alternatives under evaluation. Possible research approaches include surveys, experiments, observation and simulation.

Performance-monitoring research

Once a course of action has been selected and the marketing programme is implemented, performance-monitoring research is needed to answer the question 'What is happening?'. Performance monitoring is the essential element needed to control marketing programmes in accordance with plans. Deviation from the plan can result from improper execution of the marketing programme and/or unanticipated changes in the situational factors. Consequently, effective performance monitoring involves monitoring both the marketing mix variables and the situational variables in addition to traditional performance measures such as sales, share of market, profit, and return on investment.'

In other words research may be used in marketing to help identify possible threats and opportunities and clarify potential problems as the decision-maker becomes aware of them (exploratory research); to assist in solving problems once they have been identified (conclusive research); and to provide information to enable progress in the achievement of declared objectives to be measured (performance monitoring).

The use of marketing research

In 1984 Hooley and West undertook a survey to establish:

1. The current level of usage of marketing research in the UK with particular reference to differences in practice between the various product sectors.
2. The types of research currently being conducted in the UK, again relating this to product sector.
3. Expenditure levels, relating to both product sector and size of company.
4. The association between the use of marketing research and company performance.

Using a mail survey to subscribers to *Marketing* magazine (which included all members of the Institute of Marketing) a return of 1775 usable replies was achieved (14 per cent) which was supplemented by 100 in-depth interviews with senior managers who were primarily non-responders to the mail survey. The researchers concluded that their findings represented 'an overstatement of the commitment of UK marketing managers and senior executives to market research'.

Tables 1.1 and 1.2 indicate the level of use of a market research agency while Table 1.3 summarises the method or source of market research employed. More recent data largely confirm these findings.

Of particular interest, however, was the finding that there was 'a clear association between conducting marketing research and improved company performance both in terms of profit margin achieved and self-assessed performance'. The authors conclude:

> While the research cannot prove that the higher levels of usage have caused better performance the high level of association found does indicate that strong inferences can be drawn. The relationship between usage of marketing research and performance suggests that those companies with zero or low usage could significantly improve their performance by making better use of marketing research.

The authors also concluded that a major obstacle to the expansion of usage amongst industrial firms and small and medium sized companies (the low users) was 'a genuine fear of the costs of marketing research and a lack of belief that the benefits to be gained will outweigh these costs'. The author believes that this fear stems largely from ignorance and one of the purposes of this text is to demonstrate that there is a wealth of information and advice available on the costs and benefits of conducting marketing research. Indeed, as we attempt to show when discussing the expected value of information in Chapter 4, the real question is not whether you can afford to undertake marketing research but whether you can afford *not* to.

TABLE 1.1   Conduct of marketing research related to product category

Does your company conduct marketing research or commission marketing research from an agency?	All companies (%)	Consumer		Industrial		
		Durables (%)	FMCG (%)	Repeat (%)	Capital (%)	Services (%)
Yes	61.7	61.4*	79.9	52.6	50.2	60.2
		(100)†	(129)	(85)	(81)	(98)
No	38.3	38.6	20.1	47.4	49.8	39.8
		(101)	(52)	(124)	(130)	(404)
Number of companies	1651	215	349	348	207	532
No reply	124					

Chi-square = 73.4
Degree of freedom = 4
Level of significance = 0.001

* Percentage figures relate to column percentages

† Figures in brackets are index figures based on the 'all companies' column

TABLE 1.2   The use of a market research agency

Does your company employ the services of a market research agency?	All companies (%)	Consumer		Industrial		
		Durables (%)	FMCG (%)	Repeat (%)	Capital (%)	Services (%)
Yes	36.2	37.0	60.3	26.8	25.4	30.6
		(102)	(166)	(74)	(70)	(85)
No	63.8	63.0	39.7	73.2	74.6	69.4
		(99)	(62)	(115)	(117)	(109)
Number of companies	1690	216	356	351	209	558
No reply	85					

Chi-square = 120.7
Degrees of freedom = 4
Level of significance = 0.001

Table 1.3   Method or source of market research employed

Method or source used frequently	All companies (%)	Consumer		Industrial		
		Durables (%)	FMCG (%)	Repeat (%)	Capital (%)	Services (%)
Company records	70.0	72.7	76.7	72.6	67.9	64.5
		(104)	(110)	(104)	(97)	(91)
Secondary sources	56.6	57.9	59.6	54.7	55.0	56.1
		(102)	(105)	(97)	(97)	(99)
Surveys of consumers	27.9	19.0	42.1	20.8	18.7	30.3
		(68)	(151)	(75)	(67)	(109)
Qualitative research	25.6	19.9	39.0	19.1	22.0	24.7
		(78)	(152)	(75)	(86)	(96)
Field experiments	18.4	17.1	25.0	17.4	12.0	17.7
		(93)	(136)	(95)	(65)	(96)
Surveys of distributors	17.2	23.1	17.7	19.9	13.9	14.0
		(134)	(103)	(116)	(87)	(81)
Laboratory experiments	13.1	9.3	22.8	12.3	4.8	12.0
		(71)	(174)	(94)	(37)	(92)
Number of replies	1690	216	356	351	209	558
No reply	85					

Summary

It was Francis Bacon (1561–1626) who observed, 'Nam et ispa scientia potestas est' which may be translated as *Knowledge itself is power*. He was, however, only partly right. While the absence of knowledge is ignorance, its possession will only confer power if it is used to advantage. One of the distinguishing features of the case method of instruction in business schools is that all the participants (competitors) start off with essentially the same information yet they will not all draw the same conclusions from the information available nor decide upon the same courses of action to solve the problems contained within the case study. It would seem therefore that knowledge/information are necessary but not sufficient conditions for decision making and competitive success.

The need for information has become increasingly acute in recent years as a consequence of environmental change and increased international competition. Paradoxically, however, the development of computers and information technology mean that we have moved from a condition of information scarcity to one of information overload. Notwithstanding this proliferation of information the decision-maker is still faced with the need to define his problem and identify and select the most relevant data which will enable him to solve his problem within the inevitable pressures of time and cost. The purpose of marketing research is to assist him in this task.

In this book we shall look first at where marketing problems arise and how to define them so as to make them amenable to resolution. Thus Chapter 2 is concerned with *Problem Definition and Specification*. In Chapter 3 we pose the question '*What do we know?*' and consider the sources of published, and other, information which already exist that may help solve the problem we have identified.

Despite the enormous and ever-growing body of published or 'secondary' information most of it will have been collected for a different purpose than that which has given rise to our own particular problem. Thus an information 'gap' will exist between what we know and what we need to know, and Chapter 4 is concerned with defining this information gap precisely as a first step in determining how to close it. This consideration will also raise the question as to just how much information is worth and how we should set about acquiring it (in-house or bought-in?).

Given an agreed problem definition and a clear understanding as to the kind of additional information required to solve it the question becomes how do we acquire this information?. Chapter 5 seeks to answer this question by reviewing the three basic approaches to data collection – observation, experimentation and the sample survey. For purposes of marketing research observation and experimentation have limited application and the survey emerges as the most suitable and widely used methodology. Accordingly Chapter 6, *Sampling*, provides an extensive commentary and evaluation of the general theory underlying the conduct and execution of various kinds of sample survey.

To ensure that the data collected by sample surveys is accurate, relevant, reliable and comparable as between one respondent and the next it is necessary to design clear and meaningful questions and combine these into carefully constructed and tested questionnaires — the subject of Chapter 7. These questionnaires may be administered by a variety of methods and these — personal, mail and telephone surveys — are compared and contrasted in Chapter 8.

Given the new information, one is faced with the problem of analysing it and Chapter 9 is intended to provide a broad examination of the main statistical techniques which the user is likely to encounter — univariate, bivariate and multivariate. As with the preceding chapters, the purpose is not to provide instruction for practitioners in how to execute various types of analysis but rather to help the user of research findings determine how appropriate each method is to the available data and how to interpret accurately the output of the various kinds of analysis.

In most cases the user will be presented with a formal report and Chapter 10 examines the structure and content of a satisfactory report. It also provides extracts from the codes of conduct of the various professional bodies spelling out the clients' rights in terms of coverage and the standards expected.

A great deal of marketing research is undertaken on a regular or even continuous basis and Chapter 11 describes some of the main *Syndicated Services* available for purchase off-the-shelf or on regular subscription.

Chapters 12 and 13 look respectively at *Information Technology and Marketing Research* and the development of a *Marketing Information System*. Given the new technology, and the importance of information as a competitive weapon, it will be argued that all but the very smallest firms need a formal MIS.

References

American Marketing Association, (1961) *Report of Definitions Committee of the American Marketing Association* (Chicago: American Marketing Association).

Baker, Michael J. (1984) *Macmillan Dictionary of Marketing and Advertising* (London Macmillan).

Baker, Michael J, (1985) *Marketing: An Introductory Text*, Fourth edition (London, Macmillan).

Brech, E.F.L. (1953) *Principles of Management*, 2nd edition (Longmans).

British Institute of Management (1970) *Marketing Organisation in British Industry*.

Chisnall, Peter M. (1986) Third edition, *Marketing Research* (Maidenhead: McGraw-Hill).

Galbraith, John Kenneth (1956) *American Capitalism: The Concept of Countervailing Power* (Boston, Mass.: Houghton Mifflin).

Galbraith, John Kenneth (1958) *The Affluent Society* (Boston, Mass.: Houghton Mifflin).

Hart, Norman A., and Stapleton, John (1977) *Glossary of Marketing Terms* (1977).

Green, Paul E. and Tull, Donald S. (1966) *Research for Marketing Decisions* (Englewood Cliffs, New Jersey: Prentice-Hall).

Hooley, Graham J. and West, Christopher (1984) 'Untapped Markets for Marketing Research', *Journal of the Market Research Society*, vol. 26 (24), pp. 335–52.

Keegan, Warren J. (1984) *Multinational Marketing Management*, Third edition (Englewood Cliffs, New Jersey: Prentice-Hall).

Kinnear, Thomas C. and Taylor, James R. (1987) *Marketing Research, An Applied Approach*, Third edition (New York: McGraw-Hill).

Kotler, Philip (1983) *Principles of Marketing*, Second edition (Englewood Cliffs, New Jersey: Prentice-Hall).

Levitt, Theodore (1960) 'Marketing Myopia', *Harvard Business Review*, July–August 1960, pp.45–56.

Maslow, Abraham H. (1970) *Motivation and Personality*, Second edition (New York: Harper & Row).

Nader, Ralph (1966) *Unsafe at any Speed* (Pocket Books).

Naisbitt, John (1984) *Megatrends* (Futura Publications).

Packard, Vance (1957) *The Hidden Persuaders* (Pelican Books).

Packard, Vance (1960) *The Wastemakers* (New York: McKay).

Parasuraman, A. (1986) *Marketing Research* (Reading, Mass.: Addison-Wesley).

Piercy, Nigel and Evans, Martin (1983), *Managing Marketing Information* (London: Croom Helm).

Rostow, Walt W. (1962) *The Stages of Economic Growth* (Cambridge University Press).

Sloan, Alfred (1963) *My Years at General Motors* (Doubleday).

Tull, Donald S. and Hawkins, Del I. (1987) *Marketing Research*, Fourth edition (New York: Macmillan).

CHAPTER 2

Problem recognition and specification

Introduction

In the preceding chapter it was argued that accelerating technological change and increasing international competition have resulted in the need for a radical re-orientation in the conduct of business. No longer can producers depend upon natural population growth to create an ever-expanding market for basic goods and services largely undifferentiated from one another. Today's consumer is better educated, better informed and better off — all of which encourage much greater discrimination between the relative merits of products in both direct and indirect competition with one another. Consumer sovereignty means that we cast our money votes daily in the market place and the consequences for the producer who has neglected to capture the precise nature of his prospective customers' needs is that he will secure few, if any, votes leading, inevitably, to failure of the firm.

Faced with such a possibility, it is clear that producers must have a much greater concern for the consumers' needs and base their production and distribution decisions upon an accurate understanding of the nature of demand. To secure such an understanding, it will be necessary to undertake research and the balance of Chapter 1 was taken up with a description of the scope, function and characteristics of marketing research as inputs to marketing decision making. In this chapter we shall look more closely at the nature of marketing decision-making and seek to establish how formal marketing research can improve both the recognition and solution of marketing problems.

Marketing decision-making

Marketing decisions are difficult for at least three basic and inter-related reasons.

1. Many marketing problems are more or less unique.
2. Buyers can think for themselves.
3. Most marketing problems are very complex.

In recent years a great deal of empirical research has attempted to identify what are the factors critical to success in business. The findings point unequivocally to the conclusion that there is a multiplicity of critical success factors (CSF) but that their contribution to and importance in explaining 'success', varies dramatically according to the precise context in which a business decision was taken and executed. In other words a successful strategy tends to be highly situation specific to the extent that while one can draw general conclusions about more and less successful solutions to marketing problems, one cannot make assertions concerning outcomes with the confidence of the scientist depending upon the laws of nature.

In part the reason for this lack of predictability is contained in our second reason – buyers can think for themselves. Not only can they think for themselves but they learn from experience and will continuously adjust their behavioural response to maximise their own perception of 'satisfaction'. In that this depends upon the consumption of a very extensive and varied combination of goods and services, the relative importance of which will vary over time (the family life cycle), the difficulty of predicting behavioural outcomes other than in broad generalisations, is apparent. Taken together these two factors lead inevitably to the conclusion that marketing problems are very complex.

So, of course, are many other dynamic decision-making situations such as playing chess or flying an aeroplane. The lesson to be learned from examining experience in such analogous situations is that successful chess players and pilots combine knowledge, understanding and a structured analytical approach in addressing the problems which confront them. Of course, the difference between competence and brilliance will tend to depend upon insight, intuition, creativity and judgement but the surprising conclusion to be drawn from analysis of much managerial decision making is that many managers depend too much upon 'judgement' based upon insight and intuition, but without the benefit of a benchmark of structured analysis against which to test the likely success of their decision. In other words, many managers take uninformed decisions and get them wrong when a more deliberate and structured analysis would suggest a preferred course of action. How else can one explain the findings of the National Industrial Conference Board that over 50 per cent of all new product failures were attributable to the absence of adequate market research?

In part the manager's unwillingness to invest in formal information gathering and analysis may be because he believes that his status, and part of the mystique of being a successful manager is because the practice of management is an art or craft which demands skills that cannot be learned from textbooks. After all, if we could routinise decision making then we could develop appropriate software and leave it all to our computer. The problem is that until such time as we can create an artificial intelligence with the same capability as a human's intelligence, then we cannot provide the judgement which is necessary when formal analysis leaves a problem unresolved with several possible courses of action available to the decision-maker. In other words, formal approaches to problem definition and solution are an aid to, not a substitute for, managerial judgement. To ignore such an aid can only be considered as negligent behaviour and one of the purposes of this book is to show how the formal and judicious use of marketing research can greatly improve the quality of marketing decisions and enhance the likelihood of success.

The need for marketing decisions

The need to take a decision arises when one recognises the existence of a problem to which there are two or more alternative solutions. In other words we are faced with a choice and we need to decide which of several possible courses of action will lead to the most satisfactory outcome to the perceived problem. In general terms such decision making may be classified as falling into one of three mutually exclusive states – certainty, risk and uncertainty. Under conditions of certainty the decision-maker will have no difficulty in selecting the preferred course of action in terms of his declared decision criteria as all the options will be known and capable of comparison in terms of these criteria. However, to be in this happy position one will need to collect and make explicit all the facts relevant to the problem which clearly requires one to have a formal means for gathering and analysing information.

However, the exhaustive collection of all information may be neither possible nor worthwhile – in which case the decision-maker will have to accept either risk or uncertainty as to the correctness of his decision. Estimating the value of information is itself a question of decision making and gives rise to mixed feelings between academics and practitioners. One of the distinguished reviewers of the outline to this book (who is both an academic and practitioner) questioned the inclusion of a discussion of EVPI (the expected value of perfect information) on the grounds that while it appears in many textbooks he has never come across it in practice. In my view this simply confirms the point made above, that managers often exercise judgement to the neglect of techniques which could well improve the quality of that judgement by making explicit what factors need to be taken into account and their relative

26   *Research for marketing*

importance one to another. For the judgemental decision-maker Pamela Alreck and Robert Settle provide a useful checklist of factors which help determine the value of information which is reproduced as Table 2.1.

TABLE 2.1   Factors determining the value of information

Factors indicating high information value
1. The cost of selecting a 'bad' alternative (go error) or failing to select the best alternative (no-go error) would be relatively high.
2. There is a very high degree of uncertainty about which alternative to choose, based on existing information.
3. Survey research information is likely to reduce a substantial portion of the uncertainty.
4. There is high likelihood that survey research will be effective at reducing the uncertainty.

Factors indicating low information value
1. The cost of making either a go or no-go error would be relatively small.
2. There is relatively little uncertainty about the decision, based only on existing information.
3. Survey research information will remove only a small portion of the uncertainty about the decision.
4. There is no way to be sure that survey research information will be effective at reducing uncertainty.

Source: Pamela Alreck and Robert B. Settle, *The Survey Research Handbook* (Homewood, Illinois: Irwin 1985).

However, questions such as these can only provide a crude guide as to the action to be taken and any problem with a 'high information value' would clearly merit some further clarification and investigation to determine precisely just what would be involved in collecting and analysing more data.

As to the difference between risk and uncertainty this largely depends upon whether or not one can make precise (quantitative/statistical) statements about the probability of given outcomes. If, for example, we know that 75 out of every 1000 eggs are likely to be infected with salmonella or listeria then we can state confidently that the likelihood of contracting one or other of these diseases is 0.075 or approximately one in thirteen. What we cannot say, of course, without further information is which particular eggs are infected or who is likely to contract the disease. However, the ability to quantify risk precisely is particularly helpful in areas such as assessing premiums for spreading the cost of a risk between all those likely to be exposed to it (insurance) or the degree of investment in further quality control measures upon a production line.

In risk situations one is able to make an objective estimate of the probability of an event; under uncertainty the best one can attempt is a subjective qualitative assessment of the likelihood of any given occurrence. That said, theoreticians such as Raiffa and Schleiffer have shown clearly how one can use such decisions to develop rigorous analyses of uncertain decisions which also incorporate a sensitivity analysis to allow for one's intrinsic attitudes to risk and uncertainty. Such analyses make use of Bayes' theorem and are collectively described as Bayesian analyses. An example of such an analysis is contained in the companion volume to this book *Marketing Strategy and Management* at pages 221–7.

The question of the conditions under which a given problem/decision can be made is only likely to become apparent after one has recognised that a problem exists and given some thought to the relative importance and nature of the problem. Such recognition is invariably the consequence of a process which has been classified as a hierarchy of effects model of decision making. As Table 2.2 indicates there are several different hierarchy of effects models. However, these models are essentially the same and agree on the sequence of events from problem recognition to solution differing only in the number of steps or degree of precision which they incorporate.

TABLE 2.2   Hierarchy-of-effects models

	Strong (AIDA)	Lavidge and Steiner	Rogers	Engel, Kollat and Blackwell
Conative (motive)	Action	Purchase Conviction	Adoption Trial	Purchase process
Affective (emotion)	Desire Interest	Preference Liking	Evaluation Interest	Evaluation and search
Cognitive (thought)	Awareness	Knowledge Awareness Unawareness	Awareness	Problem recognition

Source: Baker, Michael J. (1984) *Marketing: An introductory text*, Fourth edition (London: Macmillan).

A full description of hierarchy-of-effects models is contained in *Marketing* (pp. 71–3) and it is sufficient here to describe their general import.

As we approach the millennium it is claimed that we are moving from an era of information scarcity to an era of information overload. In the course of the average day it has been estimated that we are exposed to at least 1500 advertising messages alone and it is obvious that if we were to give only 10 seconds to each we would waste over half a working day in the process. Fortunately we are equipped with an inbuilt defence mechanism known as selective perception which performs the chore of monitoring incoming information for us and decides that the great majority is unimportant or of no immediate relevance and prevents our conscious mind from considering the matter further. But if the cue or stimulus (bit of information) is particularly strong, or our subconscious has been 'programmed' to recognise it, then our subconscious will trigger conscious awareness of the cue to enable it to be given further consideration. On average about six advertisements a day survive this screening or filtering process. The success rate of more focused communications (direct mail or the telephone versus media advertising) is likely to be higher but, in every case evaluation of the possible decision can only occur once we have been moved from unawareness to awareness.

Given recognition of the existence of a possible problem, even if it occurs in the positive guise of a better means of satisfying a need for which one already has a solution, then the decision maker will seek to evaluate the implications of a possible change of behaviour in such detail as appears appropriate. For a low risk, low involvement decision − shall I buy a new snack product − probably the quickest and simplest way to gain the necessary information is to spend 20p and physically try the product − after all, it is your taste buds which will decide whether you will like it or not. Conversely, with a high risk, high involvement decision such as the purchase of a major durable good or a sub-assembly for inclusion in a piece of industrial equipment, one will seek to ascertain more about the essential properties of the new product (performance factors and cost−benefit) before even contemplating a trial let alone a purchase.

As I have argued in proposing a composite model of buyer behaviour (see, for example, *Marketing Strategy and Management* pp. 130−8), if the formal and objective evaluation phase points clearly to a preferred solution, then the decision maker has no problem. But, what happens if at the end of careful analysis one is unable to discriminate between two or more alternative solutions to a problem? Clearly one has a choice to make and the decision will require one to accept a degree of either risk or uncertainty in committing oneself to a course of action. Thus decision making is the outcome of a process which may be characterised as 'successive focusing' and represented diagrammatically as a funnel (see Figure 2.1). Of course, a decision may be made at any stage of the process to discontinue it and it is possible to skip a stage or give it only cursory attention in coming to a final decision, e.g. secondary research (see Chapter 3) may produce a satisfactory answer and eliminate the need for further data collection through primary research.

Strictly speaking, marketing research is concerned with the formal search and analysis process but in identifying how problems arise it is useful to be aware of the earlier stages which are sometimes referred to collectively as environmental scanning. The importance of environmental analysis in strategic marketing planning is the subject of Chapter 4 in *Marketing Strategy and Management* and will not be considered in detail here. In brief, environmental scanning may be thought of as the firm's early-warning system through which

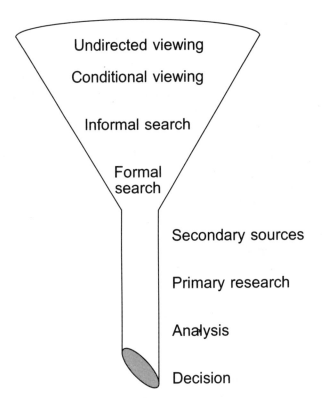

FIGURE 2.1   Successive focusing

it monitors changes in its environment which may represent threats or opportunities to its future well-being (OT in the classic SWOT analysis). Francis Aguilar examined the nature and extent of environmental scanning in his doctoral dissertation of the Harvard Business School (subsequently published as *Scanning the Business Environment*) and identified the four modes of scanning which give rise to formal marketing research. These he defines as:

Undirected viewing − general exposure to information where the viewer has no specific purpose in mind with the possible exception of exploration. 'AWARENESS'.

Conditional viewing − directed exposure, not involving active search to a more or less clearly identified area or type of information. 'SELECTIVE ATTENTION'.

Informal Search − relatively limited and unstructured effort to obtain specific information or information for a specific purpose. 'KEEPING AN EYE ON THINGS'.

Formal search — deliberate effort — usually following a pre-established plan, procedure or methodology — to secure specific information or information relating to a specific issue.

Thus, marketing research represents a deliberate and structured effort to provide answers to the problems faced by managers. As noted in Chapter 1 these may be dichotomised usefully into continuous and *ad hoc* problems — continuous where one needs to monitor actual against planned performance, e.g. sales, market share, and *ad hoc* when one identifies a new problem such as the entry of a new competitor or product to the market, a change in the price of inputs or the management of outlets which calls for specific data not available from routine sources. Given recognition of a problem, the manager will then need answers to at least the following questions:

1. What information do I need?
2. Where is it available?
3. How can I collect it?
4. What is it worth?
5. Once I've got it how do I interpret it?
6. How can I combine the 'facts' with my own subjective judgement and experience in reaching a decision?

The answers to these questions are the subject of the remainder of this book but, before attempting to answer them in detail, it will be helpful to provide an overview of the normative approach to marketing research.

Steps in the research process

Given recognition of the existence of a marketing problem, and assuming it cannot be solved by reference to existing information, then solution of the problem will usually involve a process incorporating some or all of the following stages.

1. Problem identification
2. Problem specification
3. Exploratory research
4. Problem confirmation/re-specification
5. Statement of information needs
6. Search of secondary sources
7. Restatement of information needs
8. Development of a research design

9. Instrumentation
10. Data collection
11. Data processing, reduction and analysis
12. Drawing of conclusions
13. Formulation of recommendations
14. Reporting findings.

An alternative diagrammatic version of the research cycle appears as Figure 2.2.

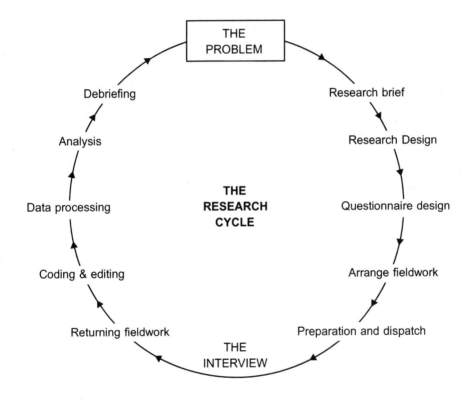

FIGURE 2.2   The research cycle

Source: Ellen Roberts, 'Birth of a Survey', *Survey*, Sprint 1987.

Problem identification was the subject of the preceding section so we will consider first some of the issues involved in problem specification.

It was Rudyard Kipling who penned the little verse which provides the key to problem specification.

'I had six faithful serving men,
They taught me all I knew,
Their names were Where and What and When
And How, and Why and Who.'

These then are the six basic questions which we normally must answer in solving a problem and provide a basic framework for spelling out what is known, what it is desired to know and the nature and extent of the gap between them. The purpose of research is to close or at least narrow this gap so that a better informed decision may be taken.

Having developed a preliminary problem specification the next stage in the process will usually be to undertake some exploratory research to establish whether the problem is perceived in a similar light by others who are likely to be involved in and/or affected by the outcome, i.e. is it a real problem and, if so, how important is it, i.e. how much effort is to be given to its solution? Given clarification of these issues the problem statement can be firmed up and used to determine what kind of information is needed to help resolve the problem.

Although it was stated in the introduction to this chapter that no two marketing problems are likely to be exactly similar it was also argued that one can identify classes of problems which do possess similarities. It follows that once one has a statement of information needs, one should examine the published information available in secondary sources to see if it can shed any useful light on the problem. As we shall see in the next chapter there are enormous and rich sources of secondary data which, provided one takes elementary precautions to establish their validity, reliability and comparability, will prove invaluable in further clarifying the problem and the kind of information which will be necessary to solve it.

The remaining steps in the process are all the subject of detailed treatment in later chapters but it will be helpful before getting immersed in this detail to take a broad look at the distinction between quantitative and qualitative research and their use in the overall research process.

Quantitative or qualitative research?

The heading to this section suggests that there is a choice to be made between a quantitative and qualitative research method. While this is so, it is vital to stress that although the two approaches are distinctly different they are complementary and most sophisticated research designs will contain elements of both. Traditionally, however, the two approaches have been positioned as if they were polar and mutually exclusive alternatives. This polarisation is implicit in Table 2.3 which lists a series of adjectival descriptors of the two kinds of research.

TABLE 2.3   Qualitative versus quantitative research

Qualitative	Quantitative
Soft	Hard
Dry	Wet
Flexible/fluid	Fixed
Grounded	Abstract
Descriptive/exploratory	Explanatory
Pre-scientific	Scientific
Subjective	Objective
Inductive	Deductive
Speculative/illustrative	Hypothesis testing
Political	Value free
Non-rigorous	Rigorous
Idiographic	Nomothetic
Holistic	Atomistic
Interpretivist	Positivist
Exposes actors meanings	Imposes sociological theory
Phenomenological	Empiricist/behaviourist
Relativistic case study	Universalistic survey
Good	Bad
Bad	Good

Source: P. Halfpenny, 'The Analysis of Qualitative Data', *Sociological Review*, vol. 27, no. 4.

More recently, however, a more balanced approach has emerged in which both kinds of researcher admit the contribution of the other. In parallel with this trend (or perhaps because of it) there has developed a growing recognition amongst the users of research that qualitative research is essential to address questions of what, how (process) and why, while quantitative research is appropriate to answer questions of who, where, when and how (quantity).

In very broad terms one should use qualitative research:

1. To define the parameters of the market.
2. To understand the nature of the decision-making process.
3. To elicit attitudinal and motivational factors which influence behaviour.
4. To help understand why people behave the way they do.

Overall qualitative research is best suited to areas calling for a flexible approach while quantitative research is necessary to define more precisely the issues identified through qualitative methods. According to Peter Sampson

('Commonsense in Qualitative Research', *Commentary*, vol. 9, no. 1, January 1967) the areas calling for a flexible approach may be summarised as:

1. Concept identification and exploration.
2. Identification of relevant behavioural attitudes.
3. Establishing priority among and between categories of behaviour, attitudes, etc.
4. Defining problem areas more fully and formulating hypotheses for further investigation.

More recently, Wendy Gordon and Roy Langmaid (1988) have suggested that the most important areas for qualitative research are:

Basic exploratory studies
New Product Development
Creative Development
Diagnostic studies
Tactical research projects.

Exploratory studies are usually called for when seeking to identify market opportunities for new product development, to monitor changes in consumption patterns and behaviour, to help define the parameters and characteristics of newly emerging markets or when seeking to enter established markets of which one has no prior experience. Gordon and Langmaid (1988) indicate five specific types of information which may be obtained from studies of this kind, namely:

1. *To define consumer perceptions of the market or product field* in order to help understand the competitive relationships between different types of product and/or brand in any product category – from the consumer's point of view rather than the manufacturer's.
2. *To define consumer segmentations in relation to a product category or brand*, e.g. psychographics and life-style segmentations.
3. *To understand the dimensions which differentiate between brands*, specifically on the basis of rational criteria and emotional beliefs. Where objective differences can be developed between products, rationality will predispose consumers to select these which conform most closely with their own preferences or criteria. Unsurprisingly, objective differences are comparatively easy to emulate with the result that emotional beliefs have come to play an increasingly important part in purchase decisions – industrial as well as consumer.
4. *To understand the purchase decision-making process and/or usage patterns.*
5. *Hypothesis generation.*

As a broad generalisation then, qualitative research is an essential prerequisite to most quantitative research in that it will help clarify the issues to be addressed, the parameters to be defined and measured and the likely relationships between them. A review of the methodology of qualitative research and the techniques used is provided in Chapter 5.

Problem identification

Recognition of a problem may arise from many sources. In some cases they are perceived in a flash of insight when an individual recognises an accepted practice as a problem demanding an alternative solution. Thus Land's Polaroid camera eliminated the need for extended film processing and delivered instant prints while electrostatic photocopying virtually killed off spirit duplicating. Both innovations were the direct result of an inventor identifying a problem with an existing process and coming up with a better alternative solution to the problem.

But as Cooper (1961) has pointed out businesses cannot afford to wait for the flash of insight of a researcher but instead must try and anticipate the problems they are likely to meet and deal with them before they develop into major crises. To this end we set up performance measures so that we can identify any deviance between the actual and intended outcome, e.g. sales volume, profit margins, costs, market share, etc. and institute the necessary analysis to determine the source of the deviance and possible courses of action to remedy it. Equally we can anticipate possible events which will call for particular responses, e.g. a batch is rejected on quality grounds, a machine breaks down, a customer postpones delivery, export sales are subject to currency fluctuations, and devise standard operating procedures (SOPs) or contingency plans to deal with these eventualities.

Other problems will be identified as a result of the organisation and its members seeking to monitor the environment in order to pick up possible early warning of events which may impact upon them both favourably and unfavourably. Experience indicates that this kind of external monitoring is less common than the internal monitoring systems described above, many of which are routine and well established. The evidence, such as it is, also suggests that it is the absence of formal efforts to anticipate problems (changes) in their environment which result in most of the difficulties/crises experienced by firms. In other words, one must develop a formal and structured approach to the acquisition, compilation and analysis of information, both internal and external, if one is to be able to identify and resolve problems satisfactorily.

Cooper (1961) suggests a number of questions one should consider on first identifying a problem, namely:

1. *What is the situation which triggered off the problem?*
2. *What is the background of this and similar problems?* What action has been taken in the past, by whom, under what reasoning and with what effect?
3. *How does the matter relate itself to currently existing goals, plans, policies and programmes?*
4. *What are the probable consequences of even considering the matter?* What impact would any of the feasible courses of action have upon the organisation and its relationships and conditions of operation? What new problems would be created?
5. *Does attention to the problem seem warranted and reasonable within the feasibilities and capabilities of the enterprise?*
6. *Is this the best time for decision?*
7. *Is this a one-time decision or a continuing one?*

The classification of market problems

Because marketing is concerned with the interaction of buyers and sellers in negotiating exchange transactions it possesses a dynamism which is absent from many other areas where research is called for to help solve problems. While laboratory based techniques and experimentation may have a role to play, the majority of marketing problems arise from the operational management of the marketing function and so cannot be separated from it. As a consequence the number and variety of marketing problems is virtually infinite. Faced with this variety it is clear that it will be helpful if one can defined a *typology* of marketing problems as the first step in the process of deciding what research methods will offer the greatest likelihood of helping solve the problem.

In order to create a typology of marketing problems it is necessary first to decide upon some organising principle and then articulate a set of criteria which will enable the classification of individual problems into particular types or categories. Given its widespread acceptance as an organising framework within marketing, it would seem reasonable to adopt the *marketing mix* as the basis for constructing a typology of marketing problems. Unfortunately, although 'the marketing mix' is a widely accepted concept it lacks a commonly agreed definition. As noted in the *Macmillan Dictionary of Marketing and Advertising* (Baker, 1984) ' . . . there is a wide diversity of opinion among marketers on what elements compose the marketing mix. Of these alternatives perhaps the best know is that proposed by McCarthy which comprises four elements described as the 4 P's, namely product, price, place and promotion.' One of the longest is that proposed by the originator of the concept, Neil Borden, which contains 12 elements. However, several of Borden's divisions can easily be accommodated within the McCarthy structure, e.g. branding as part of the product mix, and it would seem helpful if the typology used consisted on a series of 'branches' enabling one to refine the precise definition of one's marketing problems by applying a series of increasingly narrow criteria. To this end McCarthy's scheme offers the benefits of simplicity but it is felt to be lacking in one very important respect − it gives no explicit recognition to *competition*. Accordingly, it is proposed to use McCarthy's 4 P's with the addition of competition so that our emerging typology will assume the structure below.

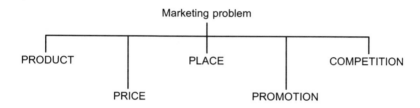

Examining the question of classifying marketing problems in one of the earlier standard texts (*Marketing Research*, McGraw-Hill, 1967) Richard Crisp suggested that another useful and practical approach would be to divide all marketing problems into two major types. These he defined as '*operating problems*' which are continuously present in almost every marketing-management situation, and *non-recurring problems*, which arise as a result of some specific development or circumstance'. This distinction is felt to be helpful as operating problems would seem to call for continuous marketing research providing inputs to an established marketing information system while non-recurring problems are of a kind which call for the development of a specific research brief and the commissioning of *ad-hoc* research designed to resolve that problem. Among the examples of recurrent operating problems cited by Crisp are: sales forecasting, monitoring sales performance, measuring industry trends, product-quality and product-line review and evaluation, evaluation of alternative promotion methods, appraisals of advertising effectiveness, etc. By contrast the major types of non-recurring problems are largely the consequence of innovation causing a step change in competition in terms of one of the mix elements, e.g. a significant product innovation making other competing products obsolescent, the concentration of retail buying power and its effect on manufacturer/retailer relationships. If then we add this additional dichotomy to our typology we obtain ten categories or types of marketing problem as shown overleaf.

Modelling the marketing research process

Every textbook includes a section in which it describes the marketing research process usually starting with problem recognition and concluding with the preparation of a report. Few, however, make explicit reference to the need for an informal investigation at the outset of the process nor for an evaluation and feed back review at the end of the process. Our own model which incorporates these stages is shown in Figure 2.3. The early stages concerned with problem recognition and specification are the major subjects of this chapter while all the subjects after problem definition are the subjects of later chapters. It will be useful, therefore, to say something now about the benefits of the informal investigation stage before proceeding to formal approaches to problem solving.

The inclusion of an informal investigation at the beginning of a marketing research study is proposed by Charles S. Mayer in his contribution to the *Marketing Handbook* (2nd edn, Albert Wesley Frey (ed.), The Ronald Press, New York, 1965) in which he argues that it serves two basic objectives:

1. To develop the hypotheses to be used in the final study;
2. To obtain a 'feel' of the market.

While the problem recognition and specification phases will undoubtedly have generated some tentative hypotheses, Mayer sees the purpose of the informal investigation as screening these for further consideration. The process may also throw up additional hypotheses not identified in the initial problem specification.

Similarly, the informal investigation enables the researcher to explore the dimensions and implications of his problem with others who may have relevant experience or views on it. While it is difficult to define precisely what is meant by a 'feel for the market' it is a readily understood concept and more likely to be developed through discussion and interaction than by sitting at one's desk with a pencil and paper.

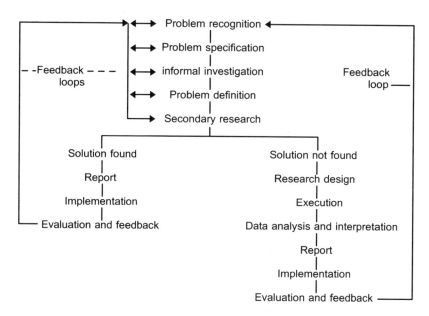

FIGURE 2.3   **The market research process**

As proposed in the model of successive focusing (Figure 2.1, p. 29) informal search occurs at the point when one believes one has identified the parameters of a problem and is seeking to test these preliminary working hypotheses by a quick and only partially structured review of the subject area. Mayer's preferred approach is to conduct a series of calls on consumers, dealers, company executives and any other key individuals whose opinions and attitudes may have an important bearing upon the problem. How many calls and of what duration and complexity is largely a matter of judgement. What is important is that it is the problem solver who is going to be responsible for defining the problem and developing the research brief who should execute this phase personally. As soon as he believes that he can define the problem in sufficiently detailed and explicit form that he can develop an operational design to solve it or communicate the problem as a research brief to a third party the informal investigation can be terminated and a structured approach set in train.

However, as the feedback loops in the model remind us, problem-solving is an iterative process in which one continuously refines one's perception of the problem in the light of new and better information, as well as possible changes in the factors which precipitated recognition of the problem in the first place. Informal investigation is necessary to test one's initial problem specification and to determine how best to proceed. Given classification of the problem then the next stage in the process must be to define it precisely and initiate research to solve it. As the model indicates, the next step is secondary research and it is to this topic which we turn in Chapter 3.

Summary

In this chapter we have been concerned with *problem recognition and specification,* i.e. what is it that triggers awareness of a perceived problem, how do we assess the relevance and importance of the problem and what steps/procedures should we follow to define the problem in such a way that we can decide how best to solve it?

In order to reach this conclusion we have looked briefly at some of the key features of marketing decision making and the factors which precipitate the need to take specific marketing decisions. Awareness of a problem does not automatically mean that it requires a solution and we looked at a model of successive focusing which suggests that decisions proceed through a sequence of stages from awareness, to interest, to information search and analysis, and to evaluation and action. Depending upon the outcomes the process may be discontinued at any stage, but if it proceeds tends to move from exploratory and largely qualitative research through to increasingly closely defined analytical and quantified research.

Following a brief examination of what may lead to problem identification in the first place, a classification, or 'typology' of marketing problems was proposed together with a model of the marketing research process which provides a structure for the chapters which follow.

References

Baker, Michael J. (1984) *Macmillan Dictionary of Marketing and Advertising* (London: Macmillan).
Cooper, Joseph D. (1961) *The Art of Decision Making* (London: Heron Books).
Gordon, Wendy and Langmaid, Roy (1988) *Qualitative Market Research* (Aldershot: Gower).

CHAPTER 3

What do we know?

Introduction

In the preceding chapters it has been argued that the role of marketing research is to reduce areas of uncertainty surrounding business decisions and that one of the first tasks to be addressed when faced with a marketing problem is to define it precisely in order to determine just what one knows and needs to know in order to solve the problem. This dichotomy between what is known and what we need to know is reflected by the distinction between primary and secondary data. In essence, secondary data is 'known' and published information whereas primary data is new information collected specifically to help solve the problem in hand *in cases where the secondary data is insufficient for that purpose.*

Two important points must be made. First, while it was stated that secondary data is 'known' this means that the data is available to the problem solver, not necessarily that he is actually aware of the data or has it to hand. Second, our emphasis upon the fact that primary data should only be collected if the secondary sources are insufficient is intended to underline the old adage that one should not seek to reinvent the wheel. It follows that the first step in solving any marketing problem should be to confirm what is already known about the subject of the problem. In doing so one will normally have recourse first to the organisation's own records and data store before extending the search to the wider domain of data sources external to the firm. The use of secondary data, its suitability and the major sources available to the researcher are the subject matter of this chapter.

The uses of secondary research

Secondary research is often referred to as *desk research* on the grounds that it can be undertaken in the office while primary data collection almost invariably requires one to go outside the office and the firm — hence *field research*. With the growing use of the telephone for survey research this distinction is no longer as clear cut as it used to be but from usage and practice it seems likely to survive into the foreseeable future. For the purposes of this book the terms desk and secondary research should be regarded as interchangeable.

Because of its association with the office and the possibly tedious aspects of identifying, reviewing and evaluating large quantities of published material, secondary research is often regarded as a clerical chore rather than a management task. As a consequence the review of published sources is frequently delegated to a junior researcher while their seniors grapple with the more demanding issues of research design and execution. While there is both sense and economy in having assistants track down sources and making preliminary assessments of their relevance, those responsible for the management of a research project cannot avoid the need to apply their experience and judgement to the organisation and interpretation of secondary data as a major influence upon any subsequent research design. That said, it is clear that the collation and evaluation of much secondary data can be formalised and included in the design of the firm's marketing information system (this is the subject of Chapter 13) which should always be the first reference point for any secondary research. Having defined the data requirements the methods of presenting it to decision makers and the interrelationships to be monitored on a regular basis then, clearly, the day to day routine can be delegated to junior personnel.

As suggested in our model of successive focusing (Fig. 2.1 p. 29) the recognition of a problem leads to an increasingly structured search for additional information with the review of published information comprising the first step of a formal attempt to solve an identified problem. According to Nigel Newson-Smith (1988) in the field of marketing such efforts can be classified as belonging to one of four categories.

1. Providing a background.
2. A substitute for a field study.
3. A technique in its own right.
4. Acquisition studies.

Providing a background to a problem is an intrinsic element of the successive focusing model which, in turn, is derived from the hierarchy-of-effects models which propose that any action is the consequence of a process in which the decision-maker moves from a state of unawareness to awareness, to interest, to evaluation and action. Once interest has been focused on a problem, information acquisition is a natural response and it is here that a review of secondary sources assumes major importance. (While it is usual to refer to published sources, in this context one should not overlook the value of consulting others who may have knowledge and experience of the problem to be addressed. Expert opinion may often help point one in the right direction much more quickly than even the most sophisticated computer search.) Whether personal or impersonal, secondary sources help avoid unnecessary repetition of prior fieldwork, they provide information concerning the population of interest so that if survey work becomes necessary one has the basis for defining and selecting representative samples, and they provide factual answers to many of the objective questions concerning market behaviour, e.g. number of consumers, sales, market shares, seasonality, etc.

While desk research is not really a substitute for field research one is sometimes fortunate enough to find sufficient information in the secondary sources to obviate the need for additional primary data collection. Given the range and specialisation of published data available, the likelihood of finding generalised market data is high. However, while published data may provide useful pointers to the consumers' possible behaviour it is unlikely that they will be able to predict their reaction to specific changes in the marketing mix.

In some cases desk research provides the only realistic solution to a marketing problem and so may be regarded as a technique in its own right. This is obviously the case if one wants to establish trends in market behaviour – longitudinal, prospective studies are clearly unrealistic which means that one must rely on historical data already in the public record. Similarly, in most advanced economies the wealth of published statistics concerning market structure and performance, often compiled by a census of all those involved, cannot help but be superior to any form of sampling by field research. (Some caveats concerning published data will be dealt with later.)

Finally, and given the increasing popularity of acquisitions and mergers, desk research is an essential element in the process, particularly when field research could reveal one's intentions prematurely. We need the following data requirements:

Company description
    Company history
    Financial structure
    Financial performance
    Ownership and directorate
    Plant location
    Production techniques
    Number of employees, etc.

Products and markets
    Competitive activity
    Advertising and marketing, etc.

Such information is widely available in company reports, share registers, financial analysis surveys, brokers reports, commercial directories, the technical press, the trade press and official statistics. While such data in the context of acquisitions and mergers are important, it is, of course, equally as important in terms of a regular competitor analysis as an input to strategic marketing planning. However, surprisingly few firms take advantage of these sources in plotting their own competitive strategy.

Table 3.1 taken from Hague (1987) provides a detailed checklist of the steps to be taken in evaluating a company using desk research methods.

TABLE 3.1 Steps in evaluating a company

Action checklist to obtain information on a company or companies

Step	Action	If unsuccessful
1	Obtain accurate name, address and telephone number from a directory or buyer's guide. Phone reception to check accuracy.	Question Directory Enquires, competitive company, distributor, known end-user in case of change of name or address. To step 2.
2	Assemble basic data on date of formation, product range, subsidiary companies, parent, number of employees, directors, financial status, etc from Kompass, Dun & Bradstreet. *Who owns whom* Build up list of distributors from adverts in Yellow Pages or buyers' guides.	Check with distributors, competitors, other companies that may know. To step 3.
3	Check for Monopolies Commission reports on the industry and industry reports published in *Financial Times*. Obtain copies.	To step 4
4	Write to company's publicity department for corporate brochure and literature.	Try sales department Try distributor To step 5.
5	Obtain largest Ordnance Survey map of factory site. Blow up to give plan of site, access, area for expansion.	Photograph site. To step 6.
6	For quoted company: write to company secretary for report and accounts.	Obtain accounts from Companies House.

	For unquoted company: obtain financial profile and microfiche from Companies House (make sure the precise name is applied for).	If 'non-trading' try to find trading company and obtain accounts. To step 7.
7	Search trade journals and all media for adverts, articles and references including local papers close to works or head office. Record management appointments.	Try abstracting service. To step 8.
8	Check with trade association if technical symposia have included papers given by company. Obtain papers.	Consider fieldwork to profile the company.

Source: Hague, *The Industrial Market Research Book.*

The advantages and disadvantages of secondary research

In their monograph *Secondary Analysis of Survey Data* (Sage University Paper S3, 1985) Kiecolt and Nathan confine their attention to the use of precollected survey data in social research but their summary of advantages and disadvantages is equally applicable to other kinds of secondary data. In introducing these advantages and disadvantages they observe:

> Secondary analysis of existing surveys allows researchers access to data from large, national samples – data that would be difficult for a lone researcher to gather. Both large and more specialised archives have been established that typically make surveys available for a modest fee. Technological advances, such as the effective storage of data in machine-readable form and the availability of statistical computing programs, as well as widespread researcher access to computers, have also contributed to the popularity of using precollected data for original research. As a consequence, secondary analysis of survey data is likely to maintain a dominant position in social science research for the foreseeable future.

With regard to the advantages and disadvantages of such analysis these may be summarised as follows:

1. *Secondary survey analysis is less costly.* A great deal of secondary data is available at little or no cost from libraries, data archives and organisations

wishing to sell marketing services, e.g. Television contractors provide compendious details of the populations they serve, their demographics, life-styles, purchase behaviour, etc. in order to encourage advertisers to place contracts with them. Even in the case of syndicated market research data, which is often highly specific and directly relevant to the marketing managers' problems, costs are comparatively modest.

2. *Secondary analysis avoids data collection problems.* Much of the content of major data archives is readily available in machine readable form and covers nationally representative samples, standard items and standard indices. A wide range of topics is covered spanning many time periods and countries.

3. *Secondary analysis is a prime source of ideas and hypotheses for further, primary research.* Many years ago when a student at the Harvard Business School the author worked on a data base compiled from a self-completion questionnaire contained in *Good Housekeeping*. The results from the survey, which were largely descriptive, were published in the magazine but the data base was then made available for further analysis by interested researchers. Data had been collected from males, females and male/female dyads on a wide range of topics. By comparing the responses of the three different 'kinds' of respondents it was possible to construct an index of influence on household purchasing decisions which indicated distinct male, female and joint areas of authority. Men were regarded as authoritative on purchases such as car batteries and tyres and responsible for over 90 per cent of all purchase decisions; women were seen as the authorities on household remedies, cleaning materials, etc (also in over 90 per cent of the cases) but most decisions on the purchase of consumer durables were 'joint' decisions with both parties playing equal roles in the decision. Given this confirmation of what most observers would have predicted, together with a validated research methodology, it was possible to adapt both the concept and the method to focused primary research for specific clients with interest in particular product fields.

4. *Secondary analysis permits the construction of trend studies.* Marketing decision makers usually want information to address current problems. As a consequence they are rarely willing to contemplate a prospective, longitudinal study in which the population of interest is surveyed on a number of occasions in order to establish trends. However, where a suitable data base exists one can work backwards to establish a trend and use a current cross-sectional study to validate and up-date this.

Of course, secondary sources also have their disadvantages, which may be summarised as: limitations.

1. *Availability.* Despite the wealth of information on archives it is seldom that it will be readily available. The more specific a data base the more likely it

has been collected for a particular purpose and the less likely the owner will release it if it has commercial and competitive value.

2. *Relevance.* This is closely associated with availability. Data in the public domain is usually fairly general in character and it is rare that one will find such data directly relevant to commercial problems.

3. *Accuracy.* Several problems exist here. First, unless there is 'complete and accurate documentation of all the data on file, it is difficult or impossible to locate needed information.' Second, there is the problem of flaws and errors in the original research design which may not be apparent in the analysis but will have a marked influence on its acceptability for future research. There is also the problem that because of its commercial value firms may be 'economical with the truth' when required to make returns which do not preserve their anonymity.

4. *Recency.* Much data has been on file for a considerable time and may not be appropriate when analysing current problems in dynamic markets.

Most standard texts (Churchill, 1987; Kinnear and Taylor, 1987; Luck & Rubin, 1987; Parasuraman, 1986) elaborate on these issues — availability, accuracy, recency and relevance — in some detail. Together with cost (both time and money) these four issues constitute the basic criteria for assessing the value of secondary sources as a solution to the practitioner's information need(s)

Rules for desk research

In *Secondary Research Information Sources and Methods* (1984) Martin Stoll sets out the following rules for desk researching:

   i) Go from the general to the particular — a review article first, then a detailed specialist one.

   ii) Use secondary sources before primary resources — then if someone has already sorted out the government or trade statistics into an intelligible table, why repeat the process?

   iii) Be methodical — look in catalogues, directories and indexes before looking in abstracts, books or periodicals.

   iv) Write it all down — make a note of all the details in full, as you go, to save backtracking.

   v) Ask a librarian — as they spend their lives doing what you may do for one day in six months, they undoubtedly know their way around the sources better, and their knowledge should be used.

This is certainly sound advice although the author's personal inclination should be to start with the librarian first. The reason for doing so is that the librarian is probably the person best able to advise as to the availability of material and help structure the remainder of one's research in line with the other 'rules'. Given the growth of on-line data bases it is now possible to conduct highly focused searches of the published literature through the judicious selection of key-words which define the central or core concepts/information in which one is interested. For example, if one is interested in establishing the contribution of marketing to competitive success then one might initiate a search by inputting the key words – marketing, competition and success and the computer will scan its memory to establish which publications, if any, occur which cite these three factors *together*. It is likely that an item which deals with all three factors is going to be fairly generalised and so will provide both an overview and introduction to the subject as well as pointers to other sources which can then be followed up.

While the precise sequence may be a matter of choice and convenience, i.e. what sources are most immediately to hand, most practitioners would agree with the sequence and procedure proposed by Luck and Rubin (1987) which is reproduced as Table 3.2.

TABLE 3.2   A sequence of steps in a secondary data search

1. Specify data requirements.

2. Determine which data are obtainable from internal sources.
   a. Specify format for reporting.

3. Seek external sources of secondary data.
   a. Libraries (use guides and compendiums of statistics).
   b. Trade publications.
   c. Data service directories.
   d. Trade associations.

4. Obtain secondary data.

5. Scrutinise data's validity.
   a. Evaluate collecting organisation.
   b. Consider objectives of the original study.
   c. Appraise.
      (1) Methods employed
      (2) Definitions and classifications.
      (3) Currency.

6. Identify data that must be obtained from primary sources instead.

Source: David J. Luck and Ronald S. Rubin (1987) *Marketing Research*, 7th edition (Englewood Cliffs, N.J: Prentice-Hall) p. 119.

It should be appreciated that in accordance with our model of successive focusing Step 1 'Specify data requirements' may well be a very broad statement initially – indeed a significant omission from the Luck and Rubin model is the absence of feedback loops as it is likely that as more information comes to hand one will want to redefine one's data requirements and initiate new searches to locate it. However, as discussed in the previous chapter, given a problem definition one has both a goal – solution of the perceived problem – and a start point – our current state of knowledge – and it is logical that one should wish to start with one's own records as they are likely to be the most accurate, accessible, relevant and least costly source available. Indeed, given the establishment of a marketing information system (MIS) of the kind described in Chapter 13, then this should automatically be the first reference point given recognition of a problem. To conclude this section we reproduce the advice given by David Stewart of 'How to get started when searching published sources of secondary data' as Table 3.3.

Internal Sources

Among the internal sources of data likely to be available to the researcher are:

Accounting records/order forms
Customer files
Sales reports
Service records
Previous market research.

In the larger company it is also possible that there will be a library containing material considered directly relevant to the firm's business.

Every company keeps track of its financial transactions with suppliers and customers and, while the information has not been collected specifically for marketing purposes, it provides a rich and usually detailed secondary source. Amongst the information to be found in account records are likely to be:

- customer location
- name(s) of contact
- type of purchase
- data and frequency of purchase
- size of purchase
- terms of trade (discounts, credit etc)
- delivery locations and types.

TABLE 3.3 How to get started when searching published sources of secondary data

Step 1: Identify what you wish to know and what you already know about your topic. This may include relevant facts, names of researchers or organisations associated with the topic, key papers and other publications with which you are already familiar, and any other information you may have.

Step 2: Develop a list of key terms and names. These terms and names will provide access to secondary sources. Unless you already have a very specific topic of interest, keep this initial list long and quite general.

Step 3: Now you are ready to use the library. Begin your research with several of the directories and guides listed in Appendix 5A. If you know of a particular relevant paper or author, start with the *Social Science Citation Index* (or *Science Citation Index*) and try to identify papers by the same author, or papers citing the author or work. At this stage it is probably not worth-while to attempt an exhaustive search. Only look at the previous two or three years of work in the area, using three or four general guides. Some directories and indices use a specialised list of key terms or descriptors. Such indices often have thesauri that identify these terms. A search of these directories requires that your list of terms and descriptors be consistent with the thesauri.

Step 4: Compile the literature you have found; is it relevant to your needs? Perhaps you are overwhelmed by information. Perhaps you've found little that is relevant. Rework your list of key words and authors.

Step 5: Continue your search in the library. Expand your search to include a few more years and one or two more sources. Evaluate your findings.

Step 6: At this point you should have a clear idea of the nature of the information you are seeking and sufficient background to use more specialised resources.

Step 7: Consult the reference librarian. You may wish to consider a computer-assisted information search. The reference librarian can assist with such a search but will need your help in the form of a carefully constructed list of key words. Some librarians will prefer to produce their own list of key words or descriptors, but it is a good idea to verify that such a list is reasonably complete. The librarian may be able to suggest specialised sources related to the topic. Remember, the reference librarian cannot be of much help until you can provide some rather specific information about what you want to know.

Step 8: If you have had little success or your topic is highly specialised, consult the *Directory of Directories*, *Directory Information Guide*, *Guide to American Directories*, *Statistics Sources*, *Statistical Reference Index*, *American Statistics Index*, *Encyclopedia of Geographic Information Sources*, or one of the other guides to information listed in Appendix 5A. These are really directories of directories, which means that this level of search will be very general. You will first need to identify potentially useful primary directories, which will then lead you to other sources.

Step 9: If you are unhappy with what you have found or are otherwise having trouble, and the reference librarian has not been able to identify sources, use an authority. Identify some individual or organisation that might know something about the topic. The various *Who's Who publications*. *Consultants and Consulting Organisations Directory*, *Encyclopedia of Associations*. *Industrial Research Laboratories in the United States or Research Centers Directory* may help you identify sources. Don't forget faculty at universities, government officials, or business executives. Such individuals are often delighted to be of help.

Step 10: Once you have identified sources you wish to consult, you can determine whether they are readily available in your library. If they are not, ask for them through interlibrary loan. Interlibrary loan is a procedure whereby one library obtains materials from another. This is accomplished through a network of libraries that have agreed to provide access to their collections in return for the opportunity to obtain materials from other libraries in the network. Most libraries have an interlibrary loan form on which relevant information about requested materials is written. Interlibrary loans are generally made for some specific period usually one to two weeks. Very specialised, or rare, publications may take some time to locate, but most materials requested are obtained within a couple of weeks. If you would like to purchase a particular work, consult *Ulrich's International Periodicals Directory*, *Irregular Serials and Annuals: An International Directory*, or *Books in Print* to determine whether a work is in print and where it may be obtained. Local bookstores often have computerised or microform inventories of book wholesalers and can provide rapid access to books and monographic items.

Step 11: Even after an exhaustive search of a library's resources, it is possible that little information will be found. In such cases, it may be necessary to identify experts or other authorities who might provide the information you are seeking or suggest sources you have not yet identified or consulted. Identifying authorities is often a trial-and-error process. One might begin by calling a university department, government agency, or other organisation that employs persons in the field of interest. Reference librarians often can suggest individuals who might be helpful. However, a large number of such calls may be necessary before an appropriate expert is identified.

Source: David W. Stewart, *Secondary Research, Information Sources and Methods* (Beverly Hills. Calif: Sage Publications. 1984) pp. 20–22. Reprinted by permission of Sage Publications, Inc. For reference to the appendix in the table, please consult the original source.

One example of the use to which such information may be put is in anticipating when customers are likely to reorder and in what quantities which provides a good start point for both sales forecasting and production planning.

Because of their nature, a detailed record of financial transactions, accounting records may be too diffuse to be immediately useful. To overcome this difficulty many firms keep customer files which contain a summary (monthly, quarterly, etc.) of transactions together with a synopsis of the data to be found on order forms and invoices. Similarly, the sales function is also likely to keep both statistical and narrative reports of customer contacts. These latter are likely to be fuller and more informative for decision makers as they will usually contain information on prospective or potential customers whereas accounting records only relate to current and past actual customers.

While sales records are compiled primarily to monitor the efficiency and effectiveness of the sales function they may well provide new insights on market opportunities, particularly to third parties who do not automatically accept the status quo as inevitable. A case in point was the analysis undertaken by a consultant of the sales records of a major carpet manufacturer which indicated strong regional biases in the type and colours of carpets sold. For example, Axminster woven carpet sales were much stronger in the north of England and comparatively low in the south, especially the south east. This pattern of sales was accepted as reflecting regional tastes despite the fact that the relative affluence of south versus north meant that the market potential of the former was significantly higher than the latter. The consultant was not persuaded that southerners are radically different from northerners in terms of carpet preferences and some primary research was commissioned to test this hypothesis. The findings indicated that while some differences do exist they are not sufficient to preclude sales of Axminster type carpets in the south and the sales force were given new, much more ambitious targets than those which they had been setting themselves based on past sales trends. The targets were achieved and resulted in a marked improvement in the firm's trading performance.

The point here applies to much of the data which the firm is likely to accumulate in the course of its daily business. People collect information relevant and useful to their own function and needs but this is rarely compared with other information within an organisation to see if this can provide a more complete picture rather than a piece in a jigsaw. For example, most functional specialists will read about their subject to keep up to date, will attend professional meetings, training courses, seminars, exhibitions, trade fairs, etc.

While reports may be written they will usually be read by the individual's line manager and possibly the personnel/training manager and filed away. Except for the very smallest firms, where the level of activity and extent of interpersonal communication is such as to make formal information gathering largely unnecessary, all organisations should have a mechanism for collating and synthesising information relevant to its business from both internal and external sources – particularly internal sources as you have the information anyway!

External sources

In the case of external sources the range and scope is enormous and most organisations will wish to take a highly selective approach to those which are to be monitored continuously. For the rest, some will be worth consulting occasionally and the majority only when they are seen as relevant to a specific and identified information need. In *Marketing* (4th edition) we group external sources into five main categories as follows:

1. Government – domestic and foreign
2. Universities and non-profit organisations
3. Trade associations
4. Academic and professional journals, the trade press
5. Commercial research organisations.

A brief summary of each of these follows.

Government (official) sources

All governments need and collect a vast amount of data much of which is subsequently published. The quality of this data varies from country to country and the user should seek professional advice concerning the accuracy and reliability of foreign data sources (one's own government will usually be quite willing to offer such advice!). The British *Government Statistical Service* (GSS) enjoys the highest of reputations and the following provides a resumé of the services which it offers

> The GSS comprises the statistics division of all major departments plus the two big collecting agencies – the Business Statistics Office and the Office of Population Censuses and Surveys – and the Central Statistical Office which coordinates the system. In sum, it is the greatest concentration of statistical expertise and by far the largest single provider of statistics in the country.

While the GSS exists to service the needs of government a great deal of the information it collects is directly relevant to business (especially marketing) and available in a highly usable form. The following checklist summarises two areas which might be of use to a business firm in a marketing context.

Marketing
— Look at your industry's *Business Monitor, Ministry of Agriculture Information Notice or Housing and Construction Statistics* to compare your own performance against general sales trends and to watch for opportunities for diversification.

— From a variety of sources you can check the number of potential customers in a given sector and compare characteristics with your own customers to highlight possible weaknesses in marketing strategy.
— If you are in consumer lines, trends in expenditure are available from *National Food Survey* and the *Family Expenditure Survey*.
— For test marketing, the *Census of Population* can provide very localised data on numbers of consumers.
— Many statistics are available on a regional or area basis, for example *Regional Trends*, and can assist in determining quotas for area salesmen.
— Watch the foreign competition by looking at the import figures available from agents appointed to compile and market the Customs and Excise Bill of Entry Service data.

Social Change
Firms should also be aware of major changes that are taking place in society which may in time affect the market for their goods and the environment in which they operate. Each year, *Social Trends* records trends and distributions in all areas of social concern – population, households, education, health, housing, environment and leisure are just a few examples. *OPCS Monitor* and reports on the *General Household Survey* also provide valuable information in the field.

Perhaps the most important point to recognise at the outset is that each department prepares and publishes its own statistics (via the HMSO). Following the earlier advice of working from the general to the particular the user would be well advised to start with the free *Government Statistics, a Brief Guide to Sources* or the *Guide to Official Statistics* (HMSO, £21.85 in 1989) which is available for reference in most major libraries. These listings should point the researcher towards those publications which relate specifically to his problem which may be consulted at the Statistics and Market Intelligence Library, the Business Statistics Office or most local libraries, or purchased from HMSO. To get some feel for the type of information available the newcomer might like to acquire *Key Data* which provides an excellent overview compiled from various sources for a modest £3.50 (1989). The scope of this overview is indicated by Table 3.4 which is the Table of Contents.
  If a review of the detailed information does not provide direct answers to the problem then the researcher should write or phone the appropriate department using the addresses/telephone numbers given in the free *Government Statistics – A Brief Guide to Sources*. (This is also reproduced in *Key Data*.)
  A source of particular value to the businessman is *Business Monitor* which:

• Collects information on supply industries and monitors their trends.
• Identifies product categories which are increasing or decreasing.
• Provides performance indicators and trends against which one can compare one's own progress.

TABLE 3.4   **Key data contents page**

CONTENTS

Source: *Key Data* (HMSO, 1988).

A word of caution – data are provided by you and your competitors so you must draw your own conclusions as to its accuracy and reliability!

Universities and non-profit organisations

Universities are pre-eminently vast repositories of knowledge (so too are other institutions of higher learning but universities tend to have the most comprehensive libraries). While most universities engage in and publish research of their own their individual contributions tend to be minor compared with the vast explosion of new information and knowledge which is occurring world wide. However, to enable individuals to pursue original and relevant research it is essential that they be familiar with the current state of the art and it is for this reason that academics and university libraries are an excellent start point for establishing 'what do we know'. It is here you are most likely to find Government publications as well as the academic and professional journals together with expert librarians familiar with abstracting services and on-line data bases of the kind discussed earlier. Further, with the growth of management education in the UK in recent years many new Business Schools have been established accompanied by the setting-up of specialist libraries and information centres which contain extensive collections of company and syndicated data sources, e.g. Henley (Centre for Forecasting), London Business School, City University Business School, UMIST, Warwick, Strathclyde University Graduate Business School Information Centre, etc. An example of the kind of help you will get is provided by Table 3.5 which is a copy of the leaflet given to first-time users of Strathclyde's Business Information Centre.

Trade associations

Trade associations are usually an excellent source of general information on the broad issues of importance to their members. However, as membership of a trade association is usually voluntary much of the information collected is less complete than would be found in the relevant *Business Monitor* as well as suffering from possible accuracy and reliability problems of the kind alluded to earlier. That said, data from trade associations is likely to be more focused and specific and will usually provide good coverage of the firms competing in a particular industry or market.

Analogous to trade associations are the professional bodies such as the Chartered Institute of Marketing, the Market Research Society, the Institute of Purchasing & Supply, the British Institute of Management, Confederation of British Industries, etc. All these organisations provide information services to

56 *Research for marketing*

TABLE 3.5 Strathclyde University's marketing information leaflet

---

Desk research should be the first step in any marketing research project. You will have to provide the effort, but this leaflet aims to provide some of the knowledge — by considering some relevant areas and listing some of the main sources.

HOW LARGE IS THE MARKET?

BUSINESS MONITOR *series is the principal source for detailed product information. Other statistical sources include:*
MONTHLY DIGEST OF STATISTICS SCOTTISH ABSTRACT OF STATISTICS
BRITISH BUSINESS (38) A-Z OF U.K. MARKETING DATA (RD314.1 A-Z)
MGM MARKETING MANUAL OF THE U.K. (in B.I.C. at RD314.i MIR)
Useful sources for overseas data are the Euromonitor Publications:
CONSUMER EUROPE (RD339.4709 CON) CONSUMER MARKETS IN ... (RD339.47)
EUROPEAN MARKETING DATA AND STATISTICS (RD314 EUR)
INTERNATIONAL MARKETING DATA AND STATISTICS (RD310 INT)

WHERE IS THE MARKET?

CENSUS OF PRODUCTION REPORT PA 1002 *gives information on geographical distribution of manufacturing industries, while PA 1003 gives the size distribution of companies.* BUSINESS MONITOR SDA 25 *covers the retail trade, publishing the annual retailing inquiry results.* REGIONAL TRENDS *gives the main economic and social statistics for U.K. regions.*

WHO ARE THE COMPETITORS?

British companies can be identified by any of the following:
KOMPASS (RD380.1025 KOM)   KEY BRITISH ENTERPRISES (RD380.1025 KEY)
SELL'S DIRECTORY OF PRODUCTS AND SERVICES (RD380.1025 SEL)
SCOTLAND'S NATIONAL REGISTER OF CLASSIFIED TRADES (RD380.1025 SCO)
SCOTTISH COUNCIL LIST OF MANUFACTURING COMPANIES IN SCOTLAND (IN B.I.C. AT RD338.0025 SCO)
For more detailed company information, consult the EXTEL BRITISH COMPANY CARD *services or the company annual reports in B.I.C.*

Overseas company sources include:
STANDARD & POOR'S REGISTER OF CORPORATIONS (IN B.I.C. AT RD338.7402 STA)
EUROPE'S 15000 LARGEST COMPANIES (RD338.7409 EUR)
PRINCIPAL INTERNATIONAL BUSINESSES (RD338.7402 DUN)

WHAT ARE THE TRENDS?

Possible sources to consider:

ECONOMIC TRENDS	EUROPEAN TRENDS (338.984.4(4))
FAMILY EXPENDITURE SURVEY	GENERAL HOUSEHOLD SURVEY
MARKETING IN EUROPE (658.83(4))	RETAIL BUSINESS (658.87)
SOCIAL TRENDS	MINTEL MARKET INTELLIGENCE (B.I.C.)

IS THERE A SURVEY OF THE INDUSTRY?

Market research surveys tend to be expensive. Consequently, few are held in the library. Check the online catalogue under your specific subject to identify what the library may hold. JORDAN INDUSTRY SURVEYS *and* KEY NOTE *market research reports, kept in the B.I.C. are industry and market sector reports giving market background, economic trends, prospects and company performance.*

Frequent surveys appear in the financial press. The best and most up-to-date index to identify these in RESEARCH INDEX. *This is a fortnightly index arranged in two sections covering industrial and commercial news, and companies.*

TABLE 3.5 – *contd*

ARE THERE ANY ASSOCIATIONS WHICH MIGHT HELP?
DIRECTORY OF BRITISH ASSOCIATIONS (RD068.41 DIR) *will identify trade associations and professional institutes in the UK and outline their activities and publications.*

WHAT ABOUT A TRADE DIRECTORY?

All British industry, trade and professional directories can be identified using
CURRENT BRITISH DIRECTORIES (DO16.05 CUR)

ABSTRACTS AND INDEXES

BUSINESS PERIODICALS INDEX (DO16.65), MARKET RESEARCH ABSTRACTS (DO16.6588)
ANBAR MARKETING AND DISTRIBUTION ABSTRACTS (DO16.65/6), RESEARCH INDEX (DO16.65)
THE TIMES INDEX (DO16.0721), THE NEW YORK TIMES INDEX (DO16.0714)

GUIDE TO SOURCES

A great variety of published information sources exist. The following guides may help you in your search.

Market Information
MARKET RESEARCH SOURCEBOOK (RD658.83 WAL)
PRINCIPAL SOURCES OF MARKETING INFORMATION, BY C. HULL (DO16.6588 HUL)

Market Research Surveys
MARKETSEARCH (DO16.6588 MAR)
PUBLISHED DATA ON EUROPEAN INDUSTRIAL MARKETS (DO16.6588 IND)

Statistics
GUIDE TO OFFICIAL STATISTICS (DO16.3141 CEN)
SISCIS: SUBJECT INDEX TO SOURCES OF COMPARATIVE INTERNATIONAL STATISTICS (DO16.31 PIE)

Companies
EUROPEAN COMPANIES: A GUIDE TO SOURCES OF INFORMATION (DO16.3387 HEN)
MULTINATIONAL CORPORATIONS: THE ECSIM GUIDE TO INFORMATION SOURCES (DO16.6581 MUL)

*   *   *   *

MITCHELL LIBRARY, North Street, Glasgow.

This library is part of the City's public reference collections. The commercial section exists to meet the needs of the City's business community and provides printed material on all aspects of economics and commerce. It has a good collection of trade directories and journals and, in addition to many of the sources already noted, it takes:
MCCARTHY CARDS – *a card service on which are reproduced extracts from the press covering companies and industries.*
MONTHLY INDEX TO THE FINANCIAL TIMES

*   *   *   *

You will have realised by now that there is no single source for marketing problems. Familiarise yourself early on with how the library works. There are other library guides to help you – as well as the library staff.

N.B. Where no classification number appears in this leaflet next to a title, it is shelved in the Government Publications Section on level 5.

Compiled by Christine D. Reid, 9/88

members and while these may vary in terms of both quantity and quality they invariably provide a useful jumping-off point at little or no cost to members.

Another source of this kind which is often overlooked but which is a particularly useful source of local information is the Chamber of Commerce. While these vary considerably in size and activity level an approach at the early stages of a secondary information search is always worthwhile.

Commercial research organisations

Commercial research organisations frequently publish standardised reports on specific topics or issues for the use of multiple clients. This *syndicated research* is the subject of Chapter 11 and will not be considered further here. Similarly, the conduct of primary research on behalf of a client is beyond the scope of this chapter but is a central issue in the next chapter which considers the merits of buying-in primary research rather than doing it oneself.

Summary

In this chapter we have examined the role of secondary or desk research as the recommended first step in addressing marketing decision problems of the kind identified in Chapter 2. On the premise that very few problems are truly unique it makes good common-sense to see if one can find how others may have addressed similar kinds of problems in the past. The obvious source of such information is the published record and the knowledge/experience of others who may be willing to share this with you formally or informally. While the emphasis in this chapter has been upon published data the problem solver will often find personal sources more 'user friendly' if for no other reason that one can interact directly with them in a manner which is rarely possible with impersonal, published sources.

On the other hand, one needs to know the questions to ask as well as of whom to ask them and published sources will often provide essential background to seeking personal advice (Purists may consider consulting others to be primary research which merely confirms the fact that writers seek to impose structure on a subject to enable a 'logical' presentation which is rarely a reflection of the dynamic reality.)

On balance the consideration of the advantages and disadvantages associated with secondary research suggests that low cost and comparatively easy access will mediate concerns as to the accuracy, reliability and relevance of published information and so reinforces the view that secondary research should always precede formal primary research (as opposed to informal personal inquiries).

As with most things an organised approach and procedure are most likely to yield worthwhile results and three 'models' of increasing degrees of detail were considered as a guide to actually undertaking secondary research.

To conclude the chapter we reviewed some of the major internal and external sources of information available with some indication of their possible use.

On occasion the researcher will be lucky and find the solution to his problem as a result of his secondary research. In most cases, however, while the secondary information will shed considerable light on the decision maker's problem and help clarify the issues involved it will rarely provide a complete answer to his specific concern. There will exist an 'information gap' and it is to this we turn in the next chapter which is concerned with defining this and deciding how to close it.

References

Churchill, Gilbert A. (1987) *Marketing Research-Methodological Foundations*, 4th edn (New York: Holt, Rinehart & Winston).

Hague, P.N. (1987) *The Industrial Market Research Handbook*, 2nd edn (London: Kogan Page).

Kinnear, Thomas C. and Taylor, James R. (1987) *Marketing Research: An Applied Approach*, 3rd edn (New York: McGraw-Hill).

Luck, David J. and Rubin, Ronald S. (1987) *Market Research*, 7th edn (Englewood Cliffs, NJ, Prentice-Hall).

Newson-Smith, Nigel (1988) 'Desk Research', Chapter 1 in Robert Worcester and John Downham (eds) *Consumer Market Research Handbook*, 3rd rev. edn (McGraw-Hill).

Parasuraman, A. (1986) *Marketing Research* (Reading, Mass.: Addison-Wesley).

Stoll, Martin and Stewart, David W. (1984) *Secondary Research: Information Sources and Methods* (Beverly Hills, California, Sage).

CHAPTER 4

What do we need to know?

Introduction

In the preceding chapter we explored the ways in which secondary or desk research could be used to help solve marketing problems. Given the nature of secondary data, namely that it was collected at some time in the past to help clarify and/or solve someone else's information need, it would be surprising if it exactly satisfied the requirements of another decision-maker with a newly identified problem. This being so it is likely that a 'gap' will exist between what is known and what the problem-solver believes he or she needs to know to come to a decision.

Clearly, the nature and extent of an information gap will be situation specific and so cannot be dealt with directly in a book of this kind. However, there are four issues which need to be addressed, which are common to all such considerations, and these will form the subject matter of this chapter, namely:

1. What is involved in defining and developing a research brief to close the information gap?
2. What is the information worth?
3. Should the work be undertaken in-house or bought-in?
4. If it is to be bought-in how should one set about selecting an agent?

Defining and developing a research brief

In many fields of inquiry it is expected that the person defining a research problem will be the person responsible for its solution. This assumption is fundamental to the whole concept of doctoral research and is central to the idea of project-related work which has become an integral part of many formal educational qualifications at both undergraduate and postgraduate levels. In the case of the latter the purpose of project work is to give the student some exposure to the purpose, nature, procedures and techniques of research so that they will be able to judge the quality and acceptability of research undertaken by others, and of the problems to be addressed and overcome. Project work also provides some initial skills training and provides a foundation for more sophisticated research training if this is desired.

To some extent, however, this experience is a double-edged weapon for in the process of exposing the novice to the research process it may also give them the impression that it is a comparatively straightforward albeit sometimes demanding exercise. Later chapters in this book provide an overview of methodology and techniques. It is to be hoped that these will serve the dual purpose of demonstrating that, while being nothing to be afraid of, the professional aspects of research are just that and require knowledge, application and skill if they are to be deployed effectively.

The message we are seeking to communicate may be summarised in four basic propositions:

1. There is no mystery to the conduct of scientific research, but
2. Its effective practice requires knowledge, skills and experience.
3. Users need sufficient understanding to be able to judge if these are present and being exercised, but
4. They should not attempt to design research procedures unless they have pursued formal education and training themselves, including the successful execution of real projects under supervision.

In other words we are proposing that decision makers will normally work with professional researchers in solving particular problems rather than seek to solve them entirely by themselves. This view was expressed some years ago by Andrew Ehrenberg (1964) who challenged the proposition that the market researcher should be restricted to 'describing the facts' and argued that researchers must play a much more active role to ensure the successful commissioning and execution of research. In doing so the researcher will be called upon to exercise judgement and selectiveness 'in reaching agreement on a research brief, in devising the ensuing research procedures, in carrying them out, and in analysing and condensing the final results'.

Probably the first area where the researcher will be called upon to exercise judgement is in clarifying the precise problem which is to provide the substance of the research brief. It will be recalled that in general terms marketing problems tend to possess a number of common characteristics which, while not necessarily distinguishing them from other problems, certainly call for particular care. Among these characteristics may be numbered:

1. Many marketing problems are multidimensional and very complex and so cannot be expected to yield direct one to one relationships of the kind found in the experimental sciences.
2. Many marketing problems are more or less unique in the sense that they call for a decision on a combination of factors and circumstances that are unlikely to be encountered again in precisely the same form.
3. A large proportion of marketing problems concern future decisions and so contain greater uncertainty than those concerned with current decisions, e.g. with production or distribution.
4. The substance of market research is frequently concerned with how buyers will respond to given marketing 'treatments' but exposure to the 'treatment' may lead the buyer to modify their behaviour both during and subsequent to the research.

Given these characteristics it is unsurprising that marketers may have difficulty in formulating research briefs which capture the essence of the problem which they wish to solve. That said, the growth of marketing education and the increasing professionalism of marketers has resulted in the emergence of a cadre of managers sufficiently versed in the technical aspects of social science research that they can communicate effectively with professional marketing researchers. (One of this book's objectives!) However, Ehrenberg's (1964) advice on the relation of the research brief to the marketing problem still holds good. Namely, the research brief must:

a) mean the same thing to all concerned,
b) not ask for irrelevant information,
c) define the relevant population(s) to be sampled,
d) state the right variables to be measured,
e) give some indication of the required accuracy of the main results,
f) give at least an order of priority for the required accuracy of the various specified breakdown analyses,
g) not prejudge the selection of research techniques and procedures.

Remember, the purpose of the research brief is to enable the professional researcher to propose what he considers the most cost effective way of providing an answer or answers to the marketer's problem, i.e. the *brief* results in the *proposal*.

In developing a brief to address a marketing problem he wishes to solve the marketer should provide the researcher with at least the following background information:

1. *Background to the problem*, i.e. who the sponsor is, the products he makes and the markets he serves, the nature of competition and the event(s) which have precipitated identification of the problem.

2. *Nature of the problem*: what precisely is the issue or problem the marketer has identified, e.g. loss of market share in an existing market; uncertainty as to the positioning of a new product; identification of gaps or niches in particular markets; implications of withdrawing a product from the market, etc.
3. *What information is needed?* What information does the sponsor believe he needs to reduce or eliminate the uncertainty concerning the appropriate action to be taken? eg usage patterns; lifestyle/psychographic profiles of existing segments; perceptual map? etc.
4. *What does the sponsor intend/want to do with the information provided?* In some cases research is wanted as background to help inform a decision, in others it is expected to give a clear go–no go indication. This has major implications for the techniques to be used, the extent and quality of the data to be collected and the degree of precision required of the analysis. Experience suggests this is the area where misunderstanding is most likely to occur in that sponsors frequently want precise answers where none in fact can be given, e.g. point estimates of demand.
5. *What are the time and budgetary constraints?* Some sponsors are reluctant to give a firm budgetary indication but in the absence of this the researcher, is left with the classic 'how long is a piece of string' problem. One solution is to provide a range, e.g. £50 000 to £80 000 and ask the researcher to show what the additional benefits would be if the base budget is exceeded.

The purpose of developing a research brief may be summarised briefly as being:

1. To ensure both parties share a common understanding of the problem to be solved.
2. To force the client to make his needs and ideas both clear and explicit.
3. To ensure the agent develops a design, and uses procedures, and techniques which will address directly the client's needs.
4. To make it possible to solicit and compare objectively the proposals of more than one agent.
5. To provide a reference point in the case of any dispute as to what was to be undertaken, by whom, when, with what intended outcome and at what cost.
6. To provide a reference point for comparing actual outcomes with desired objectives.

On occasion the client may bridle at the preparation of a formal proposal on one or other of the following grounds:

1. 'There's no time.'
2. 'The problem is so obvious it doesn't need stating formally.'
3. 'You did a study like this for us three years ago – just repeat it.'
4. 'I've told you what I want doing – just get on with it.'

Few if any professional market researchers – internal or external – would accept such a brief and rightly so. If the client cannot specify what his problem is precisely, it's highly unlikely that anything you do will be satisfactory. Further, as we have tried to demonstrate in earlier chapters, the clear specification of a problem is a necessary although not sufficient condition for its solution.

However, on the same basis that patients often consult their doctor on the grounds that they feel unwell and that they can describe the symptoms to him for diagnosis and prognosis so it may be that a firm recognises it is losing competitiveness owing to loss of market share, declining margins, increased complaints etc., but it may be unclear as to the cause or causes, of its problems and call in the researcher to help diagnose the situation. Faced with such a problem the researcher may well have to develop a research brief for his client. However, this is still essential for how, otherwise, will the parties be able to determine whether the action taken has satisfied the predetermined objectives. Hague (1987) in the *Industrial Market Research Handbook* provides a very helpful checklist to guide the researcher in this task and this is reproduced as Table 4.1 below.

TABLE 4.1   Checklist to guide a researcher when taking a brief

---

History
How long has the company been established?
How long has it concentrated on its present product range?
What was the company's product range originally, and 10, 20, 30 years ago?
Has the company always been sited in its present location?
What factors have influenced its location?

Company background
What is the principal business of the company?
What are its subsidiary activities?
What is its total turnover: (a) UK, (b) export?
Describe any holding companies/subsidiary companies.
How many employees are there at the establishment?

Product details
What are the important products in the range (by size, capacity, shape, material, etc.)?
What proportion of the total turnover in these products does each of the above groups account for?
To what extent are the products standard/custom built?
What proportion of an assembled product is made in-house or bought out?
How important are spares in terms of revenue *v* profit?
Are any of the products built under licence?

Pricing
What are the prices for each of the important products (are these prices trade or retail)?
How do prices compare with those of the competition?
Is there a published price-list?

What is the discount policy?
What power does the salesman have to alter prices?
How sensitive are sales in the product thought to be?

Sales force
Number of representatives?
Are they a general or a specialised sales force – in what way are they specialised?
How many calls a day do they make?
Do the reps bring back orders or are they sent in independently?
Are agents used in the UK – if so, where and why?

Markets
What are the major markets for the products?
What is the proportion of total sales to each of these markets?
Are any markets known for the product where the company currently does not/cannot sell?
Which markets are believed to offer the greatest scope for expansion of sales?
Who are the major customers? What share of sales do the top 20 account for?

Decision makers
Who are the key personnel in a company who decide whether this type of product should be bought? What roles do they play?
Who are the key decision makers in a company who decide who the supplier of the product should be? What role do they play?
What do decision makers look for from suppliers?
PROBE price, quality, delivery, sales service.

Quality
Where does the product fit against the competition's in its quality?
What are the special features of its quality?
Where is it weak on quality?
How long will the product last?
When it finally fails, why will it do so?

Delivery
What is the current delivery period?
What is the competition's delivery?
What is the ideal delivery?

Competition
Who are the most important competitors? Where are they based?
What is their rank order/market share?
What are each company's (including the sponsor's) perceived strengths and weaknesses?
To what extent do competitors rely upon this market for their turnover and profit?

Distribution
How is the product distributed?
What proportion goes direct/indirect? What is the policy which leads to this split (e.g. size of account: original equipment manufacturer *v* replacement etc.)?
What are distributors' margins?

What other products do distributors sell?
Do distributors actively sell or just take orders?
Who are the main distributors:
  (a) used by the company?
  (b) not used by the company?
What is the average size of a direct account and distributor account?

Promotion
How big is the promotional budget?
How does this break down between:
  (a) media, (b) exhibitions, (c) PR,
  (d) print, (e) direct mail, (f) others?'
Which media are used? Which are most successful?
What proportion of sales leads comes from promotion? How many? What is their quality?
Which exhibitions are attended? What is their perceived value?

Other data
Full details of names (with initials) of persons present at briefing; date of briefing; address of company; address to which proposals should be sent.
How any copies of the proposal are required — to be sent separately or *en bloc*?

Source: Paul N. Hague, (1987) *The Industrial Market Research Handbook*, 2nd edn (London: Kogan Page).

The importance of the research brief is that it forms the basis of the agreement between client and researcher. Where this is a formal and contractual agreement between two organisations then it is especially important that it satisfy certain minimum criteria and most of the professional research bodies provide specific advice on this to both members and prospective clients alike.

What is information worth?

As noted earlier, when asked to review the proposal for this book a distinguished practitioner queried why the author intended to address this issue particularly in terms of the *expected value of perfect information* (EVPI) on the grounds that in all his experience he had never come across anyone who actually did this. In Chapter 2 we reviewed some guidelines from Alreck and Settle (1985) for assessing the value of information which might have satisfied this critic as broadly based subjective questions which would be very helpful in deciding whether there was a prima facie case for spending time and money on acquiring further information. Of course, the crux of the issue is that if there is a prima facie case one is still left with the question as to precisely how much should one spend?

As with most innovations there is a delay in the take up and adoption of any idea or methodology which seeks to replace the current way of doing things. In the case of management practices the delay between introduction and take-off is frequently of the order of a generation or 25 years. Possibly this is because it takes those equipped with these ideas this length of time to climb sufficiently far up the corporate ladder to have a significant impact on corporate cultures and 'the way we do things around here'! Marketing itself was rediscovered in the 1950s but it was the 1980s before it really 'took-off' – statistical techniques for assisting decision making under uncertainty were pioneered at the Harvard Business School in the late 1960s by Raiffa and Schlaiffer – their time may well be at hand! Whether or not the techniques proposed by the Bayesian analyst ever become commonplace (although this seems more likely with the development of user-friendly software for PCs) no professional decision-maker can afford to ignore the potential which these methods offer for combining judgement and information to arrive at decisions consistent with the decision maker's overall attitude to risk.

In *Marketing Strategy and Management* several pages (216–27) are devoted to a discussion of Bayesian analysis, its role in defining problems and specifying alternatives, the development of decision trees and the assignment of probabilities to the perceived alternatives. This discussion will not be repeated here. However, it is worthwhile repeating that the three concepts central to the Bayesian methodology are:

(1) the identification of alternatives;
(2) the assignment of probabilistic expectations to the alternatives; and
(3) the use of expected value (utility) as the decision criterion.

The decision of whether to invest in the acquisition of additional information prior to taking a decision on a course of action is a classic situation for the application of the technique. An excellent discussion of the issues supported by a worked example is to be found in Michael Barron and David Targett's paper 'Sales Forecasting, Market Research and the Value of Information' (*Marketing Intelligence and Planning*, vol, 4, no 3, 1983).

Barron and Targett begin by pointing out that market research is not usually needed for its own sake. 'It is simply a means to an end and that end is generally a business decision.' Further, most market research information is indirect in the sense that it cannot make the decision for you, it can only inform the decision to be made.

If information is direct it is extremely easy to judge its value. For example, correct advice saying 'Do this and you will earn an extra £1 million' is clearly worth £1 million. However, when the link between the advice and the pay-off is less direct, it is much more difficult to work out its value. Hence it becomes much more difficult to decide whether the information is really worth the cost and delay involved.

Viewed in isolation the key criteria for assessing information are accuracy and quantity, with more always being perceived as being better than less. This perception may well account for the widespread phenomena of 'information overload' and 'paralysis by analysis' reflected in the ever-growing piles of computer print out that accumulate on the decision-maker's desk not to mention the direct mailshots that fill his dustbin. To control this disease one must recall that quantity does not necessarily equate with quality, that price or expenditure is not the same as value, and that in most situations more is worth less owing to the operation of the law of diminishing returns. Against this background frustrated decision makers may well question whether the acquisition of still more information is really worthwhile particularly when the need to make a decision is pressing and that, after all, is what they are paid for. Perhaps it is this mind-set which has led to the short-term strategic decision making horizon for which UK and USA businessmen have been so roundly criticised in recent years? After all the shorter the time horizon the more likely it becomes that the outcome will be similar to prevailing conditions and the less the risk involved.

Barron and Targett argue that 'In order to find out how good information needs to be it is necessary to look closely at the interrelationship between the decisions that have to be made and the information which influences those decisions.' In doing so two obvious principles need to be taken into account. First, decision making is concerned with resolving uncertainty and, second, the value of information must be judged against the level of one's existing and prior knowledge. Thus the value of additional information is relative to the improvement in overall knowledge and the reduction in perceived uncertainty which this achieves. To illustrate this point Barron and Targett take sales forecasting as an example for here the decision maker has past sales records from which to extrapolate and will probably come up with an estimate of likely sales levels for the coming year given various assumptions about inflation, competition, etc. In their example the sales manager estimates that the likelihood of sales falling between £40–£50 million is 71 per cent which, of course, is equivalent to saying there is a 29 per cent chance it will be more or less than that. While many of the factors which will affect this out-turn may be outwith the sales manager's control there clearly would be considerable value in firming up this forecast even if only to eliminate some of the less likely out-turns. So, what is information worth?

'The value of information will inevitably change depending on the circumstances.' Unfortunately, as Barron and Targett go on to observe ' . . . the precise relationship between the quality of the information and the associated decision is fairly complicated, and the formal mathematical theory can make it seem even more difficult than it really is.' To clarify the relationship they provide a second worked example of a food company which is considering substituting a cheaper ingredient in one of its products. The problem is that while the change will save £2 million if customers detect this they are likely to switch to other competing brands which could cost up to £14 million. In the absence of any information it is estimated that about 20 per cent of customers might notice the difference so that one can draw a decision pay-off table as in Table 4.2 below.

TABLE 4.2 Decision pay-off table

Actual outcome	Estimated probability (%)	Change ingredient (£)	Do not change ingredient (£)
Customer can detect the difference	20	−14m	0m
Customer cannot detect the difference	80	2m	0m
Expected monetary value (EMV)		−1.2m	0m

The key figure in this table is the EMV for it indicates that if 20 per cent of the customers switch brands the firm will lose 20 per cent of its £14 million current profit = £2.8 million. Because of this reduction in sales volume only 80 per cent of the anticipated savings of £2 million will accrue which is equivalent to a gain of £1.6 million. Thus the overall result of the change will be a loss of £1.2 million which is the EMV. This same information can be used to calculate the value of perfect information (EVPI).

The easier and more appealing method if calculating EVPI is to ask whether such information would change the original decision not to change the ingredient because a loss of £1.2m was anticipated. Suppose new information indicates that customers will not notice any difference which means we can change the ingredient and save £2 million. But our current information suggests that the likelihood of customers *not* noticing is only 80 per cent or .8 so the expected value of this gain can only be £2 million × 0.8 = £1.6 million. The same result would, of course, have been obtained if we had combined the probability of 20 per cent noticing the change × £0 million = £0 million plus 80 per cent × £2 million who would not = £1.6 million. Either way the maximum value of any additional information, ie. 'perfect information' can only be £1.6 million. Barron and Targett conclude:

It also illustrates one of the most important results of information theory. This states that the value of any information system is the *expected value of the gains from any changed decisions*. The corollary, which is even more important, says that if there is no possibility of changed decisions, the information system has no value. [Our emphasis]

The authors continue to develop these arguments with further examples but now is the time to test whether you have acquired the secondary data research skills discussed in Chapter 3 and can acquire the original source if you feel this additional information has value for you!

With a little practice the identification of alternatives and the assignment of initial probabilities based on one's extant knowledge will become fairly straightforward and will provide an extremely useful yardstick for making decisions as to how much time and effort it would be worth expending to improve on the status quo. Without such an analysis it is difficult to see how one can estimate what information is really worth in any given situation.

In-house or bought-in?

In a survey of critical success factors and corporate performance Baker and Hart (1989) found that comparatively few of their sample had an in-house market research function (about 42 per cent). The position improved when all sources of marketing research were taken into account to 58 per cent utilisation. (A result very similar to that reported by Hooley and West and discussed in Chapter 1.) In light of the frequently confirmed finding that the major cause of new product failure is inadequate understanding of the market, it is difficult to understand why firms seem so reluctant to use marketing research. This lack of expenditure on marketing research is even more difficult to understand when considered against other marketing expenditures such as personal selling, advertising and promotion.

However, as competitive pressures increase and firms struggle to maintain their position it seems likely that the value of marketing research will be 'discovered' in much the same way that marketing itself was seized on as a panacea for difficult trading conditions as supply capability began to outstrip effective demand in the 1950s. As with so many other management 'fashions', however, its true value will only be achieved if it is fully integrated into top management decision-taking – if it is regarded as a service function and left to its own devices it will have little or no impact as was the case with marketing and strategic planning departments when detached from main line decision making.

If experience with strategic planning is heeded then the most effective solution as to the location and management of marketing research is that senior managers with responsibilities for policy formulation and decision making will assume 'ownership' of the marketing research function and appoint a team of in-house specialists to service their information needs and be responsible for the establishment and maintenance of the firm's marketing information system. The size and scope of this in-house facility will depend very much upon the size of the firm and the nature of its business. The larger the firm and the more extensive its interface with ultimate consumers the greater the potential and value of keeping research in-house. Even here, however, the economies of scale available from syndicated research, omnibus surveys and the use of an established field interviewing operation will dispose the firm to buy in certain services. Conversely, small firms operating in stable markets may find that a single person is sufficient to maintain the MIS to help develop research briefs and assess agency proposals where specific *ad hoc* pieces of research are deemed desirable.

Specialist texts provide information and advice on the establishment of an in-house marketing research function. While this is beyond the scope of this book now that you know how to establish the value of alternative courses of action at least you will be able to structure the problem and decide how much it is worth to set up your own market research function! However, even if you do you will still need to use the services of a professional agency from time to time and it is this we examine in the final section of this chapter.

Selecting a market research agency

If the manager decides that he will require external assistance in closing his information gap then he will have to identify and commission a suitable agent to execute the research on his behalf. The UK is fortunate in that it possesses one of the largest and most skilled market research professions in the world – indeed, it is probably true to say that this is the one aspect of marketing where the UK leads the USA in terms of the development of specialised methodologies and techniques. However, this sophistication is a double-edged weapon for the first-time research buyer for it means that he is faced with a plethora of organisations from large full-service agencies to small 'boutiques' specialising in a particular technique or approach. How then does one set about selecting a suitable agency?

Most textbooks, like this one, will offer generalised advice as to what to look for in an agency, how to develop and agree a research design, how to assess the quality and skill exhibited by the agency in executing the research design and how to assess the final report submitted by the agent. All this is very valuable in terms of the how, what and when of market research but is less helpful in addressing the practical questions of who should I approach? Where will I find them? and why should I prefer one agency over another? To answer these latter questions we would do well to follow the general advice offered in terms of all secondary research — namely, work from the general to the particular, be methodical and consult directories and indexes before looking at detailed and specialist information, seek the advice of others with prior knowledge and experience, document all the advice and then follow-up with the sources/agencies which seem most relevant to your research problem. Following this advice lead the author to identify and acquire four key information sources in addition to the handbook of the Market Research Society of which he is a member.

1. The Key Note Guide *Buying Market Research* first published in 1989 by Key Note Publications Ltd.
2. The Handbook of AMSO - the Association of Market Survey Organisations.
3. The Handbook of ABMRC - the Association of British Market Research Companies.
4. The guidelines of the ICC and Esomar.

The Codes of Conduct and Guidelines of the Societies and Associations give first-class advice of what to look for when commissioning an agency and the code of practice to which member agencies are expected to adhere in performing marketing research for their clients. However, before turning to this detailed advice (the particular!) it will be helpful to say a little more about the organisations and publications referred to above.

The Market Research Society (MRS):

> is the incorporated professional association in the United Kingdom for those using survey techniques for marketing, social and economic research. Founded some 40 years ago, it has grown in size and stature alongside the profession it represents and now, with approximately 6,500 members, it is the largest body of its kind in the world. (1989 *Yearbook*).

Whereas AMSO and ABMRC are trade associations, MRS is a professional society comprised of individual members many of whom, of course, work for the specialist research companies. However, as a cursory glance at the membership list reveals, MRS draws its membership from academe, from the public sector and private commercial organisations representing the full spectrum of business activity. MRS has a strong commitment to both formal academic education through its diploma scheme and to professional formation and development through a wide-ranging programme of specialised seminars, and regular meetings. Like the other bodies it has a code of conduct which is monitored by the Professional Standards Committee and also a Technical and Development Committee responsible for the conduct of technical studies and investigations and the dissemination of their findings to members and interested parties. The society issues a range of publications including the *MRS Yearbook* containing the code of conduct, list of members and a detailed listing of organisations providing market research services. The *Newsletter* is issued monthly. The *Journal of the Market Research Society*, a scholarly and refereed journal, and *Survey* a magazine concerned with the value and applications of market research appear quarterly. All these sources and *Market Research Abstracts* are referenced extensively throughout this text and constitute an invaluable source of current information about the profession and practice of market research.

AMSO is an association of 31 of the largest UK research organisations accounting for nearly 80 per cent of UK turnover. Its members include the best known firms in public opinion polling such as Gallup, MORI and NOP, and in the provision of syndicated services (AGB, Nielsen, BMRB, etc.).

AMSO publishes a handbook which is free on application which provides background information on the Association together with profiles of each of the members – address, turnover, main areas of research, data collection techniques/methods and directors' names, together with a description of other distinguishing characteristics/features. The handbook also contains useful advice on commissioning research, getting value for money, scope of services available much of which has been incorporated in our treatment of these topics.

ABMRC was founded in 1982 and now has over 100 members. Unlike AMSO members they do not have to be full-service companies although a number of members satisfy this criterion. As well as representing the professional and commercial interests of its members ABMRC is concerned with promoting confidence in marketing research among both clients and the public at large. Among its major efforts to support these ends ABMRC operates a Code of Business Practice, which provides additional protection to clients over and above that offered by the MRS, and is responsible for an interviewer card scheme which is intended to reassure members of the public about interviewers bona fides.

The International Chamber of Commerce ICC is the world business organisation. It acts to promote the greater freedom of world trade, to harmonise and facilitate business and trade practices, and to represent the business community at international levels. Paris based, the Chamber is represented by National Committees in 55 countries and has members in over 40 others.

Together with ESOMAR the ICC is the sponsor of the Guidelines and Code of Practice cited earlier in the chapter.

Summary

In this chapter we have attempted to provide answers to four specific questions:

1. What is involved in defining and developing a research brief to close the information gap between what we know, based upon past knowledge and experience and the outcome of any secondary research, and what we believe we need to know to solve our problem?
2. What is the information worth? While the use of formal techniques to assess the value of more and better information is limited it is anticipated that the increase in competition coupled with the potential for information overload will predispose more managers to make use of proven techniques for answering this question.
3. Should the work be undertaken in-house or bought in? Here the evidence suggests that all companies should have an operational marketing information system (MIS) but, beyond that, the decision will depend very much upon the size of company, the nature of its products and the markets in which it is working.
4. If research is bought-in how should one set about selecting an agent? On this topic some basic advice is provided but this is also a subject to which we return in several later chapters in reviewing methodology and techniques.

In Chapter 5 we shall now turn to look at the problems associated with developing a research design by considering the alternative methodologies available to us.

References

Alreck, Pamela L. and Settle, Robert B. (1985) *The Survey Research Handbook* (Homewood, Ill.: Richard D. Irwin).

Barron, Michael and Targett, David (1986) 'Sales Forecasting, Market Research and the Value of Information', in *Marketing Intelligence and Planning*, 4 (3) (19) pp. 12–31.

Ehrenberg, A.S.C. (1964) 'What Research for What Problem?', *Research in Marketing* (Market Research Society) pp. 46–66.

Hague, Paul N. (1987) *The Industrial Market Research Handbook*, 2nd edition (London: Kegan Paul).

CHAPTER 5

Developing a research design

Introduction

In the preceding chapter we addressed the question of the information gap between what we know, based upon experience, knowledge and a review of relevant secondary sources, and what we believe we need to know in order to solve the problem which we have defined as calling for solution. In the course of this examination we looked at the value of information and explored the issue of whether we should seek to carry out primary or field research on our own behalf or buy it in from a professional marketing research agency. Irrespective of that decision consideration must be given to the manner in which the primary research is to be carried out either as the basis for undertaking the work oneself, or as the basis for briefing an agent, or for assessing proposals if no guidance is given to prospective agents as to a preferred approach.

In this chapter we consider first the scientific approach to problem solving. Next we look at the three basic approaches to collecting primary data – observation, experimentation, and survey – and then take stock of qualitative research methodology building upon the earlier discussion in Chapter 2. Finally, we consider the role of longitudinal studies as an alternative to the more commonplace one-off or cross-sectional analysis.

The scientific approach to problem solving

In the opening paragraph of the first chapter of what is widely considered to be the definitive text for research students in the social sciences, Selltiz *et al.* (2nd edn, 1959) state unequivocally:

The purpose of research is to discover answers to questions through the application of scientific procedures. These procedures have been developed in order to increase the likelihood that the information gathered will be relevant to the question asked and will be reliable and unbiased. To be sure, there is no guarantee that any given research undertaking actually will produce relevant, reliable, and unbiased information. But scientific procedures are more likely to do so than any other method known to man.

Many of the chapters of this book are taken up with describing some of these procedures, their strengths and weaknesses and possible applications. However, before looking at them it will be helpful to define the nature of the scientific method itself.

At the outset it is necessary to recognise that while social science research in general, and marketing research in the particular, follows the same basic process as pure scientific research and is based upon the same procedures of observation and experimentation, it differs significantly in that, as well as information, social science research is concerned with subjective, human values. The point about any research is that it is triggered by a desire to know more about a phenomenon and it appears possible that more information on this may be obtained through observation and experimentation. In the pure sciences where one is dealing with objective data then the cycle of scientific research would follow the sequence illustrated in Figure 5.1 which is derived from Popper (1968).

In the pure sciences the process of research is predominantly intellectual and prompted by the desire to improve and increase knowledge and understanding of the world in which we live. Intellectual curiosity also underlies applied and social science research but here the dominant motivation is usually practical – the desire to improve on something or even create something new with a specific end use or purpose in mind. That said, the process is largely the same albeit that the objects of social science research are often less amenable to research than other natural phenomena. In part this intractability may be due to the relative youth of modern social science compared with the modern natural sciences (in the Golden Age of the Greek philosophers and for many centuries thereafter there was no distinction between them!).

In the natural sciences research has uncovered the existence of natural laws such that it has been possible to develop theoretical explanations not just of how things are but also how, given observance of the qualifying conditions, they will be in the future. While some progress has been made in the social sciences the theoretical foundations are less secure and the ability to replicate exactly tests of one's theory and hypotheses make it difficult, if not impossible, for the social scientist to predict outcomes with the same accuracy and reliability as the pure scientist.

Of course, pure science does not stand still either, which is why the research cycle is common to them both. At the outset one recognises the existence of a

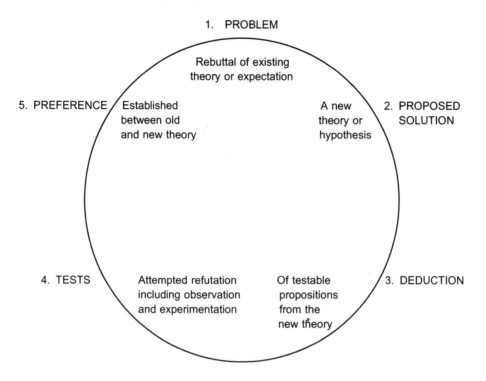

1. PROBLEM

5. PREFERENCE

2. PROPOSED SOLUTION

4. TESTS

3. DEDUCTION

Rebuttal of existing theory or expectation

Established between old and new theory

A new theory or hypothesis

Attempted refutation including observation and experimentation

Of testable propositions from the new theory

FIGURE 5.1   The cycle of scientific research

problem because one's existing knowledge and/or experience is insufficient to guide or inform one exactly how to proceed. Faced with a problem one is most likely to speculate or *hypothesise* as to the answer by drawing on past knowledge or experience and extrapolating from it. In cases where one has strong feelings about the likely outcome then one may formulate positive hypotheses while, where one is uncertain and can anticipate several possible outcomes then one would formulate a null hypothesis. Selltiz *et al.*, (1959) cite Cohen and Nagel (1934) who stated:

> We cannot take a single step forward in any inquiry unless we begin with a *suggested* explanation or solution of the difficulty which originated it. Such tentative explanations are suggested to us by something in the subject matter and by our previous knowledge. When they are formulated as propositions, they are called *hypotheses*.
>
> The function of a hypothesis is to *direct* our search for the order among facts. The suggestions formulated in the hypothesis may be solutions to the problem. *Whether* they are, is the task of the inquiry. No one of the suggestions need necessarily lead

to our goal. And frequently some of the suggestions are incompatible with one another, so that they cannot all be solutions to the same problem.

Given the research hypothesis (or 'theory') then one will proceed to deduce a series of further working hypotheses (testable propositions) as the basis for determining precisely what information is required to enable one to test them. It is these propositions which will largely govern the approach taken to data collection and the precise questions asked, and of whom if the data cannot be obtained by observation alone. Data collection is the subject of Chapters 6 and 8 while Chapter 9 addresses the question of how do we analyse and interpret our data in order to decide whether we can draw acceptable conclusions and come to a decision on our original problem. First, however, one must develop a research design and to do so will have to decide between observation, experimentation or a sample survey (or some combination of them) as the most appropriate means of securing the data necessary to test our hypotheses and, hopefully, solve the problem which initiated the cycle. It is to this we turn in the succeeding sections.

Observation

In Chapter 2 we suggested that while marketing research is not a sufficient condition for competitive success, in the medium to long term it is certainly a necessary condition for continued survival. This conclusion may be reached by considering the explanations offered for marketing failures where a lack or absence of marketing research is most frequently cited as the primary cause. Alternatively, the reasons advanced for marketing success often cite the identification of a marketing opportunity unrecognised by competitors. Either way keeping one's finger on the pulse of the market-place is seen as an essential and continuing concern of the firm's management. In our discussion of successive focusing (pp. 28–30) it was suggested that this activity could be conveniently subdivided into two components – scanning and marketing research. Observation has a vital but somewhat different role to play in both activities. Observation is the very essence of scanning but is primarily concerned with maintaining an awareness of the environment in order to be sensitive to changes within it. By contrast observation within marketing research is a scientific technique – indeed it is the basis of the scientific method – which is characterised by a much more structured and systematic approach than that called for in a scanning mode.

Fundamentally, the distinction between scanning and observation as a scientific technique is that scanning is only partly structured and is intended to maintain an awareness of information, actions and events which may have a bearing upon the decision makers' judgement and/or action. On the other hand, observation consists of the systematic gathering, recording and analysis of data in situations where this method is more appropriate – usually in terms of objectivity and reliability – and able to yield concrete results (eg. the flow of persons in a shopping centre) or provide formal hypotheses about relationships which can then be tested by experimentation or survey analysis. Hence, scanning is often a precursor of observation and may result in the formulation of tentative hypotheses leading to formal observation and the development of conclusions or formal hypotheses for further testing.

Although observation may be regarded as a technique in its own right it is probably used most often as an element of one or other of the other two methods. In experimentation observing and recording behaviour may well be the single most important technique while in survey analysis interviewers will frequently record factual information both to reduce the burden on the respondent (eg. type of property, make of consumer durable) and to ensure accuracy where the respondent may be unsure about the correct answer (make of tyres on your car). A simple inspection will immediately provide an accurate factual answer. Similarly, a meter can record precisely what channel your TV is tuned to while questions asking you to recall this at some later date could result in considerable response error.

A major advantage and disadvantage of observation as a research method is that it is very largely a 'real-time' activity. With the advent of low cost video cameras it is true that one can record events for later analysis but this is certainly not possible for *participant observation* where the direct involvement of the observer is an essential part of the methodology. Participant observation is particularly suited to the gathering of qualitative data where one is seeking to establish the behaviour of the subjects in a particular context (family decision making, board meeting, etc.). However, unless the observer is unknown to those he is observing, which is often difficult to achieve, there is always a danger of influencing the very behaviour one is seeking to monitor owing to the control or Hawthorne effect. Similarly, another danger is that by becoming a participant the observer will change his own attitudes and/or behaviour and so introduce bias into his observation. (For an extended review of the uses and problems which relate to participant observation the reader should consult Moser and Kalton (1971).)

A recent example of the value of an observation study is provided by Stephen Brown in his article 'Information seeking, external search and "Shopping" behaviour' (*Journal of Marketing Management*, 1988, vol. 4, no. 1, pp. 33–49). As the author notes in his introduction 'Few topics in consumer research have generated as much discussion as pre-purchase information seeking'; but, that said, there is a clear difference between the research findings which show that consumers do not 'shop around' and the retailers belief that they do. Brown suggests that both interpretations may be correct but reflect a different perspective. Thus, retailers observe how consumers behave, while the great majority of academic researchers survey consumers and invite them to recall and reconstruct their actual behaviour. But, in doing so, most respondents focus solely upon the purchase decision and ignore or forget their antecedent behaviour when they were acquiring information and evaluating it prior to making a shopping expedition. To overcome this deficiency Brown undertook a week long observation study in a shopping centre and observed the behaviour of 70 groups of shoppers from their time of entry to their time of departure. While only regarded as an exploratory study Brown identified three main types of shopping behaviour, leisure shopping (17 per cent), chore or purposeful shopping (41 per cent), and mixed activity (42 per cent) from which it was inferred that consumers use the occasion of shopping trips to gather information on products which they are not purchasing, presumably for future reference should it be required, i.e. 'shopping around' in the retailer's sense is incidental to the main purpose of the trip. To test this hypothesis Brown proposes a much more rigorous design incorporating both observation and face-to-face interviewing underlining the importance of using observation to help formulate hypotheses and then combining it with other approaches to test those hypotheses.

In sum, observation is usually the first step in the scientific method. Having identified a problem observation (successive focusing) allows one to define those areas or issues whose detailed examination may provide a solution to the problem.

Experimentation

In Chapter 2 when we discussed the nature of decision making in marketing it was stated that the dynamic and complex nature of most marketing problems meant that they were not readily amenable to the experimental approach used so widely in the physical sciences. However, some specific marketing problems are suited to an experimental design which, if properly controlled, will yield better and often less expensive data than can be obtained from a survey.

In an experiment the researcher usually seeks to control all the variables so that by varying one while holding the others constant he can determine the effect of the input or independent variable upon the output or dependent variable. It follows that a basic requirement for the conduct of an experiment is that one must be able to specify all the relevant variables. It is also implied that one has a theory which can be stated as a hypothesis or hypotheses about the nature of the relationship between the variables, e.g. if two identical objects carry different prices then prospective buyers will perceive the higher priced object to be of higher quality. Alternatively, one may hypothesise that the colour of a product's packaging will influence the consumer's perception of it without any specific hypothesis about what colour will have what effect.

In a nutshell, experiments are usually undertaken to determine if there is a causal relationship between the variables under investigation. Moser and

Kalton (1971) avoid a detailed philosophic discussion of the nature of causality but provide a useful guide to its determination. If A is a cause of the effect B then normally there would be an association between A and B. Thus, if smoking causes lung cancer one would expect that more smokers than non-smokers would contract the condition. All the statistical evidence points to this conclusion but some will seek to dismiss or ignore it on the grounds that smoking is neither a *necessary* nor *sufficient* condition for contracting lung cancer. A sufficient condition would mean that all smokers would invariably get lung cancer while a necessary condition would exist if people only got lung cancer after smoking. Clearly, neither of these conditions obtain as there are many non-smokers who catch lung cancer. That said, the degree of association between smoking and lung cancer is so high, i.e. we can measure how many smokers and non-smokers get lung cancer and will discover that the likelihood of a smoker getting the disease is x times as great as a non-smoker, that the Government now insists that tobacco products should carry a formal health warning that 'Smoking can cause lung cancer, bronchitis and other chest diseases'.

Evidence of causality is also to be found in the sequence in which events occur, it being obvious that a subsequent event cannot be the cause of an antecedent event. That said, while an antecedent event may be the cause of a subsequent event we will have to apply other tests of causality to determine whether in fact this is the case. In addition to tests of association we will also have to determine if there are any intervening variables which may influence the apparent relationship (or even disguise it by masking the relationship or making it disappear). Moser and Kalton (1971) exemplify the problem in terms of the observed association between the income of the heads of households (I) and their conservatism (C) as measured by some suitable index. While C may increase or decrease in parallel with I (or vice versa!) and we may measure the degree of association through the calculation of the coefficient of correlation we cannot impute any causality to the relationship without also determining the time sequence – did I precede C or vice versa – and whether or not there are any intervening variables such as education, occupation, age or whatever, that might explain the relationship better. The more the possible number of intervening variables the more complex the task of determining whether or not they have any bearing upon the relationship. It follows that in designing experiments one must have a particular concern to determine the degree of association, the sequence of events and the possible effect of intervening variables.

To address these problems three broad kinds of experiment are available, all of which require the establishment of a control group against which to compare the experimental group, namely:

1. After-only design.
2. Before-after design.
3. Before-after design with control group.

In an after-only design the experimental group is exposed to the independent variable which it is hypothesised will cause a particular effect and their subsequent behaviour or condition is compared with that of the control group which has not been so exposed. For example, a new 'cold' remedy is administered to 100 volunteers and the progress of their cold compared with that of the 100 members of the control group who must be as closely matched as possible with the experimental group in terms of age, sex, physique, general state of health, etc. If the experimental group show a dramatic improvement then, assuming no intervening factors, we may assume there is a causal relationship between remedy and cure and express this in quantitative terms of the degree of association established.

Before-after designs are commonplace in marketing where the experimenter is seeking to determine the effect of a specific factor on people's attitudes and/ or behaviour. In these cases the same people are used as both the control and experimental group. Suppose one wishes to assess the effect of a change in a marketing mix variable – price, packaging, product performance, advertising, etc. – upon a group of consumers, the first step must be to establish a benchmark of their current attitudes/behaviour. Given the benchmark the group is then exposed to the modified marketing mix (always bearing in mind you can only vary *one* factor at a time) and their attitudes/behaviour measured again. Because of the experimental effect (see below) it would be dangerous to assume that all change detected is a direct consequence of the variation in the mix variable – that said, if change occurs it is reasonable to assume that, in part, this is owing to the change in the independent variable.

The third design – before-after with control group – is generally recognised as the best of the three options in that it combines elements of both the preceding types and, most importantly, has established a benchmark for the control group before exposing the experimental group, i.e. one can quantify the similarities between control and experimental groups and not merely assume their similarity as is the case with the after-only design.

In all experiments the primary concern must be for *validity* and Moser and Kalton (1971) cite Campbell and Stanley's (1966) checklist of the twelve most frequent threats to validity. The first eight of these refer to internal validity and are:

1. *History*. Here the problem is to ensure that some extraneous factor, including prior experience, is not the cause of an observed outcome. The establishment of a control group and clear definition of the antecedent beliefs and status is the major defence against this source of invalidity. Even so, the fact that many experiments are not instantaneous but involve the passage of time may allow some external event to influence the experiment.
2. *Maturation*. Independent of any specific environmental event the passage of time is likely to influence respondent performance, e.g. fatigue, boredom

or, in the case of experiments designed to measure long-term effects, ageing itself. Before-after designs with control groups offer the best protection against this source of invalidity.

3. *Testing.* Given that we learn from experience it is unsurprising that the mere act of participating is likely to result in modification of our attitudes/ behaviour if for no other reason that it gives salience to something which previously had been of little or no importance. Once again the before-after with control design enables us to assess the effect of this factor.

4. *Instrumentation.* The conduct of experiments frequently involves the use of more than one test instrument, e.g. questionnaire, or the interpretation of test scores which involves judgement. The potential for bias is obvious and can only be guarded against by careful testing of instruments and the establishment of objective measures wherever possible.

5. *Statistical regression.* For a variety of reasons discussed in some detail by Campbell and Stanley (1966) there is a natural tendency for test subjects to gravitate towards the mean score on a given test when tested more than once. Whether this is because poor performers try harder and high performers become complacent or, as in the case of say the Delphi forecasting technique 'deviants' gravitate towards the security of the average is a matter of speculation – the existence of the phenomenon is not!

6. *Selection.* Experimental design demands that experimental and control groups should be as near identical as possible. Patently, to claim that the inhabitants of Slough (a favoured location for test markets) are the same as the inhabitants of, say, Aberdeen because the demographic structure of the towns' populations are similar (an after-only design) is a travesty of reality as anyone familiar with the two towns will appreciate.

   Before-after designs help overcome some of the problems of bias due to selection as the same persons are being studied throughout. That said, many of the other threats to validity – maturation, testing, etc. – will be more acute. Specialist texts, such as Moser and Kalton (1971) provide extensive advice on how to minimise these problems which are beyond the scope of a practitioner orientated book of this kind.

7. *Experimental mortality* quite simply means that some of the subjects will 'die' or drop out during the course of the experiment and so may threaten its validity.

8. *Selection maturation* is a problem which occurs when persons volunteering for an experiment may possess a quality absent in non-volunteers and it is this which leads to the observed effect or outcome.

In addition to the eight sources of internal invalidity cited, Campbell and Stanley (1966) also give examples of four sources of external invalidity, i.e. the extent to which the findings can be generalised and applied to other persons. One example of this is reactivity. *Reactivity* describes the interaction effect of testing as a result of which the 'subjects' behave differently than they would otherwise have done. A classic example of this is the so-called 'Hawthorne effect' in which the performance of both experimental and control groups improved largely because of the awareness of the groups that they were being monitored.

According to Moser & Kalton (1971):

> Often in designing studies the demands of internal and external validity compete; the stronger the design is made in internal validity, the weaker it becomes in external validity. In general, surveys are strong on external validity but weak on internal, while for experiments it is the other way round.

The authors provide extensive advice for controlling the effects of extraneous variables (pp. 220–24) but these are of primary interest to the specialist and will not be considered further here.

Some examples of an experimental approach to solving marketing problems are to be found in Chapter 11 which describes syndicated marketing research services especially those dealing with Hall tests.

Survey research

While observation and experimentation both have an important role to play in marketing research it is the survey which is the best known source of primary data collection, not only in marketing but the social sciences in general. Undoubtedly this owes a great deal to their widespread use in polling opinion on political issues or other matters of current interest and concern such as health and food, or the effects of environmental pollution. What then is a survey?

Moser and Kalton (1971) devote over 500 pages to the subject of *Survey Methods in Social Investigation* but decline to offer a definition on the grounds that:

> such a definition would have to be so general as to defeat its purpose, since the terms and the methods associated with it are applied to an extraordinarily wide variety of investigations, ranging from the classical poverty surveys of sixty years ago to Gallup Polls, town planning surveys, market research, as well as the innumerable investigations sponsored by research institutes, universities and government.

In the *Macmillan Dictionary of Marketing and Advertising* Baker is less restrained and asserts that a survey is 'The evaluation, analysis and description of a population based upon a sample drawn from it.' In the *Marketing Handbook* (1965) Mayer adds to this attempt at a definition when he states 'The essential element in the survey method is that the data are furnished by an individual in a conscious effort to answer a question.' Thus Mayer sees the essence of surveys as posing questions ('the questionnaire technique') and goes on to add:

> The survey method is the most widely used technique in marketing research. Some people go so far as to regard the questionnaire technique as being synonymous with marketing research. Unfortunately, the method is so universally employed in this field that many researchers use the survey technique when one of the other methods, the observational or experimental, is more appropriate.

Tull and Albaum (1973) support all three of the preceding views when they write:

> *Survey research* is a term that is susceptible to a variety of interpretations. As most often used, it connotes a project to get information from a sample of people by use of a questionnaire. The question may be designed to obtain information that is retrospective, concurrent, or projective with regard to time. They may be asked in a personal interview, by telephone, or sent to the respondent by mail.

Tull and Albaum stress that surveys are concerned with understanding or predicting behaviour and offer as their definition: 'Survey research is the systematic gathering of information from (a sample of) respondents for the purpose of understanding and/or predicting some aspect of the behaviour of the population of interest.'

Consideration of these definitions indicates that surveys are concerned with:

- Fact finding
- By asking questions
- Of persons representative of the population of interest
- To determine attitudes and opinions; and
- To help understand and predict behaviour.

Much of the remainder of this book is concerned with the design and execution of surveys, but before getting immersed in the detail of methodology and techniques it will be helpful first to provide an overview of the survey method. This we shall attempt in the remainder of this chapter which will consider:

> The purposes for which surveys are used
> The advantages and disadvantages of survey research
> Issues and topics suited to surveys.

The purposes of survey research

Mayer identifies three kinds of survey, which he classifies as *factual, opinion* and *interpretive,* each of which is seen as having a distinctive purpose.

As the name implies factual surveys are concerned with securing hard, quantitative data on issues such as usage, preference and habits, e.g.:

> How much beer do you drink?
> What is your preferred brand?
> Where do you normally drink beer? etc.

In other words, such surveys are concerned with actual behaviour while in opinion surveys the objective is to get respondents' views upon the topic under consideration. Such opinions are almost always qualitative and may or may not be based upon actual experience. For example, a teetotaller may have quite strong perceptions about brands of beer without ever having consumed them. However, consumers' attitudes and beliefs based upon past knowledge and experience are of particular value in helping to plan future strategy, eg. in designing a new product, developing a copy platform or selecting a distribution channel. As with factual surveys, a major purpose is to try and quantify the strength and direction of opinion as a basis for future decision making.

By contrast interpretive surveys are used in circumstances where the respondent is asked to explain why they hold particular beliefs or behave in a particular way rather than simply state what they do, how, when and where, etc. Interpretative surveys are often the first step in primary data collection when the researcher is trying to get a feel for the topic under investigation and will often involve the use of projective techniques such as picture and cartoon tests, word and object association tests, sentence completion tests, and role playing. Depth interviewing and focused group interviews are also widely used; often to define the questions to be used in a formal questionnaire for use in the factual or opinion survey.

Alreck and Settle (1985) also identify three basic reasons for undertaking a survey but classify them in terms of the need(s) of the survey sponsor, namely:

1. They may want to influence or persuade some audience.
2. They may want to create or modify some product or service for a particular public.
3. They may focus directly on understanding or predicting human behaviour or conditions because this is the focus of their academic or professional work.

In the case of direct interpersonal communication the sender of a message has immediate feedback as to whether the message has been understood, can clarify any misunderstandings or elaborate on points where further information is required, and gets a direct response from the receiver. Such a situation exists when personal selling occurs. However, the costs of personal selling are such that most marketers have to communicate indirectly with an audience, possibly comprising tens of millions, through some impersonal channel of communication. In order to determine the needs and wants of prospective customers, their buying behaviour, media usage, etc. the marketer will need to undertake research. The findings of such research then become an essential element in the development and implementation of the marketing plan. Surveys have a major role to play in this activity. They are also vitally important in gauging the audience's reaction to the product or service as a basis for future modification and improvement. Surveys of both an audience and a specific clientele can serve this purpose with the former most suited to undifferentiated products in mass markets and the latter to differentiated products in segmented markets.

By contrast to these surveys which have a practical objective − to provide information on which to base decisions − surveys of other populations are usually undertaken for theoretical reasons to enhance understanding. While such information may well be used as an input to decision making this is not its primary purpose. Table 5.1 summarises the multiplicity of surveys identified by Moser and Kalton (1971), the great majority of which are undertaken from a background of intellectual curiosity rather than to provide inputs to the solution of particular problems.

TABLE 5.1   A taxonomy of surveys

1. Classical poverty surveys (Booth, Rowntree, Bowley, Ford, etc.)
2. Regional Planning Surveys
3. Government Social Surveys
4. Market, audience and opinion research
5. Miscellaneous:
   - Population (Census)
   - Housing
   - Community studies
   - Family life
   - Sexual behaviour (Kinsey)
   - Family expenditure
   - Nutrition
   - Health
   - Education
   - Social mobility
   - Occupations and special groups
   - Leisure
   - Travel
   - Political behaviour
   - Race relations and minority groups
   - Old age
   - Crime and deviant behaviour

Source: Adapted from Moser and Kalton (1971).

es and disadvantages of survey research

In an article, 'The use of the survey in industrial market research' (*Journal of Marketing Management*, 1987, vol. 3, no.1, pp. 25–38) Susan Hart confirms that the survey is the most usual form of primary research undertaken and attributes its popularity to the following factors:

(i) The objectives of most research require factual, attitudinal and/or behavioural data. Survey research provides the researcher with the means of gathering both qualitative and quantitative data required to meet such objectives (Kerlinger, 1973; Kinnear and Taylor, 1987).

(ii) One of the greatest advantages of survey research is its scope: a great deal of information can be collected from a large population, economically (Kerlinger, 1973; Babbie, 1973).

(iii) Survey research conforms to the specifications of scientific research: it is logical, deterministic, general, parsimonious and specific (Babbie, 1973).

Alreck and Settle (1985) consider that the main advantages of surveys are that they are:

Comprehensive
Customised
Versatile
Flexible
Efficient

By 'comprehensive' Alreck and Settle mean that the method is appropriate to almost all types of research (cf. Mayer's factual, opinion and interpretive categories of survey). The other four advantages are closely interrelated and boil down to the fact that one can design surveys to suit all kinds of problems and budgets. Naturally, 'dipstick' or 'quick and dirty' research where a limited budget and time pressures dictate only limited sampling using judgemental methods will lack the credibility (and validity) of the properly designed survey in which carefully designed and tested questionnaires are administered professionally to a statistically representative sample of the population. That said, virtually any research is better than none and there is considerable evidence to show that diminishing returns set in early in terms of the insights gained from research and also in terms of the confidence one can attribute to one's findings. Given then that the essence of marketing is that one should seek to determine the precise needs of prospective customers, a pragmatic approach which seeks to acquire additional information consistent with available researches is to be preferred to no research on the grounds that it lacks the rigour called for in the experimental sciences. As will become apparent when discussing techniques and methodology in later chapters such rigour is attainable, the question is whether it is possible, necessary and/or worthwhile.

Of course surveys also have their disadvantages and Hart (1987) cites the following:

(i) The unwillingness of respondents to provide the desired data. The overriding concern here is of the non-response error which can invalidate research findings.

(ii) The ability of respondents to provide data. In studying managerial decisions, it is important to target individuals in the organisation with the knowledge and experience of the subject under examination.

(iii) The influence of the questioning process on the respondents. Respondents may give the answers they think the researcher will want to hear, thus distorting the accuracy of the data.

Response errors, accidental or deliberate, may be reduced significantly through careful design and execution. The subject is addressed in greater detail in Chapter 7 which is concerned with questionnaire design.

Issues and topics suited to surveys

From the above discussion, and particularly Table 5.1, it is clear that surveys can be used to gather data on virtually any problem which involves the attitudes and behaviour of people in either their individual capacities or as members of various kinds of social and organisational groupings. Within the domain of marketing research Alreck and Settle (1985) distinguish eight basic topic categories, namely:

Attitudes
Images
Decisions
Needs
Behaviour
Life-style
Affiliations
Demographics

Of course, these categories are neither mutually exclusive nor independent but to the extent that they often require different treatment and measures the classification provides a useful guide to survey planning.

Alreck and Settle subscribe to the cognitive–affective–conative (CAC) model of attitudes and see attitudes as a predisposition to act. They also assert that attitudes precede behaviour. In other words if you can define and measure attitudes you should be in a good position to predict behaviour. However, many researchers prefer the expectancy-value (EV) model developed from the work of Heider, Rosenberg and Fishbein which does not seek to establish a link between attitude and behaviour and so can accommodate problems of the kind touched on earlier when examining the purposes of survey research – namely, the teetotaller who may have strong positive attitudes towards brands of beer but with no intention of translating his attitude into behaviour. The point we are seeking to make is that one must be careful not to assume a causal relationship between attitude and behaviour, albeit that the notion of consistency in both CAC and EV models indicates that if behaviour does occur it is most likely to be consistent with the pre-existing attitude – if one exists! Either way an understanding of underlying attitudes will clearly be of great value to the marketing planner.

Image is defined in the *Macmillan Dictionary* as: 'Consumer perception of a brand, company, retail outlet, etc. Made up of two separable but interacting components, one consisting of the attributes of the object, the other consisting of the characteristics of the user.' The most important word in this definition is *perception*. Objectively it is possible to list all the attributes of a product or service but the importance assigned to these attributes is likely to vary from individual to individual. It is for this reason that in personal selling the seller will invite the potential buyer to list and rank order the specific attributes he is looking for in the intended purchase so that, in turn, the seller can focus on those elements of importance to the particular buyer. But in mass markets, or when composing copy in support of personal selling, one must seek to determine the image of the object under consideration and then define clusters of attributes which correspond to worthwhile segments in the market place. Surveys offer this potential, particularly through the use of scaling devices which are described in more detail at pp. 145–9.

Given knowledge of people's attitudes and some insight into their image of different products or services the next thing the marketing planner would like to know is how they actually choose between alternative courses of action. Elsewhere *(Marketing Strategy and Management*, Chapter 5) I have proposed a simple, composite model of buyer behaviour which incorporates elements of the economic, psychological and sociological models and argued that, when faced with a need, the consumer will consult his store of past experience (learned behaviour) to see if he has an acceptable solution. If not, the decision-maker will seek to acquire relevant information on performance attributes and cost-benefit data on possible solutions to his need. This information will then be evaluated in terms of the decision-maker's own perceptions and preferences and a choice made of the item which best satisfies these. If the marketer is to influence this process then he requires knowledge of the information used by consumers and the evaluative criteria applied in order to arrive at a preferred solution. Survey research offers a means to acquire this information.

Needs is a word often used loosely by the marketer and as if it were synonymous with *wants, desires, preferences, motives* and *goods. The Macmillan Dictionary* makes it clear that only if there is no choice will needs and wants become synonymous otherwise needs represent basic requirements such as food, shelter, clothing, transportation, entertainment, etc. (cf. *Marketing Myopia* by Ted Levitt) while *wants* comprise highly specific means of satisfying these basic needs. *Desires* are largely synonymous with wants but the term implies rather more commitment to a given solution than *preference. Motives* have a connotation of action in that people are seen as being motivated to do something usually to achieve a *goal* which is satisfaction of the need through behaviour. Scaling provides a means to documenting all of these dimensions through survey research.

According to Alreck and Settle (1985), 'The measurement of *behaviour* usually involves four related concepts: what the respondent did or did not do; where the action takes place; the timing, including past, present, and future; and the frequency or persistence of behaviour.' Such data is factual and readily acquired by standardised questionnaires using what, when, where and how often questions, usually with multiple choice answers provided to speed up completion. Of course such questions are frequently combined with others designed to measure the other categories of topics and may be regarded as a benchmark against which to assess them.

While it is convenient for purposes of data collection and analysis to identify clear-cut factors or variables such as attitudes, images, etc. actual behaviour is the outcome of the interaction of all these factors. In order to capture this complexity many researchers prefer to use composite measures which describe behaviour in the round. Life-style is such a construct – and is concerned with 'Distinctive or characteristic ways of living adopted by communities or sections of communities, relating to general attitudes and behaviour towards the allocation of time, money and effort in the pursuit of objectives considered desirable' (*Macmillan Dictionary*). Validated batteries of items for inclusion in life-style research are widely available and usually cover four main dimensions – activities, interests, opinions (hence AIO research) and possessions. The identification of subgroups or segments with similar life-styles has been greatly improved with the development of multivariate analysis techniques utilising the full capabilities of modern computers.

Behaviour is strongly mediated by the social context in which it occurs. It follows that an understanding of the nature of social interaction is central to an understanding of actual behaviour. In this context *affiliation* in terms of the membership of both formal and informal groups is a rich source of data of particular value in predicting likely behaviour. For example, membership of a referent group may exercise a significant influence on what is considered an acceptable dress code (IBM and blue suits, students and jeans), place in which to live, type of holiday, car, etc. Similarly, an understanding of the composition of a group and relationships within it may provide useful guidance when introducing a new product to the market place by helping to identify the opinion leaders (those to whom other group members turn for information and advice), and concentrating one's selling effort on these individuals. Survey methods are very appropriate to research of this kind.

Alreck and Settle's final category, *demographics*, is perhaps the most obvious and easily measured dimension associated with consumer behaviour. In addition, most governments collect copious data on the structure and composition of the population which provides a reliable and inexpensive base-line for other survey research.

Qualitative research methodology

When considering the issues involved in defining problems and selecting possible approaches to solve them (Chapter 2) we examined the distinction between quantitative and qualitative research. While these two approaches are often presented as if they are opposing and mutually exclusive research methodologies it was pointed out that they are in fàct complementary and supportive approaches to the conduct of research. Our discussion of the research cycle and the main techniques of observation, experimentation and sample survey in the preceding pages should have confirmed this view. However, some further elaboration will be useful here before turning to a more detailed examination of sampling and data collection techniques in the next two chapters.

Perhaps the main reason why many practitioners are suspicious of the value of qualitative research is because of its identification with motivation research and particularly motivation research of the kind developed by Ernest Dichter in the 1950s. It was Dichter's approach to motivation research and its application to business problems which was the subject of Vance Packard's *The Hidden Persuaders* in which he claimed that marketing researchers were using psychological and psychoanalytic techniques in order to discover the hidden or subconscious motivations of consumers and then using this information to persuade these consumers to purchase particular goods or services. Following on McCarthyism and the Red scare of the early 1950s anything which smacked of 'brainwashing' was clearly to be avoided. On mature reflection (and given many numerous marketing failures) it is clear that short of coercion you cannot make people do what they do not want to do. Thus, while one may debate the social implications and consequences of materialism and the acquisitive society, it is usually those who are materially well-off who seem concerned that others may be 'persuaded' to aspire to the same level of material comfort who are in the van of the critics. Fortunately, technological innovation makes it seem increasingly likely that the majority of mankind will be able to aspire to higher levels of material comfort and so share a common concern for responsible consumption. However, this is to digress from the main point which is that qualitative methods were brought into some disrepute by criticisms of some of Dichter's methods and it has taken a generation for a more balanced approach to emerge.

Experience has shown that qualitative research is particularly useful in a number of specific situations which may be summarised as:

1. Traditional preliminary exploration.
2. Sorting and screening ideas.
3. Exploring 'complex' behaviour.
4. Developing explanatory models of behaviour.
5. Enabling the decision maker to experience the world as consumers see it.
6. To define unfilled needs and means of satisfying them.

Most of these uses are self-explanatory and address the issue raised at the beginning of this chapter, namely, that social science research is concerned not only with facts but with *values*. Through using qualitative research it becomes possible to discover what some of these underlying values are for, while one may seek to infer them from observing actual behaviour, the only real way one can establish 'why?' people behave as they do is to ask them. Even then it is not easy to get respondents to give you the real reason for we all have a tendency to rationalise behaviour (hence the emphasis upon price as an acceptable reason for not making a purchase rather than by giving offence and saying the article in question was useless, ugly or what have you). There is also the well-known human tendency to want to please and so give the researcher the answer you think he is looking for.

To overcome these difficulties qualitative researchers have developed a whole battery of projective techniques so that the respondent is invited to speculate how someone else would behave in a given situation, e.g. by completing a sentence, by filling in the dialogue in a cartoon, etc. Of course, the only real basis we have for such speculation is our own knowledge and experience, attitudes and opinions, so it is hardly surprising if the projected behaviour is similar to how we would behave in the given situation. Gordon and Langmaid (1988) devote a whole chapter to projective and enabling techniques which they classify into five categories:

Association
Completion
Construction
Expressive
Choice-ordering.

Within the association procedures are to be found traditional word association tests such as 'Tell me the first thing that comes to mind when I say detergent', through the classic Rorschach ink-blot test, to the construction of brand personalities, eg. could you imagine Foster's Lager as a person and describe him to me. A further refinement is to provide the respondent with a pile of words and pictures and ask the respondent to choose those they associate with a brand name or product.

Completion procedures invite respondents to complete a sentence such as 'People who drive Porsche motor cars are . . .' or the missing dialogue in a conversation between two persons. Brand mapping, in which respondents are invited to group like brands/products according to various criteria, is also regarded as a completion technique and enables the researcher to determine how consumers see the products competing with each other in the market-place.

Construction procedures also invite respondents to construct a story from a picture (thematic apperception tests) or in response to projective questions, through bubble procedures (you write in what you think the character in the drawing/cartoon is thinking), to the classification of stereotypes, e.g. you define a category of consumer and ask respondents to specify their consumption behaviour.

Expressive procedures also involve the use of drawings and the invitation to the respondent to describe his perceptions of the person and/or context. They may also include role playing in which the respondent is asked to act out a particular activity, eg. purchasing a product or playing the part of a named brand.

Finally, choice ordering is just that and asks respondents to rank order objects in terms of specific criteria − a technique which is very useful in determining what alternatives will be provided in multiple choice questions or for coding the answers to open-ended questions.

However, projective techniques are only one approach to qualitative research and probably used less frequently than the group discussion and depth interview both of which are described in more detail in Chapter 8.

Cross-sectional and longitudinal studies

There can be little doubt that when people speak of marketing research they are concerned primarily with a specific, one-off or *cross-sectional* study designed to address a particular marketing problem which is facing them. Given my own preferred definitions that 'marketing is selling goods that don't come back to people who do' and that 'marketing is concerned with mutually satisfying exchange relationships' it is clear that one salient feature which distinguishes marketing from the production or sales orientation is that it is concerned with developing lasting relationships with specific customers *over time*. This being so it would seem sensible that a significant part of the firm's research effort should be devoted to such *longitudinal* studies — a view which is considerably reinforced when it is recognised that it costs approximately five times as much to create a new customer as it does to retain an existing one. In this section we shall examine the nature of longitudinal research by comparison with *ad hoc* or cross-sectional studies and then review its use in both the industrial and consumer setting.

What is it?

Longitudinal organisational research consists of using techniques and methodologies that permit the study, analysis and interpretation of changes that occur over a time period sufficiently long to assess meaningful change in the variables of interest, as well as to facilitate researcher and managerial understanding about causality.

In other words, longitudinal analysis is concerned with the collection of data by means of observation, experimentation or sample survey over time with the primary purpose of describing and explaining change in these objects or respondents over the period of the research.

In the social sciences generally there are numerous examples of the use of longitudinal methods particularly in the case of *cohort* or *tracking* studies in which the researchers have traced the development and behaviour of the subjects over extended periods of time. Clearly the benefit of such studies is that it provides insight and understanding of the process by which change occurs which is quite different from the large scale cross-sectional study of a population as a consequence of which one subdivides it into a set of major segments, e.g. psychographic, life-style or benefit segmentation. In the latter case one can define distinct sub-groups in terms of their present behaviour but can say little about how this developed or about what would be required to change it. Similar weaknesses may also exist in the case of data collected by continuous methods, e.g. Neilsen audit, Attwood, where the primary emphasis is upon *what* rather than *why*.

In brief, cross-sectional studies involve the investigation of one or more variables as they are at a particular point in time, while longitudinal studies require the measurement of the same variables or factors on a number of successive occasions over a defined period of time. Because of the sequential nature of longitudinal research it is possible to avoid the greatest weakness of the snapshot approach of the cross-sectional study, namely that any explanation of the data collected is *retrospective*. As an SSRC Working Party reported (1975), 'The hazards incurred when any survey shifts from description of the contemporary situation of a population sample to an overt or implicit attempt to identify causal influences retrospectively are heightened by the time-span of recall and by the salience of the subject matter.'

Small wonder then that 'helpful' respondents may well provide misleading explanations of why they behave in a particular way when faced with requests to recall past decisions of comparatively minor importance in their lives as a whole such as the difference between brand A and brand B.

Inevitably, cross-sectional or *ad hoc* studies are unable to deal adequately with dynamic behavioural changes and properly designed longitudinal surveys are necessary to monitor such change. By 'properly designed' is meant research which consists of measurement of the same objects/respondents at a series of different points in time as opposed to what often passes for a longitudinal study which is a series of cross-sectional studies at specified points in time. While this may appear to be a counsel of perfection it is one which is felt to be justified, particularly where one is seeking to establish causality and when concerned with organisational as opposed to individual behaviour where the consequences of misunderstanding are likely to be larger and longer lived. A good example of the problems and importance of establishing causality is to be found in Gordon *et al*'s (1975) study of the adoption of innovations by hospitals. It was hypothesised that increased centralisation of authority in a hospital would result in a reduction in its willingness to innovate in the purchase of new equipment but in order to test this hypothesis it is clear that one must discriminate between two quite distinct possibilities. First, where authority is decentralised it may be that innovative individuals will purchase new equipment and introduce it to the system. On the other hand, an equally plausible causal priority is that where a hospital (as a system) has acquired new equipment then it will be more dependent upon individual physicians and their expertise and so involve them. A cross-sectional study to determine the relationship between centralisation and responsiveness to change would have failed to discriminate causal priority between the two variables.

Similarly, the longitudinal study helps to reduce the possibility of making incorrect causal inferences which, as Likert (1967) has demonstrated, may occur due to the time lag between certain classes of causal and end-result variables. Longitudinal research also helps overcome what Seiler (1967) has termed the single cause habit in which, based on a single data set from a cross-sectional study, one imputes all the observed effects to single causes. In reality behaviour is invariably the outcome of a time-related process and one should seek to monitor the causal chain which results in given outcomes and so avoid unduly simplistic interpretations of events recorded by the snapshot of a cross-sectional study.

In summary, and as Kennedy (1982) has pointed out:

[the] literature would appear to advocate the use of longitudinal methods on the basis of the facts that this particular research methodology addresses the issue of causality; identifies time lags between cause and effect; permits analysis of dynamic processes; minimises the probability of hidden third-factor error and enables the researcher to monitor the actual occurrence of changes in dependent and independent variables. Longitudinal research would appear to afford the potential to eradicate problems of causality, produce more exact conceptualisation of process, develop better predictive models of growth and change and facilitate the identification of contextual constraints.

Summary

In this chapter we have taken a broad look at the issues involved in selecting a research design, i.e. the method and approach by which we seek to secure the additional information necessary to solve our problem. From this review certain broad principles emerge.

The first principle is that research is usually initiated because our current knowledge and experience appear insufficient or unsatisfactory to explain an issue of importance to us. Irrespective of whether this perception is prompted merely by intellectual curiosity or is the response to a practical problem which needs to be resolved the only satisfactory approach is to follow the so-called scientific method. In essence the scientific method requires us to formulate hypotheses as to the causes and possible solution to our problem and develop these into testable propositions.

The second principle is that in formulating hypotheses and developing these into testable propositions we would be well advised first to use observation to see if we can discover an acceptable explanation and then see if experimentation will help clarify the relationship between the phenomenon under scrutiny and the factors which appear to be associated with it. In the natural sciences where it is possible to control many of the variables which may be influencing the interaction(s) in which we are particularly interested, experimentation will often provide an acceptable solution. However, in the social sciences, where the main focus of interest is usually human behaviour, it is rare that one is able to apply sufficient controls to make experimentation successful. Further, one is usually concerned to know 'why' people behave in a particular way and inference from observed or experimental data is notoriously weak in doing this satisfactorily. Accordingly, having exhausted the possibilities of observation and experimentation most marketing researchers will wish to undertake some form of sample survey of the population in which they are interested.

The third principle is that just as one proceeds from observation, to experimentation to sample survey so one should first undertake qualitative research before attempting to quantify the direction and extent of any hypothesised relationships. In doing so projective techniques will often be found to be especially useful in clarifying the underlying motivations which influence actual behaviour.

Finally, it is clear that while one-off or cross-sectional studies may provide brief illumination of a problem it is much preferable if decision-makers and researchers keep track of issues of interest to them through longitudinal studies.

Given these principles we can now turn to look more closely at the research methods available to collect the data for testing our hypotheses.

References

Alreck, Pamela L. and Settle, Robert, B. (1985) *The Survey Research Handbook* (Homewood, Ill.: Richard D. Irwin).

Babbie, E. R. (1973) *Survey Research Methods* (Belmont, California: Wadsworth).

Campbell, D. T. and Stanley, J.C. (1966) *Experimental and Quasi-experimental Design for Research* (Chicago: Rand McNally).

Cohen, M. R. and Nagel, E. (1934) *An Introduction to Logic and Scientific Method* (New York: Harcourt).

Gordon, G., Kimberley, H.T. and MacEachran (1975) 'Some Considerations in the Design of Effective Research Programs on the Diffusion of Medical Technology', in W. J. Abernathy, A. Sheldon and C.K. Prahalad (eds), *The Management of Health Care* (Cambridge: Ballinger).

Gordon, Wendy and Langmaid, Roy (1988) *Qualitative Market Research: A Practitioners' and Buyers' Guide* (Aldershot: Gower).

Hart, Susan J. (1987) 'The Use of the Survey in Industrial Market Research', *Journal of Marketing Management*, 3 (1), pp. 25–38.

Kennedy, A. M. (1982) *Longitudinal Research Methods: Applicability in Industrial Marketing*, Working Paper, Department of Marketing, University of Strathclyde.

Kerlinger, F. N. (1973) *Foundations of Behavioral Research*, 2nd edn (New York: Holt Rinehart & Winston).

Likert, R. (1967) *The Human Organization* (New York: McGraw-Hill).

Mayer, Charles S. (1965) 'Marketing Research Sec 24 and Statistical and Mathematical Tools Sec 25', in *Marketing Handbook*, 2nd edn, ed. Albert Wesley Frey (New York: Ronald Press).

Moser, C. A. and Kalton, G. (1971) *Survey Methods in Social Investigation*, 2nd edn (London: Heinemann).

Popper, K. R. (1968) *The Logic of Scientific Discovery*, rev. edn (London: Hutchinson).

Seiler, R. E. (1965) *Improving the Effectiveness of Research and Development* (New York: McGraw-Hill).

Selltiz, C., Jahoda, M., Deutsch, M. and Cook, S.W. (1959) *Research Methods in Social Relations*, 2nd edn (London: Methuen).

Tull, D.S. and Albaum, G.S. (1973) *Survey Research* (Aylesbury: International Textbook Co. Ltd).

CHAPTER 6

Sampling

Introduction

In the preceding chapter we reviewed the basic methodologies available to the marketing researcher and classified these as observation, experimentation and survey. All three methodologies are concerned with the systematic gathering and analysis of data with a view to informing the decision-maker and enabling him to make a better decision than would be possible in the absence of that information. But, as we have also seen, the acquisition of additional information is a resource-hungry process which requires the decision-maker to balance some element of risk or uncertainty against the time and money which would be necessary to reduce this still further. Ideally, we would like to consult everyone likely to be influenced by or to have an effect on our decision but, in practice, we will usually have to compromise. Sampling offers us a means of doing this in an acceptable way and in this chapter we shall look at the basic ideas underlying sampling, the different kinds of sample available, their various advantages and disadvantages, and the planning of a sampling operation. Such technical matters as calculating sample size, variability, error and bias will be touched on in Appendix 1 to the chapter, together with references to additional sources for those who wish to explore these issues further.

The basis of sampling

As stated in the Introduction, ideally we would prefer to consult or measure everyone or everything which has a bearing upon the problem we are seeking to solve. Technically this totality of persons or things is referred to as the *universe* or *population* and one of the first problems to be addressed in sampling is the definition of the population to be researched in precise and unambiguous terms. For example, in the case of a manufacturing process the population to be sampled for quality control purposes could be every unit of output within a given time period, while for the provision of a social service for elderly persons it could be every individual aged 65 and over in a defined geographical area.

Under some circumstances it may be possible or necessary to survey or enumerate the complete population. Obvious examples are the counting of a country's population every ten years, the construction of a register of occupiers of property for purposes of the payment of poll tax, the electoral register, etc. Similarly, in some industrial markets, where the numbers of suppliers and/or users are small, a complete enumeration or *census* may be a viable proposition. However, in the case of very large populations it has to be accepted that a complete census is often unachievable – people will have died, moved, be out of the country, etc. – with the result that in some circumstances the results from a properly controlled sample may be more accurate than an attempted census. (The difficulties associated with establishing contact with respondents are clearly illustrated in Appendix 2 which is a Technical Report from a major survey.)

Accuracy and precision are key concepts in sampling and fundamental to all good sampling design. Accuracy and precision, or *reliability*, means freedom from random error and the degree to which repeated administration of a sample will lead to comparable results between the samples *(repeatability* or *reproducibility)*. In addition to reliability the other acid test of sample design is *validity* by which is meant the degree to which the survey measures that which it purports to measure. Validity is usually assessed and expressed in terms of the presence or absence of *bias* and a number of measures have been developed to identify sources of bias and their effect on validity, some of which will be discussed in the Appendix.

The concepts of *reliability* and *validity* are a frequent source of confusion amongst students. A very clear and precise definition is offered by Martin and Bateson (1986).

1. **Reliability** concerns the extent to which measurement is repeatable and consistent; that is, free from random errors. An unbiased measurement consists of two parts: a systematic component, representing the true value of the variable, and a random component due to imperfections in the measurement process. The smaller the error component, the more reliable the measurement.

Reliable measures, sometimes referred to as good measures, are those which measure a variable precisely and consistently. At least four related factors determine how 'good' a measure is:

(a) **Precision**: How free are measurements from random errors? This is denoted by the number of 'significant figures' in the measurement. Note that accuracy and precision are not synonymous: accuracy concerns systematic error (bias) and can therefore be regarded as an aspect of validity (see below). A clock may tell the time with great precision (to within a millisecond), yet be inaccurate because it is set to the wrong time.

(b) **Sensitivity**: Do small changes in the true value invariably lead to changes in the measured value?

(c) **Resolution**: What is the smallest change in the true value that can be detected?

(d) **Consistency**: Do repeated measurements of the same thing produce the same results?

2. **Validity** concerns the extent to which a measurement actually measures those features the investigator wishes to measure, and provides information that is relevant to the questions being asked. Validity refers to the relation between a variable (such as a measure of behaviour) and what it is supposed to measure or predict about the world.

Valid measures, sometimes referred to as right measures, are those which actually answer the questions being made. To decide whether a measure is valid ('right'), at least two separate points must be considered:

(a) **Accuracy**: Is the measurement process unbiased, such that measured values correspond with the true values? Measurements are accurate if they are relatively free from systematic errors (whereas precise measurements are relatively free from random errors).

(b) **Specificity**: To what extent does the measure describe what it is supposed to describe, and nothing else?

Both reliability and validity are highly dependent upon the accurate definition of the population to be surveyed, of the *sampling unit* to be surveyed and the specification of the *sampling frame* from which the sampling units are to be selected. A sampling unit (sometimes called an *elementary sampling unit* or ESU) is the specific individual or object to be measured in the survey. While the ESU will be drawn from the defined population its definition need not necessarily be precisely the same. For example, the population may be all households with a satellite television receiver but the actual ESU might be specified as a particular member of that household in terms of age, sex, viewing habits or whatever. As noted, the sampling frame is a defined population from which the sample is to be drawn and so must be accurate, adequate, up to date and relevant to the purposes of the survey for which it is to be used. Ideally one would like a list such as the electoral register (even though we know this will be partially incomplete in terms of the population of persons aged 18 and over living in a given geographical area), the companies in a particular industry, the members of an organisation and so on. In recent years many companies have come into existence specifically to offer such lists to persons or organisations wanting to reach a clearly defined audience and these may provide an excellent sampling framework, particularly for mail surveys. In other circumstances one may wish to use location as the basis for a sampling frame, eg. town, local government district, etc. and then sample from that area on a selective basis; or an airport for travellers, shopping centre for shoppers and so on.

Given a sampling frame and having defined the sampling unit the next step is to determine the most cost-effective way of selecting specific sampling units from the sampling frame. Basically the choice rests between a *probability based* or *random* sample or some kind of *non-probability* based design. Probability based sampling in its strictest sense means that every member of the defined population has a known and non-zero chance of being included in the sample. Where this condition is satisfied then one can make unequivocal statements about the accuracy and validity of the findings from the survey by reference to the degree of error and/or bias which may be present in it, as measured by well understood statistical methods. Similarly, if the purpose of the survey is to test hypotheses rather than estimation, e.g. the incidence of television viewing in a population, then one may use tests of significance to estimate the confidence one can place that a given hypothesis is correct, e.g. the likelihood that firms using marketing research will be more successful than those which do not is 0.95 i.e. the association between using marketing research and success is such that we would expect this relationship to hold good in 95 cases out of every 100 observed. There are several kinds of probability-based sample in addition to the 'pure' or simple random sample and these will be described in more detail in the following section.

In the absence of a sampling frame one cannot draw a probability based sample and so will have to resort to some judgemental or non-probabilistic method. Such sampling is often referred to as *purposive* and alternative approaches will be reviewed below.

Sampling techniques

The main sampling techniques available to the marketing researcher are summarised in Table 6.1.

TABLE 6.1   Sampling techniques

A. Probability-based samples
- Random samples – unrestricted and simple
- Stratified samples
- Cluster samples
- Systematic samples
- Area
- Multi-stage

B. Non-probability based or purposive samples
- Judgement
- Quota
- Convenience

Random samples

An *unrestricted* random sample is one in which every unit has an equal chance of selection and where the selected unit is replaced before another is drawn, i.e. the same unit could occur more than once in a sample. Unrestricted random sampling is the kind to which most statistical theory refers and is suited more to static populations of inanimate objects than to dynamic populations of human beings. Even so the requirement for replacement makes it unsuited to most real-life sampling operations of the kind used to assess and control quality in manufacturing industries. Accordingly, simple random sampling is generally preferred and has the added advantage that it 'produces more precise estimators' (Moser and Kalton, 1971).

In the New Collins *Thesaurus* (1985) 'random' is shown to have the connotations of 'accidental, adventitious, aimless, arbitrary, casual, chance, desultory, fortuitous, haphazard, hit or miss, incidental, indiscriminate, purposeless, spot, stray, unplanned, unpremeditated'. It is unlikely that any procedure described by any of these words could meet the requirements of a true random sample that every member of a population should have an equal chance of selection and so avoid the problems of selection bias. To achieve true randomness two procedures are available – the lottery method in which each unit is assigned a number which corresponds to a ticket a sample of which is then drawn from a box or urn, and the random number method in which one selects the numbers from a table of random numbers. As anyone who has bought a lottery ticket knows the draw does not often convince one that the tickets were thoroughly mixed before drawing! Because of the practical problems of achieving a satisfactory mix most researchers use tables of random numbers such as those prepared by Kendall and Smith or Fisher and Yates.

However, this procedure will only ensure a true random sample if the numbers have also been assigned to the sample units in a random way. As Moser and Kalton observe no ordinary list is constructed in a random fashion. 'Whether it is in alphabetical order, or seniority order or, as is often the case with lists of the general population, in street and house number order, there is invariably some systematic arrangement.'

The great advantage of random sampling is the ease with which the sampling error may be calculated. Because of this the statistical efficiency of the method is seen as a benchmark against which to compare the efficiency of more complex methods and is assigned a coefficient of 1.0. That said, its disadvantages are almost overwhelming in the applied field of marketing research, namely:

1. The need to identify every single sampling unit.
2. The need to enumerate the sampling units.
3. The need to establish physical contact with the selected sampling units in order to measure or question them.

Stratified samples

To overcome these technical difficulties a number of *restricted* approaches to random sampling have been developed of which *stratified* sampling is one of the most popular. According to Mayer (1965):

> Stratification is simply the process of splitting the population into strata (or smaller populations) according to factors that are correlated with the factor under study. The only requirement for stratification is that each item in the population must fall into one and only one stratum. Efficiency is gained through stratification by creating relatively homogeneous strata. The greater the correlation between the stratifying variable and the factor under study, the more efficient stratified sampling will be. Having set up strata, a simple random sample is drawn from within each stratum. The correct representation of the related factors in the sample assures a lower overall sampling error.

From this description it is clear that defining the strata is critical to the sample design. Ideally sampling units within each stratum should be as homogeneous as possible and each stratum should be distinctive from all the other strata. For example, we could stratify the population in terms of age, sex and education or use a composite factor such as socio-economic grouping or stage in the family life-cycle. If the subject of our survey is to do with shopping behaviour then perhaps we could stratify on the basis of food and non-food and further sub-divide or stratify in terms of independents and multiples. In these cases one already has an a priori basis for stratification but in others this may not be readily apparent and some exploratory research may be necessary to help define meaningful segments or strata for investigation.

In determining the representation of sampling units two approaches are possible described as *proportionate* and *disproportionate*. As the term suggests, in the case of proportionate stratified sampling the amount of the sample drawn from each stratum is proportionate to that stratum's share of the total population, whereas in the case of disproportionate sampling one varies the proportion within each stratum in accordance with a criterion or criteria which reflects the variability within the strata. Suppose, for example, that one wishes to sample the opinions of employees about the desirability of a buy-out from the current owners and that the workforce comprises 700 manual workers, 150 technicians, 125 clerical and administrative workers, and 25 managers. Given a sample size of 200 then we would survey 140 manual workers, 30 technicians, 25 clerical workers and 5 managers using a proportionate design which, theoretically, is what we would expect from a truly random design but with the improvement that by stratifying the population we have eliminated the possibility of any variation between the strata. While this is a technically satisfactory answer it is clear that by adopting a disproportionate sampling methodology we could greatly improve the quality and usefulness of the data for the same expenditure of effort. Given a sample size of 200 we would probably want to survey all 25 managers, all key technical and clerical workers up to a maximum of 105 and survey only 1 in 10 of the manual workers totalling 70 in all.

While a disproportionate sampling procedure increases the complexity of the statistical calculations necessary to arrive at an unbiased sample estimate, the improvement in efficiency (quality of output) is well worth the effort, for in addition to being able to make statements about the population as a whole, one can make statements about each of the strata individually.

Stratified sampling is used extensively for continuous research activities such as the Neilsen retail audit or the household consumption survey where the researcher has a sound knowledge of the population and the basic strata which comprise it. Even so the economics of data collection may make it unduly expensive to sample some strata on a truly random basis and the researcher will look for a more cost-effective method such as that offered by *cluster* sampling.

Cluster sampling is similar to stratified sampling in that both techniques require the researcher to sub-divide a population into a set of mutually exclusive and exhaustive sub-groups. However, the methods differ in that in cluster sampling one samples the sub-groups whereas in stratified sampling one selects a sample from within each sub-group. It follows that in a cluster sample each sub-group should be a microcosm of the total population while in a stratified sample each stratum represents a subset or segment of the population each different from the other. The advantages of the cluster sample are that one does not require a precise sampling frame and that it can be used where the population is widely distributed geographically. Because of this advantage cluster sampling is frequently used in conjunction with a geographic frame when the method may be referred to as *area* sampling. For example, one wishes to conduct a survey of the use of fertilisers by farmers in the UK then one approach would be to identify types of farming area — arable, pastoral, mixed, hill, etc. — choose geographic locations to reflect varying climatic conditions and then interview every farmer within a radius of two miles of points selected within each area as the appropriate cluster. Similarly, with a household survey one might divide a town up into a number of areas each containing the same number of households and interview each householder in a sample drawn from all the areas. While cluster sampling is economically more efficient than other forms of random sample it is statistically less efficient in that the standard error of the estimate is likely to be larger.

Another form of random sampling which is widely used is the *systematic sample*. This method has advantages over simple random sampling in that it is not necessary to number every unit in the sampling frame. Instead one divides the population by the required sample size to determine the sampling interval ('k') and then selects a random starting point whereafter every kth item is selected systematically, e.g.

Population = 2000, sample = 200

$$k = \frac{2000}{200} = 10$$

Random start = 7, therefore sample = 7, 17, 27, 37, 47 . . ., 1997

On reflection, it is apparent that a systematic sample may be regarded as a one-stage cluster sample in the sense that in the above example we have really divided our population into 10 clusters and decided to sample the 7th cluster. Had we started at 5(15, 25, 35, . . ., 1995) then we would have sampled the 5th cluster. In addition if there is no order in the list from which the sample is drawn a systematic sample would also qualify as a simple random sample. When drawing a systematic sample care must be taken to ensure that there are no hidden patterns or periodicities in the data as these could result in severe bias, eg. a sample is drawn of daily sales receipts – if one numbers the days of the week 1–7 we would expect significant differences in the pattern of sales on a day to day basis such that selecting any day as representative would lead to distorted results.

While it has been convenient to describe the various types of probabilistic samples as if each could be executed as a single procedure, in reality most sampling is undertaken in a series of steps defined as *multi-stage* sampling. A multi-stage approach was implicit in our earlier example of a cluster sample of farmers' use of fertiliser. While there may exist a complete listing of the UK population of farmers, drawing a simple random sample could easily result in a widely dispersed and difficult to contact group of farmers. By stratifying farming into broad types – arable, pastoral, mixed, hill, etc., and selecting areas of the country where each is dominant, e.g. arable – Norfolk, Vale of York, Ayrshire, etc. one is able to focus one's interviewing effort in a highly cost-effective way. Multi-stage sampling is widely used in national surveys of this kind particularly when seeking to obtain information from the whole population of the country, e.g. voting intentions, opinions on an issue such as security at airports, etc. It is also the basis of omnibus surveys although the actual selection of respondents for these may not always satisfy the random requirements of a probabilistic methodology to the satisfaction of a purist.

While the above description covers the main types of probability based sample, several other procedures are available (replicated, multi-phase, etc.), but are of more interest to the technician than the manager. Of more interest and importance to the manager and practitioner are a number of non-probability based sampling procedures which form the subject of the next section.

Non-probability based or purposive samples

The obvious benefit of probability-based sampling procedures is that they allow one to draw inferences about the population from which the sample was drawn and state these with a known degree of confidence that any similarly chosen sample would yield the same results as that given by the present sample. The major drawback is that such procedures can be difficult, complex, time consuming and expensive to execute. Clearly, there is a need for a simpler methodology which can assist and inform decision making albeit that it lacks the precision and accuracy of the probability based survey. This need is largely met by judgemental approaches in which a sample is selected for a particular purpose (hence purposive sampling) with the two main techniques being *quota* and *convenience* sampling.

The essential difference between quota and random sampling is that in the case of quota sampling the interviewer selects respondents in accordance with some predetermined criteria such as age, sex and occupation, while in the random sample the respondents are selected (using the same criteria) by an objective methodology independent of the interviewer, While both approaches might yield very similar results the potential for bias in a quota sample is obvious − interviewers tend to select the most accessible individuals both physically and in terms of their willingness to participate. Consider, for example, a survey of airline passengers. Such persons are more likely to co-operate while killing time prior to departure than they are when going to an appointment on arrival but their views on arrival might be more relevant. (Just to complicate matters the people with most time to kill are least likely to be important business people!)

The real problem is that while bias may exist in all survey research we cannot *quantify* it when using non-probability based samples and so do not know what allowance we should make for it. That said, a great deal of bias can be eliminated by using carefully specified and defined quota controls and using experienced interviewers. By doing so it is possible to obtain data which may be of greater practical use to the marketer than that from a random sample owing to the greater focus on the particular types of respondents in whom he is interested. For example, if one is seeking feedback from persons who have used a new product it is unlikely that one has a sampling frame from which to select a random sample. But, for a quota sample, one would specify 'use/ experience' as a basic criterion for selection.

The quota method, according to J. Desabie (1966), is based on the following principle:

> Given that the various characteristics of a population are not independent of each other, a sample which is identical to the base population with respect to the distribution of certain base characteristics will not differ significantly from the base with respect to the statistical distribution of the other characteristics.

In other words, if you select a quota from a population provided the quota reflects the population in terms of factors such as age, income, education, occupation, etc. then it is reasonable to infer that other attributes discovered in the quota will reflect their distribution in the population.

Stocks (1973) quotes a number of definitions in his 'Review Paper on Quota Sampling Methods' which remains a basic reference on the subject. Thus Yates (1953) defines the quota method as: '. . . a variant of purposive selection. Interviewers are given definite quotas of people in different social classes, of different age-group, etc. and are instructed to obtain the requisite number of interviews in each quota.' Collins (1972) offers a similar definition when he states:

> In this form of sampling, the interviewer received, instead of a list of names and addresses, a quota to fill. This will instruct her to conduct a set number of interviews with people in various categories, e.g. six interviews with women aged under 35 in the AB social grades.

Moser and Kalton (1971) offer a more extended definition when they observe that:

> A wide variety of procedures go under the name of quota sampling but what distinguishes them all fundamentally from probability sampling is that, once the general breakdown of the sample is decided (e.g. how many men and women, how many people in each age group and in each 'social class' it is to include) and the quota assignments are allocated to interviewers, the choice of the actual sample units to fit into this framework is left to the interviewers. *Quota sampling is therefore a method of stratified sampling in which the selection within strata is non-random.* [Emphasis added.]

From these definitions it is clear that the reliability of a quota sample will depend very much upon the interviewer selecting respondents who correspond to the profile defined in the instructions for selecting a sample. Stocks (1973) cites several eminent statisticians who have criticised quota sampling on the grounds that the sampling variability of quota samples is several times as large as that found in random samples. Obviously the solution is to ensure that interviewers are properly briefed and supervised! The University of Strathclyde's Advertising Research Unit Fieldwork Guide gives precise instructions on the matter:

Quota sampling

This is used when we want to obtain a given proportion of respondents in all social classes, sex and age groups. This is usually designed to match the overall proportion of respondents in all classes, sex and age groups. Your instructions will include a quota sheet stating how many men and women in each class, sex and age group are to be interviewed.

If the quota is INTERLOCKING, it will be necessary to ensure that *each* respondent fits the quota according to *all three* criteria, e.g. if you have to interview a male aged between 25 and 34, of social class C2, it is not adequate to interview a man aged 38 of social class C2.

If the quota is PARALLEL, it is not necessary for each respondent to fit all three criteria simultaneously. Instead, you will be told the number of interviews to obtain, and within that total you will have to get a certain number of men and women, a certain number in each age group, and a certain number in each social class. The combination of the three criteria is not significant.

Of these two methods of quota sampling, the interlocking quota is the more effective in minimising error due to sampling in an on-going survey.

Method of finding quota

a) First deal with the class. Tour the area to find the streets where the property looks as though it will produce the classes you need. Council houses or houses close together in rows near the factories, etc., will be C2Ds. Middle class homes are usually in better suburbs.

b) When you are getting towards the end of your quota, you will have to ensure against wasting time interviewing someone of the wrong age or class. You will have to modify your opening and say 'Good morning . . . we are interviewing a cross section of people in different occupation groupings and different age groups. It's a survey among women in the 16–24 age group. Does that include you/is there anyone in that age group in the household?' If not, ask if they know anybody nearby who does fit. If she does fit, you can then ask the occupation of the head of the household. 'I have to interview people in all sorts of occupations. Would you tell me what is the occupation of the head of household?'

c) After conducting a successful interview at an address, you always leave five houses before making the next call, unless otherwise instructed. Although the interval may vary, you never interview next door neighbours. If at the end of an interview, the respondent suggests that you interview his/her friend, you should avoid doing this.

d) Keep a constant check that you have the right kind of respondents for the quota. If someone is out of quota, write O/Q in at the top of the questionnaire and tell your Supervisor. He/she may ask you to conduct a replacement interview so that you remain in quota.

You should not, however, discard the questionnaire which is out of quota, as it may well still be used.

e) Keep a tally of the number of interviews you have conducted on your Quota Sheet. It is important that you mark off each interview on your Quota Sheet immediately after it is completed so that you can see at a glance what type of respondents you still need to find. This also avoids the problem of doubling up on some interviews.

(See sample Quota Sheets, Figure 6.1 and Figure 6.2.)

Provided specific instructions such as these are followed then it is reasonable to accept Desabie's assumption that quota samples will yield reliable and valid

Interviewer name .A.B. SMITH.... Number of days .....5.............

Interviewer code ....OO.I............. Area ..GLASGOW.......

AGE	SEX & SOCIAL CLASS	NUMBER	TALLY CHECK	AGE	SEX & SOCIAL CLASS	NUMBER	TALLY CHECK
10 – 15	Male ABC1	2	✓✓	35 – 44	Male ABC1	1	✓
	C2				C2	1	✓
	DE	2	✓✓		DE	1	✓
	Female ABC1				Female ABC1		
	C2				C2	2	✓✓
	DE				DE		
16 – 24	Male ABC1			45 – 54	Male ABC1	1	✓
	C1				C1		
	DE				DE	4	✓✓✓✓
	Female ABC1				Female ABC1		
	C2	2	✓✓		C2		
	DE				DE	3	✓✓✓
25 – 34	Male ABC1			55 – 64	Male ABC1		
	C2	3	✓✓✓		C2		
	DE				DE		
	Female ABC1				Female ABC1	2	✓✓
	C2				C2		
	DE	1	✓		DE		

FIGURE 6.1   Sample interlocking quota sheet

Interviewer name .A.B. SMITH.... Number of days .....5...........

Interviewer code .....OOI............ Area ..GLASGOW......

SEX	Male	15	✓✓✓✓✓✓✓✓✓✓✓✓✓✓✓
	Female	10	✓✓✓✓✓✓✓✓✓✓
AGE	10 – 15	4	✓✓✓✓
	16 – 24	2	✓✓
	25 – 34	4	✓✓✓✓
	35 – 44	5	✓✓✓✓✓
	45 – 54	8	✓✓✓✓✓✓✓✓
	55 – 64	2	✓✓
SOCIAL CLASS	ABC1	6	✓✓✓✓✓✓
	C2	8	✓✓✓✓✓✓✓✓
	DE	11	✓✓✓✓✓✓✓✓✓✓✓

FIGURE 6.2   Sample parallel quota sheet

data that is representative of the population from which the sample is drawn. This expectation will be enhanced as the number of interlocking criteria is increased. Stocks (1973) proposed that the Market Research Society should adopt the following for its Code of Practice.

Quota set in terms of:	Age
	Social class
	Working Status
	Geographical location, i.e. particular street
	Type of business
	Product usage
Place of interview:	Home
	Street
	Work
Time of day of interview:	Daylight
	Evening
Weekday or weekend:	Weekday
	Saturday
	Sunday
Type of interviewer:	Working individually
	Working as a team.

Where the marketer has extensive experience of his customer, quota sampling may become very close to stratified sampling and the only issue is whether one selects respondents randomly or on the basis of judgement. Certainly, this is true of many aspects of household consumption where there is extensive documentation of the population in terms of its composition, e.g. socio-economic classifications, and its location, e.g. ACORN. As in all other cases the trade-off is between time/money and accuracy/reliability such that each case will have to be taken on its merits in terms of the perceived risk involved in the decision.

Another form of sample which involves neither probabilistic methods nor judgement is the *convenience* sample where the researcher takes a purely opportunistic approach and seeks information from a readily accessible sub-group of the population. A classic example of such a sample was that drawn by Hastorf and Cantril whose paper 'They saw a game' had a major impact on defining the nature of selective perception. Following a major incident on the field between two college football teams the researchers interviewed spectators leaving the game and discovered that depending upon which team the respondent supported there were quite different interpretations of the incident itself. Sampling the opinions of a class of students or attendees at a management conference are also examples of convenience sampling and can prove very valuable in helping to develop hypotheses which may then be tested by a more rigorous survey design if so desired. This is also true of quota sampling which may be an essential piece of exploratory research to provide information to define strata for subsequent random sampling.

Given the variety of survey methods available what factors should the manager take into account in planning a sample survey? These are issues which will be addressed in the final section of this chapter.

Planning a sample survey

The planning of a sample survey may be conveniently divided into seven steps, namely:

1. Define the purpose and objectives of the survey, i.e. what do you want to learn from the survey?
2. Define the relevant population or universe.
3. Identify the sampling frame and the elementary sampling unit (ESU).
4. Select a sampling procedure.
5. Determine the sample size.
6. Select the sample units.
7. Data collection.

The purpose or object of the survey was covered in the preceding chapter when considering which of the three basic approaches – observation, experimentation, or sample survey – was the most appropriate to use. However, while the purpose should give a broad indication of the population to be surveyed it rarely defines it sufficiently precisely for the purposes of drawing a sample. An obvious requirement is that the population should comprise persons who possess the information which the survey is intended to secure and time spent in defining precisely what this is will greatly improve the overall efficiency of the final survey. Of course, the precision with which one can define the intended respondents will depend very much upon how much one already knows about the subject under investigation. For example, if one manufactures controls for use in a process industry such as steel or pulp and paper making it is likely that one will have a complete listing of all the firms in these industries and so can easily define the universe. On the other hand if one operates a chain of international hotels almost anyone could be a potential customer and it will be necessary to specify precisely the 'product' – business traveller, conference business, tour operator, etc. – in order to begin to define the population. Even so it is unlikely that one will come up with a sufficiently comprehensive listing that one could be confident that every single firm or individual who qualifies as a sampling unit is included within it. As we have seen, cluster sampling is the only probabilistic approach which does not require a list of the population as the basis for drawing a random sample but all populations, e.g. business travellers, are not suited to this method. It follows that one will often breach the rules of probabilistic sampling owing to an inability to identify fully the population from which a sample is drawn, but this does not seem to occasion too much concern in the case of many surveys which claim their results are representative of the population. Within reason it should not bother the practitioner either, but it does underline the spurious accuracy which statistical analysis can confer upon dubious data.

Selection of a sampling procedure will depend upon a number of factors not least of which is the existence or otherwise of a listing of the population as discussed above. Tull and Hawkins (1987) suggest seven criteria for judging which type of survey to use, namely:

1. Complexity
2. Required amount of data
3. Desired accuracy
4. Sample control
5. Time requirements
6. Acceptable level of non-response
7. Cost.

Although these criteria are proposed in relation to the method of gathering data, i.e. by personal, mail, telephone or computer interview, they are equally applicable to the selection of a sampling procedure. Indeed, the selection of a sampling procedure will be influenced significantly by the preferred method of data collection and vice versa so that both will need to be considered together. (Data collection methods are discussed in Chapter 8.)

As a working generalisation the more complex a subject the more likely it is one will use personal interviewing and the less likely one will use a probabilistically based sample. With complex issues qualitative research using in-depth interviews is usually more appropriate although these may form the basis for simplified and structured questionnaires that can be administered to large samples.

Similarly, with the amount of data. The more information required the greater the likelihood that a respondent will discontinue an interview and so bias the results. Personal interviewing can help reduce this but its cost will restrict the number of interviews compared with other methods and so may incline one to a stratified or cluster sample in preference to a simple random sample. Conversely, where one only wishes to address a limited number of fairly straightforward questions a simple random sample would be preferred because of its greater accuracy and precision.

Sample control, time and cost are also closely interrelated. Clearly the more rigorous the sampling procedure the greater the time and cost involved. From a pragmatic point of view the greater accuracy yielded by probabilistic methods may be unnecessary, particularly in a dynamic market which is changing rapidly, and so predispose the practitioner towards a purposive sample. Indeed a well-executed purposive sample may yield better and more timely data for decision making than a poorly executed random sample.

The determination of sample size is largely a technical issue concerned with the required reliability of the data to be collected, i.e. what is an acceptable level of error. Management invariably want little or no error until the budgetary implications of achieving this are spelled out. Much, therefore, will depend upon the overall importance of the decision for which the data is required. Given a budget, the sampling statistician will then use an appropriate mathematical formula (see Appendix 1) to select the best design and sample size. Of course, this only applies to probability based samples; for purposive samples, judgement and experience will guide the decision.

The issue of non-response is one of the major problems facing marketing researchers. Tull and Hawkins (1987) review a wide variety of sources which have addressed the topic and note that non-respondents 'have been found to differ from respondents on a variety of demographic, socio-economic, psychological, attitudinal and behavioural dimensions'. This is the crux of the issue – establishing contact and completing an interview will often yield initial response rates as low as 10 per cent (telephone surveys) 20 per cent (mail questionnaires) and 60 per cent (personal interviews) but, provided the respondents are similar to non-respondents in terms of the characteristics relevant to the survey, this will not prevent the drawing of valid conclusions provided an adequate data base is collected. Various techniques have been devised to improve response rates and will be touched on when examining the merits/demerits of the different data collection methods in Chapter 9. But, given the nature and size of the problem it is unsurprising that managers question the time and effort involved in defining a population, developing a sample frame and selecting sampling units in a random fashion when a purposive sample involving much less cost could yield virtually equivalent data.

In the final analysis, it all boils down to the risk perceptions of those responsible for taking the final decision. Personal experience suggests that senior managers who are prepared to make major investment decisions on the basis of very limited evidence will often look for unreasonable, and often spurious accuracy on issues such as market share or sales forecasts, particularly for new products. Hopefully, increased exposure to marketing research as part of their career development will encourage the next generation of senior managers to invest more research effort on strategic issues and less on tactical matters and reverse the current emphasis.

Summary

In this chapter we have reviewed the ideas underlying the use of *sampling* as a means of improving our knowledge and understanding of the larger *population* or *universe* from which the sample was drawn. Save for very small populations, as may occur in some highly concentrated industrial markets, where it is possible to survey the whole population by means of a *census* the sample survey is the only practical means of acquiring data on which one can base projections about the behaviour of the whole population.

Two broad approaches to sampling are available – *probability based* or *random* samples and *non-probability based* or *purposive* samples. In a true random sample it must be possible to list every member of the population to be surveyed and then select the *sampling units* (ESU) in such a manner that each has a known and non-zero chance of being included. A variety of techniques including *simple random samples, stratified samples, cluster-samples* and *systematic samples* were reviewed as were *judgement, quota* and *convenience* samples as non-probability based approaches.

Each technique has particular advantages and drawbacks nearly all of which require the user to compromise between costs and benefits in terms of accuracy, precision and reliability. Thus, in planning a sample survey it is necessary to balance the needs of the decision maker against the budgetary constraints. The responsibility of the researcher is to make explicit just what trade-offs are possible and what their implications are. To do this fully one must also consider carefully how the desired data are to be collected and it is to this which we turn in the next two chapters.

References

Collins, M. (1972) *Consumer Market Research Handbook* (New York: McGraw-Hill).

Martin, Paul and Bateson, Patrick (1986) *Measuring Behaviour* (Cambridge: Cambridge University Press).

Moser, G. A. and Kalton, G. (1971) *Survey Methods in Social Investigation*, 2nd edn (London: Heinemann).

New Collins Thesaurus (1985) (Glasgow: Collins).

Stocks, J. M. B. (1973) 'Review Paper on Quota Sampling Methods: Market Research Society Annual Conference Proceedings.

Tull, Donald S. and Hawkins, Del I. (1987) *Marketing Research*, 4th edn (New York: Macmillan).

Yates, F. (1953) *Sampling Methods for Census and Surveys* (London: Charles Griffin).

Appendix 1   Technical aspects of sampling

Introduction

While this book is addressed primarily to the *user* of marketing research rather than the *doer* some insight into the practitioner's art is necessary if the manager is to be able to assess the merits/demerits of the proposals submitted to him. Nowhere is the need more acute than in the cases of sample design and data analysis; accordingly the purpose of this appendix is to provide a limited overview of some of the key issues involved in selecting sampling techniques and calculating an appropriate sample size. Technically, however, these issues are more the province of the statistician than the marketer and it is to the former we should turn for detailed explanation (see reading list at the end of this appendix).

In the main body of the chapter we made reference to a number of technical terms such as error, and variability but before seeking to define and explain these it will be helpful to look first at the statistical basis of sampling.

The Basis of Sampling

Despite the difficulties of enumerating entire populations the use of sampling techniques is of comparatively recent origin. In her book *Significance Tests*, Evelyn Caulcott, dates the use of sampling and surveys using sampling methods to 'the great post-1945 expansion in the use of statistical methods generally'. Prior to this, surveys of the kind undertaken by Rowntree, who is credited with the first statistical survey in the UK in 1899 (into working class households in York) were based upon a census of the entire population under consideration. However, when Rowntree published the results of his second survey in 1941 (*Poverty and Progress*) he included an analysis of a sample of his survey (census) data from which he concluded that, given a sufficiently large group, a sample of 1 in 10 would yield data which compared favourably with a complete enumeration. The key issue, however, is how can we be sure that our sample is truly representative of the population from which it is drawn?

The answer is that *we cannot* but we can use statistical methods to enable us to infer how likely or probable it is that our sample does represent the population. The key to being able to draw inferences as to the representativeness of a sample is to be found in the concept of probability which, in everyday language, may be defined as 'one's strength of belief that an event will occur' (Greensted *et al.*, 1974). To express this 'strength of belief' it is conventional to use a scale ranging from 0 which represents certainty that an event will *not* occur to 1 which represents certainty that it will. However, when expressing the probability of an occurrence in normal speech it is more usual to express this as a percentage such as 'I'm 80% certain it will rain tomorrow' or 'There's only a 10% chance that the flight won't be delayed by air traffic control.'

Underlying both these statements is the implied assumption that they are based upon repeated observations of the frequency of rainy days and the occurrence of flight delays. If, in fact, we have made such observations then we can tabulate them as a frequency distribution such as that for flight delays shown in Table 6A.1.

TABLE 6A.1   Flight delays frequency table

Delay	Frequency	Relative frequency
0	30	30/300 = 0.100
1–10 mins	50	50/300 = 0.166
11–20 mins	70	70/300 = 0.233
21–30 mins	70	70/300 = 0.233
31–40 mins	50	50/300 = 0.166
Over 40 mins	30	30/300 = 0.100
Total	300	1.000

A table such as this allows us to make a variety of probabilistic statements concerning the incidence of flight delays, e.g. 50 per cent of flights experience a delay of more than 20 minutes; it is 90 per cent certain the delay will not exceed 40 minutes, and so on. The problem is, however, that our observations only cover a particular period of time – a sample – and the question remains 'How representative is the sample of all flight departures?'

To answer this question we need to be able to compare the sample with what we believe is the underlying distribution of all flight departure times from which our sample has been drawn. To do this we need to compare our actual frequency distribution with a theoretical *probability density function* which represents what the distribution may be assumed to look like given an infinite number of samples. In sampling theory the *normal* or *Gaussian* distribution is probably the best known and frequently used probability density function and its properties will be described after first considering the concept of probability in a little more detail.

As implied in Table 6A.1 the total probability of all the possible outcomes of an event is represented as 1 (or 100 per cent) so we can express the likelihood of any specific occurrence as a fraction of 1. Alternatively, if p is the probability of occurrence then $1 - p$ is the probability of its non-occurrence. If, therefore, we wish to create a theoretical probability density function it is conventional to start with the simplest case which considers a pair of mutually exclusive and equiprobable outcomes – the tossing of a coin. Assuming that the coin is fair (and that it does not fall on its edge!) then the probability of either a head or tail on any given toss is 0.5. Similarly, if we take a dice the probability of throwing any number between 1 and 6 is 0.116 or, conversely, the probability of *not* throwing a given number between 1 and 6 is $1 - 0.166 = 0.833$.

This is not the place to attempt an exposition of the theory of probability (which is dealt with clearly and fully in Moroney (1951) and Ehrenberg (1982)) but as everyone knows who has tossed a coin or thrown a die, while the probability of a given outcome is the same for each throw there is nothing to prevent a continuous sequence of heads or tails occurring or for us to keep throwing a 1 when we need a 6 to get started. While it may be no consolation to us if we consistently select the 'wrong' option in games of chance at least the theory of probability enables us to quantify how likely/unlikely is a given outcome such as being dealt 3 sevens in a game of black jack. However, confining ourselves to the simplest case of coin tossing then it can easily be shown that the probability of a given run of heads or tails is equiprobable so that if we were to plot the outcome of a sequence of throws we would expect the actual frequency of 'runs' of heads or tails would be distributed as shown in Table 6A.1. The reason this is so is because of the operation of the central limit theorem which:

> states that when observations are made up of irregular elements which are (i) large in number, (ii) independent of each other, and (iii) additive, the resulting variation will follow a distribution which gets closer and closer to a normal distribution as the number of elements increases. (Ehrenberg, 1982, p. 81).

Given that this is the expected theoretical distribution we can now make formal statements about the observed distribution of outcome/frequencies which represent our 'sample' of the infinite underlying distribution. To do so we need to understand something of the properties of the normal distribution.

Perhaps the first point which needs to be made is that there are several theoretical distributions including the binomial, Poisson and normal which may be used for drawing inferences from observed frequency distributions. In fact, our coin tossing example is a binomial distribution of discrete or discontinuous values but, because its mean and standard deviation correspond to those of a normal distribution in this instance, it becomes possible to use the 'simpler' and more familiar normal distribution which is appropriate for continuous data, for purposes of analysis. (The term 'simpler' refers to the method of calculation of the various distributions and is effectively redundant given the advent of powerful computers and appropriate software!).

Caulcott (1973) attributes the 'discovery' of the normal distribution to Abraham de Moivre (1667–1745) who considered it had practical applications only in relation to games of chance. However, Carl Gauss (hence Gaussian distribution) developed the curve to explain the occurrence of errors when taking repeated measurements of the same experiment or phenomenon. Analysis showed that small errors occurred fairly frequently but the larger the error the less frequently it occurred. When plotted the 'normal curve of errors' was shown to have a symmetrical 'bell' shape as shown in Figure 6A.1.

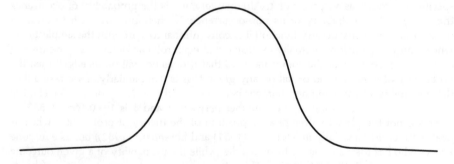

FIGURE 6A. 1   The Gaussian or normal distribution

In nature it has been found that the distribution of many kinds of continuous data approximate to the normal distribution, e.g. age, height, intelligence so that even where the approximation is not very close it is possible to describe these distributions by reference to the parameters of the normal distribution – the *mean* and *standard deviation*.

The mean of a normal distribution is the same as the median and the mode and represents the measure of central tendency while the standard deviation measures the dispersion or distribution of the data around this measure. Statistics texts provide the formula for calculating the curve of the normal distribution but, for all practical purposes, all one needs to know is that a given number of all cases will lie within 1 or more standard deviations of the mean. In theory the normal curve does not touch the horizontal (*y*)-axis admitting the possibility of the infinite nature of the data set. But, again for all practical purposes, as 99.74 per cent of all cases lie within ±3 standard deviations of the mean, knowledge of these two parameters will enable us to make highly specific statements about the likelihood that sample data are representative of the population from which it is drawn.

In Table 6A.2 are given the values for the area of the curve (number of observations) which fall within 1 and 3 standard deviations of the mean, while Fig. 6A.2 depicts these graphically.

TABLE 6A.2   Areas in two tails of the normal curve at selected values of x/σ from the arithmetic mean

This table shows:

x/σ	0.00	0.01	0.02	0.03	0.04	0.05	0.06	0.07	0.08	0.09
0.0	1.0000	0.9920	0.9840	0.9761	0.9681	0.9601	0.9522	0.9442	0.9362	0.9283
0.1	0.9203	0.9124	0.9045	0.8966	0.8887	0.8808	0.8729	0.8650	0.8572	0.8493
0.2	0.8415	0.8337	0.8259	0.8181	0.8103	0.8026	0.7949	0.7872	0.7795	0.7718
0.3	0.7642	0.7566	0.7490	0.7414	0.7339	0.7263	0.7188	0.7114	0.7039	0.6965
0.4	0.6892	0.6818	0.6745	0.6672	0.6599	0.6527	0.6455	0.6384	0.6312	0.6241
0.5	0.6171	0.6101	0.6031	0.5961	0.5892	0.5823	0.5755	0.5687	0.5619	0.5552
0.6	0.5485	0.5419	0.5353	0.5287	0.5222	0.5157	0.5093	0.5029	0.4965	0.4902
0.7	0.4839	0.4777	0.4715	0.4654	0.4593	0.4533	0.4473	0.4413	0.4354	0.4295
0.8	0.4237	0.4179	0.4122	0.4065	0.4009	0.3953	0.3898	0.3843	0.3789	0.3735
0.9	0.3681	0.3628	0.3576	0.3524	0.3472	0,3421	0.3371	0.3320	0.3271	0.3222
1.0	0.3173	0.3125	0.3077	0.3030	0.2983	0.2937	0.2891	0.2846	0.2801	0.2757
1.1	0.2713	0.2670	0.2627	0.2585	0.2543	0.2501	0.2460	0.2420	0.2380	0.2340
1.2	0.2301	0.2263	0.2225	0.2187	0.2150	0.2113	0.2077	0.2041	0.2005	0.1917
1.3	0.1936	0.1902	0.1868	0.1835	0.1802	0.1770	0.1738	0.1707	0.1676	0.1645
1.4	0.1615	0.1585	0.1556	0.1527	0.1499	0.1471	0.1443	0.1416	0.1389	0.1362

1.5	0.1336	0.1310	0.1285	0.1260	0.1236	0.1211	0.1188	0.1164	0.1141	0.1118
1.6	0.1096	0.1074	0.1052	0.1031	0.1010	0..989	0.0969	0.0949	0.0930	0.0910
1.7	0.0891	0.0873	0.0854	0.0836	0.0819	0.0801	0.0784	0.0767	0.0751	0.0735
1.8	0.0719	0.0703	0.0688	0.0672	0.0658	0.0643	0.0629	0.0615	0.0601	0.0588
1.9	0.0574	0.0561	0.0549	0.0536	0.0524	0.0512	0.0500	0.0488	0.0477	0.0466
2.0	0.0455	0.0444	0.0434	0.0424	0.0414	0.0404	0.0394	0.0385	0.0375	0.0366
2.1	0.0357	0.0349	0.0340	0.0332	0.0324	0.0316	0.0308	0.0300	0.0293	0.0285
2.2	0.0278	0.0271	0.0264	0.0257	0.0251	0.0244	0.0238	0.0232	0.0226	0.0220
2.3	0.0214	0.0209	0.0203	0.0198	0.0193	0.0188	0.0183	0.0178	0.0173	0.0168
2.4	0.0164	0.0160	0.0155	0.0151	0.0147	0.0143	0.0139	0.0135	0.0131	0.0128
2.5	0.0124	0.0121	0.0117	0.0114	0.0111	0.0108	0.0105	0.0102	0.00988	0.00960
2.6	0.00932	0.00905	0.00879	0.00854	0.00829	0.00805	0.00781	0.00759	0.00736	0.00715
2.7	0.00693	0.00673	0.00653	0.00633	0.00614	0.00596	0.00578	0.00561	0.00544	0.00527
2.8	0.00511	0.00495	0.00480	0.00465	0.00451	0.00437	0.00424	0.00410	0.00398	0.00385
2.9	0.00373	0.00361	0.00350	0.00339	0.00328	0.00318	0.00308	0.00298	0.00288	0.00279

x/σ	0.0	0.1	0.2	0.3	0.4	0.5	0.6	0.7	0.8	0.9
3	0.00270	0.00194	0.00137	0.0^3967	0.0^3674	0.0^3465	0.0^3318	0.0^3216	0.0^3145	0.0^4962
4	0.0^4633	0.0^4413	0.0^4267	0.0^4171	0.0^4108	0.0^5680	0.0^5422	0.0^5260	0.0^5159	0.0^6958
5	0.0^6573	0.0^6340	0.0^6199	0.0^6116	0.0^7666	0.0^7380	0.0^7214	0.0^7120	0.0^8663	0.0^8364
6	0.0^8197	0.0^8106	0.0^9565	0.0^9298	0.0^9155	$0.0^{10}803$	$0.0^{10}411$	$0.0^{10}208$	$0.0^{10}105$	$0.0^{11}520$

Source: This table is copyrighted by Prentice-Hall, Inc. It is reproduced by permission of Frederick E. Croxton.
Source: Kinnear and Taylor *Marketing Research* (1983) 3rd edn (New York: McGraw-Hill).

Given that we believe our population data is normally distributed then it follows that we can use the parameters of the normal distribution as the basis for determining whether the data in our sample appears to be representative of that population. Of course, if we know the mean and/or standard deviation of a population then we can compare our sample data directly with these but, more often than not, the reason we draw samples is to learn something about the population because we do not possess knowledge about the factor in question and cannot afford to survey the whole population. In such cases the process is reversed and *we infer the parameters of the population from those derived from the sample.* Naturally the confidence we can place in this inference will vary according to the variation in our sample data and the actual size of the sample itself but, as a basic proposition, hopefully it can be accepted without detailed proof. (Most statistics and some market research texts spend many pages and even chapters on worked examples to prove the relationship. Users may safely assume that the calculations are correct!)

Overall, however, we return to the point that selection of sample size is largely a matter of judgement based on a number of factors admirably summarised by Alreck and Settle in Table 6A.3.

Table 6.A3   Factors determining sample size

Factors indicating a large sample

1. The decisions to be based on the survey data have very serious or costly consequences.
2. The sponsors demand a very high level of confidence in the data and estimates.
3. There is likely to be a high level of variance among the units in the population to be sampled.
4. The sample is to be divided into relatively small subsamples during analysis and interpretation.
5. Project cost and timing vary only slightly with increases in the size of the sample.
6. Time and resources are readily available to cover the costs of data collection.

Factors indicating a small sample

1. There are few if any major decisions or commitments to be based on the survey data.
2. The sponsors require only rough estimates concerning the parameters of the population.
3. The population to be sampled is very homogeneous, with little variance among units
4. The analysis and interpretation will be based on the entire sample or only a few, large samples.
5. A large proportion of total project costs are for data collection or costs increase dramatically with sample size.
6. Budget constraints and/or time requirements limit the volume of data that can be collected.

Source: Pamela L. Alreck and Robert B. Settle, *The Survey Research Handbook* (Homewood, Ill.: Irwin, 1985).

References

Alreck, Pamela L and Settle, Robert B. (1985) *The Survey Research Handbook* (Homewood, Ill: Richard D. Irwin).

Caulcott, Evelyn, (1973) *Significance Tests* (London: Routledge & Kegan Paul).

Ehrenberg, A. S. C. (1982) *A Primer in Data Reduction* (Chichester: John Wiley).

Greensted, C. S., Jardine, A. K. S. and Macfarlane, J. D. (1974) *Essentials of Statistics in Marketing* (London: Heinemann).

Kinnear, Thomas C. and Taylor, James R. (1987) *Marketing Research: An Applied Approach*, 3rd edn (New York: McGraw-Hill).

Moroney, M. J. (1951) *Facts from Figures* (Harmondsworth: Penguin).

Appendix 2   Technical report

The study

The National Consumer Council commissioned Research Services Limited (RSL) in the summer of 1979 to undertake a survey of consumer concerns. The aim of the survey was defined as being to 'assess consumers' perceptions of the experiences and problems they face in their day-to-day lives and to explore the importance they attach to them, both in relation to other areas of life, and over time'. It was agreed that the study should cover adults aged 18 and over resident in the United Kingdom.

Development work

The development work for this study consisted of two group discussions and 14 semi-structured interviews. The aim of the group discussions was to provide the research team with a first and unprompted indication of the types of problems concerning people, and of the language used to describe them. Because group discussions can only be undertaken with a limited range of people, RSL restricted both groups to social groups C1, C2 and D, and to the age range 25–44. The first group, in Welling, Kent, was an all-male session, and the second, in Northampton was all female.

Semi-structured interviews were undertaken in London, Buckinghamshire and Bristol. Both RSL and NCC staff were involved in this work. For about half the interviews a detailed prompt list based on the RSL proposal was used: for the remainder a looser structure was used, relying more on stimulation from the informants.

The pilot study

The questionnaire developed by NCC/RSL for the pilot study consisted of pre-coded questions, each faced by a write-in page for details of informants' problems. Detailed classification data – derived from the relevant National Readership Survey questions – was also obtained. Each interview started with informants being asked to fill in a brief self-completion questionnaire containing two batteries of attitude scales to allow some evaluation of each informant's life satisfaction.

The pilot study involved a quota sample of 18 interviews, the interviewing being undertaken in three different areas of the country. Broad age, sex and social grade controls were set to ensure that a range of ages and types of people were interviewed. As a result of this development work, and of the meetings with NCC specialists, the number of questions was increased within ten of the eleven sections of the questionnaires. The final questionnaire allowed us to obtain details about approximately 1000 potential problems.

The sample

The sample was a two-stage probability sample of adults aged 18 and over, resident in the United Kingdom, and the sampling procedure was the following:

(i) all wards were stratified within Registrar-General's Planning Region in descending order of Labour vote at the 1979 General Election;

(ii) a total of 160 wards were selected with probability proportional to their current electorates; over-sampling for Scotland, Wales and Northern Ireland (see Below) was introduced at this stage; the number of wards selected were:

England	100
Wales	19
Scotland	22
Northern Ireland	9

(iii) within each ward 19 electors were selected across the total electorate by a random start equal interval procedure;

(iv) to these 'starred' elector addresses the next following address was added if this appeared to be missing from the register, in order to represent those adults who were not on the electoral registers;

(v) an interview was attempted with each 'starred' elector and with the appropriate non-elector adult at the 'second address' if issued. Movers-in, aliens and eligible people who have failed to register are selected by the Marchant–Blyth procedure.

Fieldwork

Fieldwork was undertaken in two stages over a period of one year. Forty-two areas of those originally sampled (27 in England, 5 in Wales, 5 in Scotland and 5 in Northern Ireland) were issued to the field on 20 November 1979 and 512 usable interviews completed by 20 February 1980.

A total of 118 areas (75 in England, 14 in Wales, 17 in Scotland and 12 in Northern Ireland) were issued on 12 September 1980 and 1458 usable interviews achieved by 18 November 1980.

The response rate for both stages are given in Table 6A.4:

TABLE 6A.4   Response rates for NCC questionnaire

	1979		1980	
	No.	%	No.	%
Total addresses	871	100	2555	100
less – not located	12	1	203	8
– demolished	6	1	38	1
– vacant	22	3	130	5
Total possible addresses	831	95	2184	85
total persons	895	100	2437	100
less – not known	26	3	98	4
– moved	110	12	190	8
– dead	13	1	23	1
Total possible persons	746	100	2126	100
less – no reply	63	8	167	8
– refused	96	13	250	12
– language problems	2	*	12	1
– sick permanently	15	2	44	2
– sick temporarily	6	1	14	1
– busy temporarily	25	3	73	3
– away temporarily	24	3	102	5
Total interviewed	515	69	1464	69
Total usable interviews	512		1458	

A total of nine questionnaires were rejected in analysis as being incomplete, giving a total of 1970.

The questionnaire

The questionnaire used in Stage 1 contained the following:

A self-completion attitude battery
Section   1 Housing
2 Area
3 Getting around
4 Shopping
5 Fuel and water
6 Finance and money
7 Tax and work
8 Health
9 Education
10 Welfare
11 Communications
Classification

Within the main body of the questionnaire, the sections were rotated for half the sample (i.e. sections 5–11 asked first, followed by sections 1–4).

The questionnaire used in Stage 2, although amended, was substantially the same. In addition to the section rotation mentioned above, half the sample was not asked the communications section in order to further reduce the average length of interview. Communications sections questions are based on 1204 total.

Regional oversampling

Because the NCC wished to analyse separately the experiences of people living in Scotland, Wales and Northern Ireland, these countries were oversampled (i.e. more respondents were interviewed than their true proportion of the UK population). For analysis covering the whole of the UK, the responses from people living in all regions had then to be weighted by country and by sex to represent population distribution. The numbers of respondents, both unweighted and weighted, are shown in Table 6A.5:

TABLE 6A.5 Regional oversampling

	Unweighted (i.e. actual interviews)	Weighted
Total	1970	1968
England	1198	1633
Scotland	277	187
Wales	247	98
Northern Ireland	248	50

The factors applied to the 1970 respondents were as follows:

England, men	1.43	Scotland, men	0.70
England, women	1.31	Scotland, women	0.65
Wales, men	0.46	Northern Ireland, men	0.21
Wales, women	0.35	Northern Ireland, women	0.20

The confidence limits of survey percentages

Figure 6.A3 gives the approximate 99 per cent confidence limits for any percentage contained in the consumer concerns survey report. These confidence limits are such that there is only about 1 chance in 20 of the true percentage lying outside the limits given by the observed percentage plus or minus the confidence limit.

To obtain the confidence limits for any percentage, lay a straight-edge across the chart so that it joins the size of the unweighted sample on the left-hand scale. The confidence limits can then be read off the central scale where it is cut by the straight-edge.

Example: The unweighted sample for social grade C2 (skilled manual) is 620. Among this group 26 per cent claimed to have bought floor coverings in the last 12 months.

A straight-edge laid across 620 on the left-hand scale and 26 per cent on the right hand-scale cuts the central scale at approximately 4.3 per cent.

The 95 per cent confidence limits of the reported percentage of 26 per cent are therefore approximately 30.3 per cent (i.e. 26 per cent + 4.3 per cent) and 21.7 per cent (i.e. 26 per cent − 4.3 per cent); there is only a 1 in 20 chance that the true percentage lies outside these limits.

The confidence limits of a percentage are the same for 100 minus that percentage. Thus to use the chart for percentages greater that 50 per cent (e.g. 65 per cent), subtract the percentage from 100 (e.g. 35 per cent) and then use the chart in the normal way (i.e. reading 35 per cent, instead of 65 per cent, on the right-hand scale).

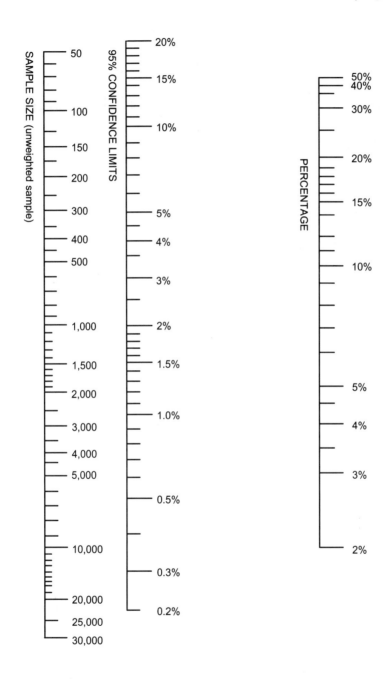

FIGURE 6.A3   95% confidence limits

Data collection – questionnaire design

Introduction

Ask a silly question and you'll get a silly answer. Trite but true. In the previous chapter we looked carefully at the means of selecting respondents from a population in order to ensure that they were representative of that population. One thing was particularly obvious – it takes time, effort and money to select an unbiased sample; yet all this investment will be squandered if one fails to design clear, relevant, meaningful and unambiguous questions for eliciting the desired information from the selected respondents. This is the subject of this chapter. First we look at the design of questions, next at the issue of scaling and finally the construction of questionnaires.

Question Design

In an earlier chapter we cited Tull and Hawkins's (1987) definition of survey research as 'the systematic gathering of information from respondents for the purposes of understanding and/or predicting some aspect of the behaviour of the population of interest'. Such information may be factual or opinion based and the researcher's ability to secure it will depend heavily upon both the structure and the sequence in which he puts questions to the respondent. In turn, the information he receives will be a function of the respondent's *ability* and *willingness* to respond (Moser and Kalton 1971). On ability it is recommended that:

the surveyor should aim to ask questions only from those likely to be able to answer them accurately; to ask about past events only if he can reasonably expect people to remember them accurately (perhaps with the aid of recall methods); and to ask their opinions only if he can be reasonably sure that they understand what is involved and are able to give meaningful answers. It is always well to remember that most survey questions are addressed to a variety of people very differently qualified to answer them.

It is also a well established phenomenon that, once committed to a survey, respondents will answer questions even when they have no knowledge at all. Churchill (1987) cites the example of a question in a public opinion survey which sought views upon a mythical piece of legislation. A total of 99.7 per cent of the population expressed firm views on the desirability of the non-existent Metallic Metals Act with only 0.3 per cent having 'no opinion'. Numerous other examples are to be found in the literature and it is common practice now to include a fictional item in a questionnaire as a control item to help establish actual knowledge or experience of the survey subject matter.

With regard to willingness to participate in a survey this has been shown to depend very much on the prospective respondent's interest in the subject of the survey and on the method of administration (mail, telephone or personal interview). As noted in the previous chapter, non-response is a major problem in probabilistically based surveys and researchers devote considerable effort and ingenuity in reducing this to an acceptable minimum. (We return to this issue in discussing the administration of questionnaires in the next chapter.)

In addition to facts and opinions research may also be used to improve understanding of motivation, i.e. *why* people behave the way they do, and also to help predict behaviour.

Question phraseology

The actual phrasing of questions is critical to the quality of the data obtained and is a topic given extensive coverage in most specialist books on marketing research techniques. A sample of some of the better known of these is summarised in Table 7.1. Tull and Hawkins (1987) suggest that there are five general questions which must be addressed to ensure that both respondent and researcher assign exactly the same meaning to a question, namely:

1. Are the words, singularly and in total, understandable to the respondents?
2. Are the words biased or 'loaded' in any respect?
3. Are the alternatives involved in the questions clearly stated?
4. Are any assumptions implied by the questions clearly stated?
5. What frame of reference is the respondent being asked to assume?

To answer these questions it will be helpful to review the major issues identified in Table 7.1.

TABLE 7.1   Issues in question phrasing

	Moser and Kalton	Alreck and Settle	Tull and Hawkins	Churchill	Chisnall
Focus or specific nature of question	√	√	√	√	√
Simple language	√	√	√	√	√
Ambiguity/clarity	√	√	√	√	
Vague or imprecise words/Vocabulary	√	√	√	√	
Leading question overemphasis/bias	√	√	√	√	
Presuming questions	√				
Hypothetical	√				√
Personalised questions	√				
Embarrassing questions Social desirability	√	√			
Questions on periodical behaviour	√				
Questions involving memory	√	√			√
Brevity/economy of language		√			√
Loaded questions		√	√		
Double-barrelled questions		√		√	
Implicit alternatives/ assumptions			√	√	

As noted earlier a major factor influencing the quality of survey data is the respondent's ability to recall information accurately or else retrieve it from readily accessible records (applicable mainly to mail questionnaires). The problem with *memory* is that if people cannot recall accurately they are likely to guess and so introduce an unknown error element into the findings.

Mayer (1965) points out that while memory decays over time the effect of *recency* may be influenced by two other 'laws of memory' – the intensity of the stimulus and the degree of association. In other words we may forget trivial or minor events almost immediately but recall major happenings clearly years after the actual event, e.g. graduation day, wedding, birth of a child, etc.

Because of the influence of association we may also recall trivial events associated with major events long after they occurred. The message for the researcher is that one cannot assume an ability to recall accurately and so should take steps to select respondents for whom the topic is important and of interest (which will also improve response rates) and design questions which will aid recall or, alternatively, elicit qualitative statements which provide an indication of the strength, frequency, etc. of the behaviour which cannot be quantified precisely. Scaling and multiple choice answers are both of use in such situations and will be discussed in greater detail later.

Converse and Presser (1986) identify three techniques which have proved useful in enhancing the validity of the reporting of the past, namely: (a) bounded recall; (b) narrowing of the reference period; (c) cueing.

Bounded recall is useful in reducing over-reporting owing to people's tendency to lose track of time and so include past events which happened before the time period under investigation. For example, in reporting the number of times my train or flight has been late in the past six months it is quite likely that I will include occasions extending over a longer period. To avoid this one should establish a baseline in an initial survey then re-interview the respondents at a later date and establish what has happened in the intervening period. Panels are particularly appropriate for collecting data in this way where one is especially interested in specific consumption behaviour over a defined period.

As the term suggests *narrowing the reference* period means inviting the respondent to report recent events rather than expecting prodigious feats of memory to recall trivial events that occurred weeks or even months ago. Converse and Presser (1986) offer the following example. 'Rather than asking "Do you get regular physical exercise?" (IF YES), How many hours of physical exercise do you usually get in a week?" one can zero in on a narrow time period and ask, "Did you get any physical exercise yesterday?" And, if yes, "How much?"'

However, such a question also raises the question as to whether 'yesterday' was a typical day. If asked on a Monday I would answer 'Yes, I swam half a mile' as I invariably do on a Sunday morning but what would I say if asked on Tuesday through to Saturday? To overcome this type of problem one can ask respondents to *average* their behaviour, e.g. Q. 'On average how much exercise do you take?' A. 'I swim half a mile on Sunday mornings, walk to the station most weekdays and go hillwalking every other weekend.'

The use of *landmarks* and *cues* is still regarded as experimental but the thinking behind them appears sound. *Landmarks* are particular events or dates which are likely to have salience as reference points, e.g. major holidays, while *cues* amount to expanded explanations of the key word on which information is being sought so that respondents will not discard answers which they think might not fall within the definition of the key word.

Several of the issues identified in the table are dimensions of the same basic requirement – understandability. Thus ambiguity arises from vague, complex or imprecise words while clarity will come from focus, brevity and the use of simple language.

Questions should be simple, intelligible and clear. It has been pointed out that, because questionnaires are usually written by educated persons who have a special interest in and understanding of the topic of their inquiry, and because these people usually consult with other educated and concerned persons, it is much more common for questionnaires to be over-written, over-complicated, and too demanding of the respondent than they are to be single-minded, superficial, and not demanding enough.

While the generally accepted wisdom follows Payne's (1951) advice that questions should be kept short and not exceed twenty words in length Converse and Presser (1986) cite examples of longer questions proving more effective in eliciting more information. Possible reasons are that longer questions may stimulate respondents to talk more, may provide the respondent with longer to think of their reply, or may stimulate wider recall on the part of the respondent.

A major source of ambiguity is the so-called double-barrelled question. For example, if we asked the question, 'Have you flown to Glasgow on British Midland or the Shuttle?', the answer, 'Yes', would certainly inform us that the respondent had flown to Glasgow but we would not know if this was on British Midland, the Shuttle, or if both carriers had been used. To obtain the information the interviewer apparently wants we would be better advised to ask:

Have you flown to Glasgow?   Yes ____
                                                               No   ____
If 'Yes' can you tell me which airline you used?
          British Midland
          Shuttle/British Airways   ____
          Other (write in) _____

Double-negative questions are also a source of ambiguity. For example, Oppenheim (1966) cites the question 'Would you rather not use a non-medicated shampoo?' (What does a negative answer mean here?)

Vague wording also leads to ambiguity even though the words themselves may be in common usage. For example, words expressing frequency such as 'often', occasionally', 'regularly', 'frequently' can mean quite different things to different people. For example, the answer 'Yes' to the questions 'Do you clean your teeth/brush your shoes/wash your car/regularly?' could mean 1 to 3 times a day/daily to weekly/weekly to monthly/respectively. Moser and Kalton (1971) counsel against the use of vague words and phrases such as 'kind of', 'fairly', 'generally', 'often', 'many', 'much the same' and 'on the whole' all of which are likely to yield equally vague answers. They also advise against 'why' and 'what' questions without some frame of reference to give focus to the question. Despite this advice many questionnaires do include such questions and derive useful information from them. To do so one needs to pre-identify the main responses one anticipates receiving, possibly with the intention of rank ordering these in terms of the spontaneous, top of the head reaction, e.g. Could you tell me why you prefer to fly British Midland to Glasgow?

More convenient schedules	_____
Better inflight service	_____
Easier check-in	_____
More friendly	_____
Cheaper	_____
Other (write in)	_____

Of course, many respondents may cite more than one reason but this can be accommodated by numbering the answers 1, 2, etc. so that one can still assess which factor first comes to mind as the major benefit offered by British Midland by comparison with other competitors – its unique selling point. Such a question can also provide a basis for probing on both the answers given and the factors not cited.

Equally confusing to respondents as non-specific questions are those which use words or phrases which are complex or not in common usage. One of the advantages cited for undertaking exploratory qualitative research through group discussions or unstructured/semi-structured interviews with individuals is that these give the researcher an insight into the vocabulary used by prospective respondents when thinking and talking about the research topic. In addition to helping to develop meaningful questions, such exploratory research may also throw up words or phrases which are particularly expressive to users and so can be used in developing a more effective selling/advertising message. The story is often told of a new floor polish developed by Johnson & Johnson which had a high resistance to traffic and so required less frequent buffing than other competitive products. Initial sales were disappointing so J & J commissioned some consumer research to help establish why their product had not achieved more success. The research showed that most users could not see any additional benefit from the new product and so preferred to stick to the safety of their current brand. Probing on the traffic resistant property revealed that this was very attractive but that housewives referred to the marking of polished floors as 'scuffing' so what they wanted was a 'scuff resistant' polish. Relaunched with this promise it was an instant success. (Perhaps the moral here is to do your research first!)

The above is an example of a word in common usage among respondents but unknown to the researcher. A much more frequent problem is that the well-educated researcher will have acquired a vocabulary which will let his peer group know he is well educated but may not be understandable to the audience to whom the research is directed. While this problem is especially acute in the case of technical terms (even when communicating with other 'experts' it is as well to define precisely what you mean by such technical terms) it is also aggravated by the use of complex words where simple ones would do. Specialist texts such as Payne's *The Art of Asking Questions* (1951) or Seltiz *et al.* (1959) *Research Methods in Social Relations* give extensive examples of the use of simple language in place of more pretentious and obscure phraseology while Gower's *Plain Words* is an essential *vade-mecum* for anyone seeking to communicate clearly with others.

An example of simpler alternatives provided by Gower is reproduced as Table 7.2.

Focus and brevity will also help to reduce ambiguity and complexity. Focus will usually be achieved by constantly reminding oneself what is the fundamental purpose of the survey, i.e. *what do we want to know*. Alreck and Settle (1985) offer three examples of the right and wrong focus but one will suffice to make the point about establishing purchase preference:

Wrong: which brand do you like the best?
Right: which of these brands are you most likely to buy?

While the first question may help establish which brand has the highest reputation it does not necessarily tell you what you want to know, i.e. taking everything into account what do you actually buy?

Brevity will usually result if one sticks to one topic or issue at a time – a practice which will help avoid double-barrelled and complex questions. In addition to improving the likelihood that the respondent fully understands the question he is being asked to answer, the use of a series of sequential questions will often prove more economical as it is possible to skip questions which cannot apply given an earlier answer, or to probe in greater detail where a respondent possesses an attribute on which more information is required. Occasionally, one will have to use more than one idea to define an issue to which one wishes a reply. Wherever possible, use a separate sentence for each point rather than a compound sentence containing several clauses but, if this is not possible careful attention to vocabulary and the avoidance of superfluous words will help make the question clear. For example, to determine the 'brand loyalty' of a British Midland flier travelling to Glasgow you might ask the following 'What would you do if you got to the airport and found that there was a 30-minute delay in your British Midland flight but there was a Shuttle leaving within that time?' This question would be better phrased as 'If your British Midland flight was delayed how long would you be prepared to wait before switching to an available Shuttle?' This is a compound question but yields better data from a simpler and more direct approach. Alternatively, you could have said: 'A 30-minute delay is announced on your British Midland flight. A Shuttle is due to leave before then. What would you do?'

TABLE 7.2 Complex and simple words

Acquaint	Inform or tell
Adumbrate	Sketch; outline; foreshadow
Advert	Refer
Ameliorate	Better; improve
Apprise	Inform
Assist	Help
Commence	Begin
Consider	Think
Desire	Wish
Donate	Give
Eventuate	Come about; happen; occur; result; turn out
Evince	Show; manifest; display
Factor	Fact; consideration; circumstance; feature; element; constituent; cause
Function (verb)	Work; operate; act
Inform	Tell
In isolation	By itself
Initiate	Begin; start
Locality	Place
Locate	Find
Major	Important; chief; main; principal
Minimise	Under-estimate; disparage; belittle; make light of
Practically	Virtually; almost; nearly; all but
Proceed	Go
Purport (noun)	Upshot, gist, tenor, substance
Question (noun)	Subject, topic, matter, problem
Purchase	Buy
Render	Make
Require	Want, need
Reside	Live
Residence	Home
State	Say
Sufficient	Enough
Terminate	End
Transmit	Send; forward
Visualise	Imagine; picture

Source: Ernest Gower, *The Complete Plain Words* (London: HMSO, 1954).

To summarise, in order to phrase questions in a manner which is readily understandable to respondents you should:

Use everyday language
Use simple words rather than complex ones
Use simple sentences rather than complex ones
Keep the questions short and to the point

Avoid double-barrelled questions
Avoid double-negatives.

Perhaps most important of all once you have designed your questions pilot test them on persons of the kind who will be included in your survey to see if the questions are meaningful to them.

Another fault to be guarded against in designing questions is the use of phraseology which 'leads' the respondent or is 'loaded' in a way which suggests a particular answer is being looked for. The problem arises most often with questions concerning people's attitudes but is also possible with factual questions. For example, if you wish to establish people's preference for a particular brand you should either list all those available or none at all. If you asked 'Which brand of baked beans, like Heinz or Crosse & Blackwell, do you buy?' it is likely that the aided recall effect of mentioning two brands will inflate the numbers claiming to buy them.

When seeking people's opinions questions which start 'Don't you agree?' or 'Do you agree?' are likely to secure agreement although subsequent words may counteract this initial invitation to support the proposition. For example, the statements 'Do you agree the Government should interfere in setting airline prices?' might yield a negative answer because of the loaded implications of 'interfere' while 'Do you agree the Government should get involved in setting airline prices?' is more neutral but has overtones that such involvement is a good thing. (Incidentally, my Thesaurus offers 'get involved' as a synonym for 'interfere'!) Numerous examples of leading and loaded questions are given in the specialist texts referred to earlier and these should be consulted for further illustrations if required. Before leaving the matter, however, it must be recognised that on occasion a leading or loaded question may be included deliberately either to bias the result in the sponsor's favour or, alternatively to help identify those with strong views in the opposite direction for further investigation. The ethics of the former are highly questionable and to be guarded against but, be warned, the practice does exist.

Many questionnaires incorporate questions which invite the respondent to 'Agree' or 'Disagree' with the statement made. This approach has been heavily criticised by numerous researchers on the grounds that it suffers from 'Acquiescence response set' whereby a proportion of all respondents will be found to agree with even directly contradictory statements. This tendency is greatest among those with least education. In order to avoid bias from this source it is suggested that one should use *forced-choice questions* in which the respondent is required to choose one of two alternatives offered by the question or statement rather than agree or disagree with a statement defining only one or other of the alternative choices. For example, the statement 'The government should offer places in higher education to all those qualified to benefit from it' would require a high level of agreement. So might, 'Young people wanting to benefit from higher education should be prepared to pay some of the cost themselves.' But, if our purpose is to determine whether our survey population is more or less in favour of fully government funded higher education perhaps we would be better advised to ask 'should the government provide free higher education for everyone qualified to receive it, or should prospective students pay some of the costs themselves?'

The previous discussion of question phraseology has identified many of the pitfalls which face the researcher in his quest for clear and unbiased responses. Careful question design will do much to reduce bias arising from confusion or lack of understanding and will also help minimise the response bias which is a function of the respondent's perceptions and predispositions. Alreck and Settle (1985) provide a very helpful summary table of the major sources of response bias and this is reproduced as Table 7.3.

TABLE 7.3   Sources of response bias

---

1. *Social desirability*. Response based on what is perceived as being socially acceptable or respectable.
2. *Acquiescence*. Response based on respondent's perception of what would be desirable to the sponsor.
3. *Yea- and nay-saying*. Response influenced by the global tendency toward positive or negative answers.
4. *Prestige*. Response intended to enhance the image of the respondent in the eyes of the others.
5. *Threat*. Response influenced by anxiety or fear instilled by the nature of the question.
6. *Hostility*. Response arises from feelings of anger or resentment engendered by the response task.
7. *Auspices*. Response dictated by the image or opinion of the sponsor, rather than the actual question.
8. *Mental set*. Cognitions or perceptions based on previous items influence response to later ones.
9. *Order*. The sequence in which a series is listed affects the responses to the items.
10. *Extremity*. Clarity of extremes and ambiguity of midrange options encourage extreme responses.

Source: Pamela L. Alrech and Robert B. Settle, The Survey Research Handbook (Homewood, Ill.: Irwin, 1985).

The descriptions of the terms are seen as self-explanatory but further detail is to be found at pages 112–19 in the original source.

The examples used to illustrate problems of question design have indicated that questions may be of two kinds — *structured* and *unstructured* or *open-ended*. The essential difference is that with a structured question one anticipates the possible answers and classifies the responses accordingly, whereas with open-ended questions one has no preconceived ideas as to the responses and only seeks to classify the data *post facto*. As a working rule of thumb unstructured questions are most appropriate in exploratory and qualitative research and enable one to develop structured questions which are best suited to survey and quantitative research.

The benefits of structured questionnaires in terms of speed of completion and analysis, accuracy and comparability of data are self-evident, always bearing in mind the sources of response bias discussed earlier. In terms of administration, structured questionnaires are ideally suited to self-completion as the respondent has a clear indication of the scope of possible answers to the question which helps ensure that he is on the same wavelength as the researcher. While one should seek to ensure that the alternatives listed are mutually exclusive and exhaustive this is sometimes neither practicable nor possible. However, it is standard practice to provide a space for 'others' with a short 'write-in' to define these. When administered personally in a face-to-face interview two basic options are available. First, one poses the question and records the spontaneous and unprompted answer of the respondent – probing for clarification if necessary. Given that the interviewer is assigning the respondent's answer to one of the predefined alternatives there is some danger of interviewer bias and this should be borne in mind both in briefing the interviewers and in interpreting the completed questionnaires. The second option is to show the respondent the possible alternatives and ask them to select the one which best fits their opinion or behaviour. Obviously, disclosing the options introduces problems of response bias but careful design and administration should keep these within acceptable limits. One advantage of the personal administration over the self-completion questionnaire is that with the former the respondent is unaware of the scope of subsequent questions and so cannot modify his responses in anticipation of these. Of course, uncertainty as to the direction an interview may take may predispose a respondent to avoid committing himself too strongly in case this causes dissonance later in the interview. We shall return to this issue in the final section on questionnaire construction.

As noted above the design of structured questions requires one to predetermine the possible alternative answers ensuring that they are comprehensive but mutually exclusive. Designing such *multiple choice* or *categorical* questions requires considerable skill and can be very time-consuming – the benefits come, of course, at the analysis stage when the pre-classified responses can be transferred directly to the survey data base for analysis. Categorical questions are best suited to factual issues where it is possible to list the known alternatives. In some cases these will be limited to only two options – 'Yes' or 'No' – although such *dichotomous* questions should always make provision for a 'Don't know' category. In other cases there will be a wide spectrum of possible answers and it will be necessary to group or classify these into an acceptable number of subgroups – usually not more than eight. Here the guiding principle is that one should opt for the minimum number of categories consistent with the level of detail required. In doing so one should also remember that it is always possible to combine or collapse categories but impossible to disaggregate them after the event. For example, in classifying respondents in terms of age the following categories might be provided

Under 16
16 – 24
25 – 40
41 – 60
Over 60

from which it is a simple matter to split the sample into persons over 40, and 40 and under. But, if you had asked: 'Could you tell me if you are over 40?', one has no means of analysing one's data to determine if there are any meaningful sub-groups or segments within these two broad groupings.

Where one is seeking to measure attitudes and opinions one is usually seeking to establish the strength and direction of the attitude. To do so the researcher will normally resort to some form of scaled measure and it is to the nature and scope of scaling techniques that we turn in the next section.

Before considering scaling methods, however, it may be appropriate to emphasise that a great deal of effort has been expended on determining what kinds of questions yield accurate, valid and reliable data. This being so the new researcher should not seek to reinvent the wheel and set out to design all of his questions from first principles of the kind which have only been lightly touched on in the preceding pages. Rather, he would be better advised to consult published compilations of survey questions.

Converse and Prosser (1986) provide the following listing.

Converse, Philip E., Jean D. Dotson, Wendy J. Hoag, and William H. McGee III (eds), *American Social Attitudes Data Sourcebook 1947-1978* (Cambridge, MA: Harvard University Press, 1980).

Gallup, George, *The Gallup Poll: 1935–1971*, 9 vols (New York: Random House, vols 1-3, 1935–1971; Wilmington, DE: Scholarly Resources, Inc., vols 4–9, 1972–1981).

Hastings, Philip K. and Jessie C. Southwick (eds), *Survey Data for Trend Analysis: An Index to Repeated Questions in U.S. National Surveys Held by the Roper Public Opinion Research Center* (Roper Public Opinion Research Center, 1974).

Martin, Elizabeth, Diana McDuffee, and Stanley Presser, *Sourcebook of Harris National Surveys: Repeated Questions 1963-1976* (Chapel Hill: Institute for Research in Social Science, University of North Carolina Press, 1981).

Miller, Warren E., Arthur H. Miller and Edward J. Schneider, *American National Election Studies Data Sourcebook 1951-1978* (Cambridge, MA: Harvard University Press, 1980).

National Opinion Research Center, *General Social Surveys 1972-1985: Cumulative Code Book* (Chicago: NORC, 1985).

Robinson, John P., Robert Athanasiou, and Kendra B. Head, *Measures of Occupational Attitudes and Occupational Characteristics* (Ann Arbor, MI: Institute for Social Research, 1969).

Robinson, John P., Jerrold G. Rusk, and Kendra B. Head, *Measures of Political Attitudes* (Ann Arbor, MI: Institute for Social Research, 1968).

Robinson, John P., and Phillip R. Shaver, *Measures of Social-Psychological Attitudes* (Ann Arbor, MI: Institute for Social Research, 1973, rev. ed.).

In addition the researcher should also consider the design of other extant questionnaires which may have addressed the same or similar issues as those of concern to him. Many such questionnaires are available in published research reports or will come one's way as a potential respondent.

Attitude measurement and scaling

While marketers have a strong interest in facts about markets and customers these reflect past events and the status quo whereas the *primary* concern of marketing planners is the future. In order to help predict how people will behave in the future it is necessary to gather information on their prevailing attitudes and the factors which underlie and condition them. As noted earlier (Chapter 5) attitude is a predisposition to act but it is no guarantee of actual behaviour. On the other hand, people rarely behave in a manner inconsistent with their attitudes/beliefs as this would create internal tension or dissonance so that favourable or unfavourable attitudes provide the marketer with valuable information for planning the most effective marketing mix.

Churchill (1987) draws on the work of Summers and Engel, Blackwell and Miniard in proposing that there is substantial agreement that:

1. Attitude represents a predisposition to respond to an object, not actual behaviour toward the object. Attitude thus possesses the quality of readiness.
2. Attitude is persistent over time. It can change, to be sure, but alteration of an attitude that is strongly held requires substantial pressure.
3. Attitude is a latent variable that produces consistency in behaviour, either verbal or physical.
4. Attitude has a directional quality. It connotes a preference regarding the outcomes involving the object, evaluations of the object, or positive–neutral–negative feelings for the object.

Given the multidimensionality of the concept it is clear that considerable thought and care will have to be given to the measuring of attitudes to ensure that the data secured from respondents is accurate and comparable. Scaling satisfies these criteria. However, as will become apparent, there are many types of scale and one of the first considerations to be addressed in selecting one is to establish its *measurement* properties. In increasing order of sophistication four kinds of scale may be identified – *nominal, ordinal, interval* and *ratio*.

In the *Macmillan Dictionary* these are defined as follows:

(a) Nominal scales. This is the weakest form of scale in which the number assigned serves only to identify the subjects under consideration. Library classification schemes employ nominal scales, as does the Standard Industrial Classification (SIC) such that members of the same class will be assigned the same number but each class will have a different number. By extending the number it is possible to achieve finer and finer distinctions, until a unique number is assigned to a specific object, e.g. a telephone number.

(b) Ordinal scales seek to impose more structure on objects by rank ordering them in terms of some property which they possess such as height or weight. As with nominal scales, identical objects are given the same number but the ordinal scale has the added property that it can tell us something about the direction or relative standing of one object to another, e.g. 1 may represent the smallest member of a group such that we can safely say that 2 is bigger than 1, 5 is bigger than 2 and 17 is bigger than 5. However, this is all we can say (other than reversing the scale) and in order to be able to draw conclusions about difference between the numbers we must know something about the interval between the numbers.

(c) Interval scales have this property in that they are founded on the assumption of equal intervals between numbers, i.e. the space between 5 and 10 is the same as the space between 45 and 50 and in both cases this distance is five times as great as that between 1 and 2 or 11 and 12 etc. However, it must be stressed that while we may compare the magnitude of the differences between numbers we cannot make statements about them unless the scale possesses an absolute zero, in which case we would have a ratio scale.

(d) Ratio scales are the most powerful and possess all the properties of nominal, ordinal and interval scales, while in addition they permit absolute comparisons of the objects, e.g. 6 metres is twice as high as 3 metres and six times as high as 1 metre.

As noted there are many types of scales all of which have been tested and are of known reliability and validity in terms of measuring what they purport and measure. Among the more important scales which will be discussed here are the Thurstone, Likert, Verbal Frequency, Semantic Differential and Stapel scales.

Thurstone scales

Thurstone scales were first introduced by L.L. Thurstone in 1928 and have been very widely used ever since. In essence, a Thurstone scale is an attempt to construct an interval scale by selecting a set of statements about a subject which range from very favourable to very unfavourable expressions of attitude towards the subject with each statement appearing to be equidistant from those on either side of it. While the scales are easy to administer and easy to respond to — the respondent just indicates those items with which he agrees — they are laborious to construct and require the collaboration of a large group of judges who are required to assess the battery of items which consist of statements relating to the subject of the survey. Each statement is recorded on a card and the judges are asked to sort these into piles with each pile containing statements expressing the same degree of favourableness towards the subject. The number of piles to be created equates with the number of points to be incorporated in the scale and is usually 7 or 9 with the central point — 4 or 5 — being seen as the neutral 'neither like nor dislike' middle of the continuum ranging from 'Dislike intensely' to 'Extreme liking' and each pile being judged as equidistant from its neighbours. Each pile is then numbered and the median value for each item is then arrived at such that half the judges score the item higher and half lower than the median value. The items are then sorted again discarding those for which there is a wide range of opinion and the remainder covering the whole range of opinions and approximately equally spaced along the scale, both as judged by the median scores. Depending upon the number of items which survive the process the researcher may wish to divide these into two sets making it possible to administer a different battery to equal halves of his sample ('split — half method').

The selected items are incorporated into the questionnaire in random order and the respondent is asked to select all the items with which he agrees and his score is calculated as the average of the values (medians) of the items selected. Obviously the advantage of this method is that the respondent does not have to judge the distance between the statements as this was done by the judges in constructing the scale. All the respondent does is select statements with which he agrees and so positions himself upon the scale without having to reflect on the degree of agreement or disagreement with each item. On the other hand Thurstone scales require a considerable degree of effort to construct them and some critics question whether the judges are representative of the ultimate respondents. Whether the effort is worth it depends upon the reliability the researcher is looking for and the time saved in administration — both of which help affect the time and effort required to develop Thurstone scales. As to representativeness the researcher should take this into account when selecting his judges in the first place.

Likert scales

These differ from Thurstone scales in that respondents are presented with a series of statements and asked to indicate their *degree of agreement or disagreement* by selecting a point on a 3, 5 or 7 point scale. Thus a 5 point Likert scale might appear as follows:

British Midland's inflight service is better than British Airways:

Strongly agree	Agree	Uncertain	Disagree	Strongly disagree
_____	_____	_____	_____	_____

(NB. Some researchers use 'Neither agree nor disagree' as the midpoint).

Data collected by using Likert scales may be presented as either a single, *summated* score or as a profile analysis.

If a single score is required then one can assign values of 1 to 5, 5 to 1 or + 2 to − 2 to reflect the level of agreement or disagreement with the sum of the individual scores being taken as a measure of the respondents' overall attitude towards the subject of the survey. In constructing the scale it is important to use items which invite the respondents to express a clear opinion, i.e. avoid neutral statements, and to vary the presentation between positive and negative statements in order to avoid the respondent getting into a mind set and automatically ticking the same box.

While a summated score has its advantages as a summary statistic its main disadvantage is that it loses the richness and detail which are obtained if one analyses the responses individually. Because each statement is a rating scale in its own right such analysis is possible with Likert scales but not with Thurstone scales. It must be remembered though that the Likert scale does not have interval properties so no conclusion may be drawn as to the distance between the scale points. (While Thurstone scales are supposed to have interval properties Moser and Kalton (1971), *inter alia*, cast doubt upon this.) However, in addition to having good ordinal properties, Likert scales have a number of advantages, foremost among which is that they are comparatively easy to construct and easy to administer especially in mail questionnaires. Some critics see ease of construction as a disadvantage and Chisnall quotes Worcester's comment that 'All the overworked research executive has to do is to think up a few contentious statements, add a Likert agree–disagree scale, and, hey presto, he has a ready-made questionnaire.' (As with all these techniques there is an extensive literature which deals with such issues in detail and those who wish to try their hands at constructing research instruments should refer to the recommended readings for further advice on the construction and wording of Likert scales.)

In addition to reporting summary scores many researchers now use profile analysis as an effective and readily understandable means of presenting their results. In the case of a profile analysis one computes the mean or median value for each item for each group that one wishes to compare either with each other or with some 'ideal' profile. For example, suppose that in our airline survey we were seeking opinions on the following factors:

Age of equipment – Modernity
Check-in efficiency
Experience
Punctuality
Scheduling – Frequency, Convenience
Cabin comfort – leg room, decor
In-flight service – food, drink, entertainment
Friendliness

We could then ask respondents to rank our two airlines using a 5 point scale along the following lines.

1	2	3	4	5
Excellent	Very Good	Good	Average	Poor

By summing the scores and deriving the average or mean score we could then plot the average score for each airline on each factor and construct a plot as in Table 7.4.

TABLE 7.4   Profile analysis of two airlines

Factor \ Rating	1 Excellent	2 Very Good	3 Good	4 Average	5 Poor
Age of Equipment					
Check-in Efficency					
Experience					
Punctuality					
Scheduling- Frequency					
Scheduling-Convenience					
Cabin Leg Room					
Cabin Decor					
In-Flight Service					
Friendliness					

―――――― = Airline A
- - - - - - = Airline B

These factors or attributes can then be listed as in Table 7.4 and the mean scores for the two airlines reported giving an immediate visual picture of how they compare with one another.

Verbal frequency scales

A major interest in nearly all research inquiries is determination of the frequency with which respondents behave or act in a given way. Such interest stems very largely from the pervasive nature of the Pareto distribution as a description of actual behaviour in the market place. Simply put Pareto's law states that a disproportionately large fraction of a given phenomenon will be accounted for by a disproportionately small percentage of the total cases. In marketing it is often referred to as the 80–20 rule from the observation that in many industries 80 per cent of the total output is accounted for by 20 per cent or less of the producers in that industry (see the concept of concentration ratios in economics). Similarly, on the consumption side there is extensive evidence to indicate that a comparatively small number of users account for a significant amount of the total consumption as can be seen from Figure 7.1.

Clearly the attitudes and opinions of those who are heavy users carry more weight than those who are infrequent or light users. Thus in our inquiry into attitudes towards British Midland and British Airways' service factors on the Glasgow–London route we would want to explore how attitudes might vary in terms of frequency of use and we would ask a question to determine this in our survey.

However, in many cases, respondents may be unwilling or unable to specify a numerical frequency when we would still like to obtain some feeling for how often they have or might behave in a particular way. In such situations a verbal frequency scale will provide some data though clearly not as substantive as that implied by a numerical frequency.

Verbal frequency scales usually comprise five alternatives, namely:

Always
Often
Sometimes
Seldom
Never

Such a scale can be used in connection with a series of separate questions, when it is a useful technique for providing variety in a questionnaire and so aids involvement, or with a battery of questions concerning frequency of behaviour on a number of related topics, as suggested in Table 7.5.

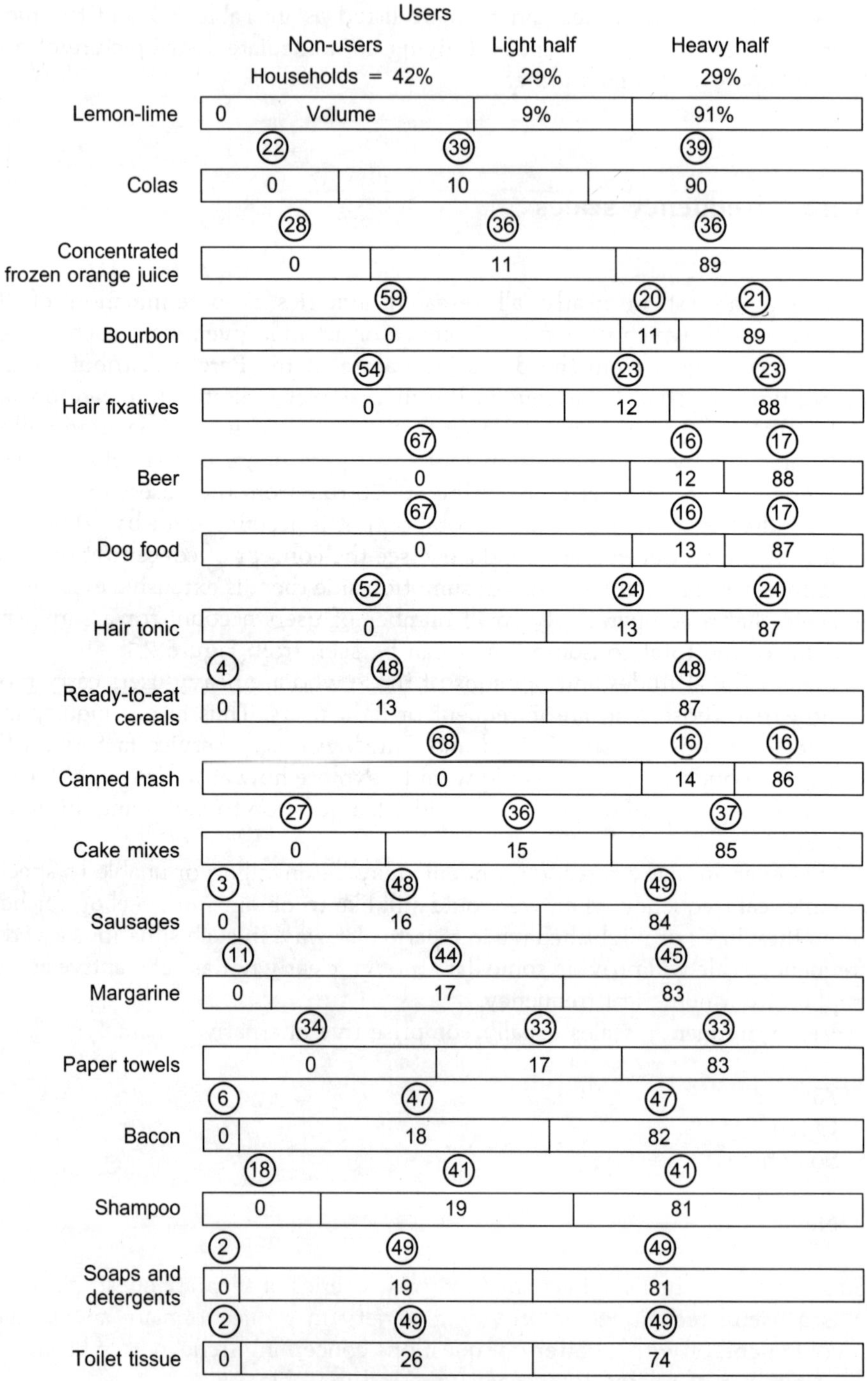

Users

	Non-users	Light half	Heavy half
	Households = 42%	29%	29%

Lemon-lime | 0 Volume | 9% | 91%
(22) | (39) | (39)

Colas | 0 | 10 | 90
(28) | (36) | (36)

Concentrated frozen orange juice | 0 | 11 | 89
(59) | (20) | (21)

Bourbon | 0 | 11 | 89
(54) | (23) | (23)

Hair fixatives | 0 | 12 | 88
(67) | (16) | (17)

Beer | 0 | 12 | 88
(67) | (16) | (17)

Dog food | 0 | 13 | 87
(52) | (24) | (24)

Hair tonic | 0 | 13 | 87
(4) | (48) | (48)

Ready-to-eat cereals | 0 | 13 | 87
(68) | (16) | (16)

Canned hash | 0 | 14 | 86
(27) | (36) | (37)

Cake mixes | 0 | 15 | 85
(3) | (48) | (49)

Sausages | 0 | 16 | 84
(11) | (44) | (45)

Margarine | 0 | 17 | 83
(34) | (33) | (33)

Paper towels | 0 | 17 | 83
(6) | (47) | (47)

Bacon | 0 | 18 | 82
(18) | (41) | (41)

Shampoo | 0 | 19 | 81
(2) | (49) | (49)

Soaps and detergents | 0 | 19 | 81
(2) | (49) | (49)

Toilet tissue | 0 | 26 | 74

FIGURE 7.1   **Annual purchase concentration in 18 product categories**

Source: Baker, *Marketing Strategy and Management.*

TABLE 7.5   Frequency of behaviour

When travelling to London please indicate how often you use the following services by checking (√) the appropriate point on the scale provided:

Services / Frequency	Always	Often	Sometimes	Seldom	Never
Bus					
Train					
Air - B. Midland					
Air - B. Airways					
Book through a Travel Agent					
Pay by cash					
Pay by Cheque					
Pay by Credit Card					
Travel Off-Peak					
Travel 'Stand-By'					

Verbal scales of this kind are very useful in helping the researcher get a feel for the salience of a topic or the likelihood of involvement in an activity. Their obvious disadvantage is that they lack the precision of numerical scales so that care must be taken not to read too much into the answers. For example, there is a world of difference between the businessman who travels to London every week and 'often' travels on British Midland and the student who travels up and down three times a year!

The semantic differential

This technique was devised by Osgood *et al.* (1957) as part of their study of semantics. The technique is straightfoward in that respondents are invited to 'place' a concept or idea on a 7 point scale anchored by a pair of polar adjectives of the kind implied by the comparison between quantitative and qualitative techniques given in Chapter 2. Although it is not known how this table was constructed it is quite possible that it was derived from a semantic differential test in which respondents were invited to indicate where they would put qualitative and quantitative research methods in terms of the polar adjectives which could be applied to research techniques.

Clearly one of the key aspects in devising a semantic differential scale is the selection of pairs of adjectives which are appropriate to the concept or object to be rated, are of interest to the researcher, and are meaningful to the intended respondents. To determine the latter it may be necessary to conduct some preliminary, exploratory research in order to establish just what are the relevant attributes. Obviously respondents can only rate the attributes presented to them. Equally, they will rate attributes which may be unimportant and so give the impression that they deserve equal attention to those that are.

Assuming one has identified a set of salient attributes then the next task is to select appropriate adjectives and their polar opposites. For example, Osgood *et al.* proposed the following:

Good   – Bad
Kind   – Cruel
True   – False
Strong – Weak
Hard   – Soft
Severe – Lenient
Active – Passive
Hot   – Cold
Fast   – Slow
Sane   – Insane

In this listing all the 'positive' adjectives come first and the 'negative' ones second. When constructing an actual scale the designer should randomise the order so as to avoid response set developing. Figure 7.2 gives an example of a semantic scale.

Indicate on the scale below which adjective best describe *qualitative* research techniques:

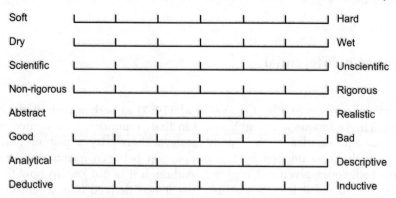

FIGURE 7.2   A semantic scale

Two derivatives of the semantic differential scale are the adjective checklist and the Stapel scale, both of which are fully described in Alreck and Settle (1985). The benefit of the adjective checklist is that one can list a very large number of adjectives and simply ask the respondent to check those which he considers appropriate. As Alreck and Settle observe 'Simplicity, directness, and economy are the major virtues of the adjective checklist.' However, the output is nominal only and gives no measure of distance between the descriptive adjective and the thing being rated as does the semantic differential. On the other hand adjective checklists may be used as an input to the semantic differential scale or combined with a numeric rating to form a Stapel scale (so called after its creator).

All three variants are particularly useful in marketing research in developing profiles of the image which a brand, product, or service has in the minds of the public at large. In turn this provides useful guidance on the development of messages, copy and unique selling propositions to enable sellers to communicate more effectively with prospective buyers.

To conclude this section it has become obvious that the researcher has a wide selection of different scales available to him to help capture the attitudes, interests and opinions of respondents. In selecting the most appropriate, one could do worse than observe the ten commandments proposed by Alreck and Settle, namely:

1. Keep it simple.
2. Respect the respondent.
3. Dimension the response.
4. Pick the denominations.
5. Decide on the range.
6. Group only when required.
7. Handle neutrality carefully.
8. State instructions clearly.
9. Always be flexible.
10. Pilot test the scales.

Questionnaire design

In a paper given at an Esomar seminar in 1973 J.M. Bowen addressed a problem familiar to all market researchers – the trade off between a desire to secure a maximum of information from a respondent and the need to keep the interview clear, straightforward and of reasonable length for ease of administration and maintenance of respondent interest. Clearly, this trade-off has a major bearing upon questionnaire design in respect of at least four elements:

Length
Complexity
Layout
Wording

In order to keep the length of a questionnaire within reasonable bounds Bowen suggests five possibilities:

1. Learn to say No.
2. Ensure the results of every question can be used.
3. Avoid duplication of information.
4. Restrict the classification data asked for.
5. Confine questions to the major issues.

The first two suggestions recognise that very often the buyers/users of research have not thought through precisely what it is they want to find out from a specific piece of research and so have a natural tendency to include anything and everything which may have a bearing upon their problem. The role of the questionnaire designer is to inquire whether a question is really necessary and, if not, exclude it. Similarly one should avoid collecting identical information in response to what appear to be different questions *except* when this is done intentionally as a test of internal consistency and a deliberate test of respondent accuracy.

The conventional wisdom with regard to classification data is that it should be left to the end of an interview so that if a respondent is unwilling to give the information (e.g. income) it will not prompt them to break off the interview. (Obviously this rule does not apply when one needs to ascertain whether the respondent conforms to the profile called for in a quota sample.) However, the fact that classification data is left to the end of the interview should not encourage the questionnaire designer to ignore the advice in 2 and 3 above.

Finally, one should avoid the temptation to try and obtain complete information when to do so might compromise the whole interview for very little improvement in one's understanding of the key issues. For example, four or five brands may account for 80–90% of total market share with a further ten brands comprising the balance. To ask a respondent questions concerning all 15 brands could be counter productive particularly if one intends to lump together all the minor brands as 'Others'.

Bowen also suggests a number of devices which may make the questionnaire *seem* shorter essentially by keeping the respondent involved and interested. The techniques proposed are:

1. Varying the type of questions asked.
2. Giving the informant things to do.
3. Use of visual aids.

4. Scattering questions on the same theme rather than bunching them.
5. Introducing interesting questions as soon as possible.
6. Making sure the questionnaire flows.

By using devices such as these one can help reduce the natural tendency of respondents to economise by using the same information more than once, i.e. they get into a 'response set' and begin to tick the same end of the scale every time without paying due attention to the actual question asked. Of course, such behaviour may arise from confusion which is a consequence of ambiguity and/ or complexity in the design of the questionnaire.

On the issue of *complexity* Bowen (and others) counsel that you should always start a questionnaire with simple questions of fact or opinion in order to overcome the respondents' concern that they make a fool of themselves by being unable to answer the questions asked. Inevitably some questions are bound to address complex issues. Many of the issues relate to the construction of scales and the choice of words which were discussed earlier in the chapter.

With regard to *layout* two distinct issues must be addressed — the order effect of questions and the actual physical layout of the questionnaire. Order effect was mentioned above in terms of varying the mix and construction of questions in order to avoid a response set developing. However, it is clear that the problem cannot be avoided entirely which makes it vital that the designer establish which is the most important issue and address this first. Bowen cites the example of a series of studies every six months designed to measure changes of image and attitude to a brand. Questions on this must precede questions on actual usage for otherwise the respondents may adjust their responses so that their preferred (most used brand) is rated better on all dimensions to all competitive brands even though this is not actually the case.

In terms of physical layout the first precept is to ask the fieldwork department's advice as they have the most direct experience of the problems which occur in administering poorly designed questionnaires. Six basic principles are proposed.

1. Make the questionnaire as clear as possible.
2. Use a legible typeface and space the questions out. Some researchers mistakenly believe that by photo reducing their questionnaire they will make it less daunting. This may encourage the respondent to start but the sheer density and illegibility of such questionnaires will often prevent a respondent from completing them.
3. Leave plenty of space for answers to open-ended questions.
4. Ensure the instructions are crystal clear — particularly where it is intended that one should skip questions following a given response.
5. Make certain all possible answers are provided for — otherwise the interviewer or respondent will be uncertain whether to classify a response such as 'pantry' as 'larder' or 'kitchen' if only these alternatives are provided.

6. Keep instructions next to the question to which they apply. Listing them separately or at the beginning of a questionnaire is bound to result in confusion.

Bowen's fourth design element is *wording* and this is discussed in some detail earlier. However, the four golden rules for questionnaire design, especially those used for personal interviews, are:

1. Think through the use of each question and relate it to the research objectives to ensure it is absolutely necessary;
2. Design the techniques and question methods used to maximise informant involvement;
3. Cater to the interviewer in the worst possible conceivable situation;
4. Pilot the questionnaire yourself.

Piloting the questionnaire

While all marketing research texts advocate the pre-testing or piloting of a questionnaire the advice is often honoured more by the breach than the observance. Research buyers should therefore insist that pretesting be built into the design and reported on – preferably before administration of the final, agreed questionnaire.

Converse and Presser (1986) suggest ten purposes of pretesting the first four of which relate to specific questions and the last six to the design of the questionnaire as a whole, namely:

1. Variation.
2. Meaning.
3. Task difficulty.
4. Respondent interest and attention.
5. 'Flow' and naturalness of the sections.
6. The order of questions.
7. Skip patterns.
8. Timing.
9. Respondent interest and attention overall.
10. Respondent well-being.

While many of these factors are self-explanatory some additional explanation may be helpful.

Variation refers to the degree of variation in actual responses to a question. Occasionally, where one is fairly certain of the distribution of the variation a highly skewed response will help confirm one's expectations but otherwise such a pattern may well suggest that the question is not detecting the expected variation in the phenomenon under investigation. Of course the difficulty here is how many times should one pretest a question to be confident the test is representative?

The importance of testing for *meaning* has already been addressed in the earlier discussion of ambiguity. Clearly, if respondents attach a different meaning to a word or phrase than that intended by the researcher then the results are unlikely to be relevant although the data itself could be highly valid and reliable. Similarly, if questions are very complex respondents are likely to simplify them and answer the question they think they were asked which might be quite different from the researcher's original intention.

Task difficulty often arises because of low salience and difficulties of recall. Approaches to reduce these difficulties have been discussed earlier and may be further assisted by offering respondents open-ended 'write-in' opportunities so that they can qualify responses or define the perspective from which they have answered the question.

Respondent interest and attention relates to both specific questions and the questionnaire as a whole and will have a significant influence on the quality of the data provided. Once a respondent is committed to a questionnaire they will usually stick it out to the end but, if you have lost their interest, it is quite likely that they will take the path of least resistance in an effort to get through the exercise. The validity and accuracy of such responses is at best questionable.

The maintenance of interest depends heavily on both question and questionnaire design. Variety in the design of questions, the 'flow' or sequence of the questions, the use of 'skip questions' to avoid questions which are irrelevant to particular respondents and the actual time required to complete an interview will all affect the quality of data. It is evident that questionnaire design is a skilled craft so that, while one may apply some 'scientific' tests to determine if basic principles have been observed, one must depend heavily upon the experience and expertise of the researcher. It should also be evident that our opening statement, that if you 'ask a silly question you'll get a silly answer', is likely to be the rule rather than the exception if questionnaire design is entrusted to an amateur. However, it is to be hoped that armed with some of the insights and issues reviewed in this chapter the user will be better placed to select a professional qualified to perform the task efficiently and effectively on his behalf.

Summary

In this chapter we have examined some of the major issues involved in designing a questionnaire. Clearly the quality of the data gathered will depend greatly upon the development of clear, unambiguous questions which convey the same meaning to all respondents and so are more likely to elicit comparable replies.

While designing questions and questionnaires is still something of an art there is extensive advice available on 'do's and don't's' for those wishing to try their hand at constructing a valid questionnaire. Similarly, there are extensive batteries of validated questions which have been thoroughly tested and shown to measure that which they seek to measure. Also, as we shall see in Chapter 12, it is now possible to buy computer software to help design both questions and questionnaires, pilot them and produce hard copy or a computer-based guide as required.

Given that much marketing research is involved with seeking to measure attitudes and opinions as a basis for both explaining and predicting behaviour, considerable attention was given to various scaling methods for distinguishing the nature and degree of such attitudes and opinions.

Finally, we looked at some of the issues involved in combining questions into a questionnaire and method for pilot testing this prior to administration to the intended sample of respondents.

In the next chapter we examine various approaches to administering questionnaires and other methods of acquiring data from respondents.

References

Alreck, Pamela L. and Settle, Robert B. (1985) *The Survey Research Handbook* (Homewood, Ill.: Richard D. Irwin).

Churchill, Gilbert A. (1987) *Marketing Research – Methodological Foundations,* 4th edn (New York, Holt, Rinehart and Winston).

Converse, J.M. and Presser, S. (1986) *Survey Questions* (Beverly Hills: Sage).

Mayer, Charles S. (1965) 'Marketing Research Sec 24 and Statistical and Mathematical Tools Sec 25', in *Marketing Handbook,* 2nd edn, ed. Albert Wesley Frey (New York: Ronald Press).

Moser, C.A. and Kalton, G. (1971) *Survey Methods in Social Investigation* (London: Heinemann).

Osgood, Charles E., Suci, George J. and Percy H. Tannenbaum, *The Measurement of Marketing* (Urbana: University of Illinois Press).

Payne, S.L. (1957) *The Art of Asking Questions* (Princetown: Princetown University Press).

Selltiz, C., Jahoda, M., Deutsch, M. and Cook, S.W. (1959) *Research Methods in Social Relations* (London: Methuen).

Tull, Donald S. and Hawkins, Del I. (1987) *Marketing Research,* 4th edn (New York: Macmillan).

CHAPTER 8

Data collection methods

Introduction

In Chapter 5 we reviewed the issues involved in selecting an appropriate research design and classified these into three categories – observation, experimentation and survey. In this chapter we are concerned primarily with the latter category and the collection of data using questionnaires, of the kind discussed in the preceding chapter, through the medium of personal interviews, mail and telephone surveys. However, the reader is reminded that the first step in developing a research design is to establish what is already known from existing published sources (the subject of Chapter 3) and that observation and experimentation will often precede any formal approach to respondents through survey research.

Interviewing

An interview is '1. a conversation with or questioning of a person, usually conducted for television or a newspaper. 2. a formal discussion especially one in which an employer assesses a job applicant' (*Collins Concise English Dictionary*). While neither of these definitions addresses directly the nature and purpose of the interview in a marketing research context they do establish the key elements, namely; an interview involves a personal exchange of information between an interviewer and one or more interviewees in which the interviewer seeks to obtain specific information on a topic with the co-operation of the interviewee(s).

Interviews vary considerably in their structure from highly formal exchanges in which the interviewer follows exactly a carefully designed and worded questionnaire, of the kind discussed in the preceding chapter, to highly informal exchanges in which the interviewer introduces the topic of interest and lets the discussion develop naturally by asking the respondent to expand or clarify points made by him. Between the former *structured* interview, which is sometimes called a *formal* or *closed* interview, and the *unstructured, informal, non-directive* or *conversational* interview are to be found three other kinds of interview. In the middle of the continuum is the *standardised open-ended* interview which consists entirely of formal open-ended questions in a predetermined sequence. In turn we can distinguish two other kinds of interview intermediate between the standardised open-ended format and the ends of the continuum. First, there is the *semi-structured* interview which is a combination of both closed and open-ended questions and second, there is the *interview guide* approach where the interviewer has a checklist of topics he wants to cover but interacts with the respondent and formulates *ad hoc* questions to get the desired information.

Clearly, unstructured and interview guide interviews are most appropriate in the early, exploratory phases of research where the researcher is seeking to gain an understanding of the topic and to formulate some preliminary working hypotheses. By the same token highly structured formal interviews ensure that each respondent is required to address exactly the same questions as all the others so that the data collected can be aggregated and analysed and regarded as representing the views of the population from which the sample respondents have been drawn. Sue Stone (1984) in her Crus Guide on *Interviews* makes the point that data derived from structured interviews is the most *reliable* whereas that obtained from less structured interviews is more *valid*. The less structured the interview the more valid the data as the respondent has more and more freedom to express precisely how they think and feel about the topic being discussed.

Madge (1953) suggests there are nine kinds of interview situation to be found in social investigation depending upon the type of person to be interviewed and the purpose of the interview itself. In terms of the type of person, Madge identifies three classes whom he labels *potentate, expert* and the *people*. A potentate is a person in a position of authority, an expert is a person who possesses special knowledge about other people or things, while people are members of a group in whom the social scientist is interested. Potentates may be regarded as opinion leaders (formal or informal) whose endorsement, co-operation and support is necessary in order for the research to proceed. For example, if one wishes to conduct multiple interviews with a firm to establish who is involved in organisational buying decisions then one will need the authority of the chief executive to proceed. Experts are persons with specialised knowledge or information of the subject of inquiry while people are persons whose attitudes, interests and opinions are at the very heart of marketing decision making.

So, with three classes of persons, three purposes and five types of interview we have a basic repertoire of 45 interviewing 'treatments' available to us. In selecting between them, however, it will be helpful to stick with the basic distinction – class of person, purpose and type of interview – and we shall review each of these in more detail in the next few pages.

Type of respondent

In the introduction to his chapter on 'The Interview' Madge quotes Roethlisberger and Dickson's observation:

> It is commonly supposed, although there is very little evidence to warrant such a supposition, that there exists a simple and logical relation between what a person says and what he thinks.

If this is so, and many would agree that it is, then the selection of respondents is as critical an issue as the selection and wording of questions and the construction of questionnaires considered in the previous chapter. This is particularly the case in terms of potentates and experts as misidentification may well invalidate the totality of the data obtained. In the case of surveys of 'people' then the problem may be addressed quite successfully through the construction of the test instrument, control of its administration and care in the subsequent analysis and interpretation of the data obtained.

After all we expect variability in our respondents and a primary objective of our research design and data collection is to ensure insofar as is possible that they are 'neutral' and do not influence or bias our respondents. Of course, the same requisites also apply to interviews with potentates and experts but, given that these types of respondents are likely to be much fewer in number than in the case with broadly based consumer surveys, identification and selection are of the utmost importance. An example will help reinforce this point.

A colleague was undertaking research into the purchase of a flexible manufacturing system and wished to compare attitudes and practice in the UK and West Germany. Although able to speak conversational German this was not sufficient to conduct semi-structured technical interviews with German engineers actually responsible for selection and purchase decisions. He found that the respondent firms were nominating their public relations personnel to participate in the interviews because they spoke more English than their engineers. The fact that the PR people knew virtually nothing about the technical issues was considered secondary to the ability to communicate with an English-speaking interviewer. In this case the researcher appreciated the problem and got the linguists to act as interpreters but he could just as easily have reported the views of the PR people as being those of the company. Users of research should be unusually careful in checking out who the respondents were and how they were selected – a point to which we will return when examining postal surveys.

Very often one will wish to interview potentates to gain access to other categories of respondents as well as to establish their own views on the survey topic. Access is probably the single biggest problem facing the researcher undertaking industrial as opposed to consumer research (although it can also be a problem in the latter area too!). This, of course, is quite understandable as information and know-how are very often the primary source of competitive advantage and the owners of such are unlikely to want to share this with others. It follows that if one is to gain access one will invariably have to convince a Chief Executive that the information supplied will be treated confidentially, that it is of no specific value and will only become so when aggregated with the replies from other respondents and also that he and his organisation will derive some tangible benefits from the published survey.

Both potentates and experts can be very helpful in the early stages of developing a research design because their position and knowledge enables them to define what the key issues are. Also, they are usually able to point one in the direction of other sources of relevant information and so help one structure the problem to be addressed. Further, in the realm of forecasting potentates and experts are probably the best source of information about likely futures if for no other reason than that it is their opinions and decisions which are most likely to influence future states. It is for this reason that the Delphi forecasting technique uses expert opinion as the basis for predicting significant future events, especially those involving technological change.

In *Marketing* we state that 'markets are people'. As the very raw material from which markets are built the attitudes, interests and opinions of people are central to the whole marketing research process. Interviewing is the basic method of eliciting and establishing these factors. Further, as we noted earlier, when discussing the relative merits of qualitative versus quantitative research, the latter tends to carry more conviction and so has increased the incidence and scope of sample surveys many of which depend upon the personal interview as a means of data collection. In addition increased access to telephones in the UK has resulted in wider use of the telephone on consumer surveys so that their incidence is now approaching that in the USA. For all these reasons there is a strong likelihood that consumer market research will involve personal interviews and the user/buyer of research needs to be sensitive to issues relating to the selection and control of interviewers as a basis for assessing the quality of a given piece of research. However, before looking at these factors in more detail we will examine more closely the type of interview as this will largely determine its suitability for different research purposes.

Type of interview

Earlier we identified a spectrum of interview types ranging from highly unstructured to highly structured. We shall now look at each of these more comprehensively with a view to establishing their basic characteristics, their advantages and disadvantages, the kind of data which they yield and any particular problems associated with their use. In that it is usual to proceed from exploratory research through to formal surveys we shall follow this order in our presentation.

Unstructured interviews

Unstructured interviews are also known as informal, non-directive or conversational. In Madge's view interviews of this kind owe their origin to the counselling techniques used by Sigmund Freud to elicit information necessary to diagnose his patients' problems and prescribe appropriate courses of treatment. While Freud's counselling techniques may seem somewhat distant from commercial marketing research, aspects of them are still to be found in the field of motivation research of the kind developed and practised by Ernest Dichter. Similarly, they helped inform the development of the methodology used in the famous Hawthorne experiments which are a classic study in the evolution of social science research methodology.

Hawthorne was the name of the Western Electric Company's plant in Chicago and it was here that Harvard Business School Professor Elton Mayo undertook his famous studies into the importance of groups in affecting individual behaviour and thereby discovered the importance of the informal organisation. In the course of these studies it was decided to conduct a series of directive interviews in which the interviewer was required to ask a series of specific questions of the employee respondents. However, considerable difficulty was experienced in keeping the interviewees on track and led to the adoption of an indirect as opposed to direct approach which was very similar to Freud's counselling methodology. Madge quotes Mayo's colleagues Roethlisberger and Dickson (1939) who described this 'new' method as follows:

> After the interviewer had explained the program, the employee was to be allowed to choose his own topic. As long as the employee talked spontaneously, the interviewer was to follow the employee's ideas, displaying a real interest in what the employee had to say, and taking sufficient notes to enable him to recall the employee's various statements. While the employee continued to talk, no attempt was to be made to change the subject. The interviewer was not to interrupt or to try to change the topic to one he thought more important. He was to listen attentively

to anything the worker had to say about any topic and take part in the conversation only in so far as it was necessary in order to keep the employee talking. If he did ask questions, they were to be phrased in a noncommittal manner, and certainly not in the form, previously used, which suggested the answers.

Twenty thousand interviews were obtained over the next two years each lasting an average of one and a half hours and led to the formulation of a code of conduct for interviewers which is entirely relevant to the use of the technique over fifty years later, namely:

1. The interviewer should listen to the speaker in a patient and friendly, but intelligently critical, manner.
2. The interviewer should not display any kind of authority.
3. The interviewer should not give advice or moral admonition.
4. The interviewer should not argue with the speaker.
5. The interviewer should talk or ask questions only under certain conditions.
   (a) To help the person talk.
   (b) To relieve any fears or anxieties on the part of the speaker which might be affecting his reaction to the interviewer.
   (c) To praise the interviewee for reporting his thoughts and feelings accurately.
   (d) To veer the discussion to some topic which had been omitted or neglected.
   (e) To discuss implied assumptions, if this were advisable.

In its purest form the totally unstructured interview can be an invaluable source of ideas and insights from which working hypotheses may be developed. However, the information obtained is largely impressionistic and it is usual for the interviewer to follow rules 5(d) and 5(e) and 'veer' or *focus* the interview in order to ensure that it covers the topic with which the interview is concerned and to clarify the basis or premises which underlie the respondents' answers. On this point Madge observes:

> The Hawthorne interviewers steered the informant on to particular topics but not away from others. If the informant responds to a topic towards which he is guided, it is fairly reasonable to infer that he would have reached that particular topic without guidance in the course of a long enough interview. The distortion is in the sectors represented, and not necessarily in the internal content of these sectors.

Given that you are willing to endorse Madge's inference then, clearly, the focused interview offers significant advantages over the unfocused kind where the analyst may well have to review large amounts of irrelevant information (especially now that most depth interviews are tape recorded!). Merton and Kendall (1946) report one of the earlier uses of a focused interview in which respondents were asked to listen to a radio programme and then interviewed on it following the 'four canons of the focussed interview procedure . . . non-direction, specificity, range, and depth and personal context.'

Non-direction is self-explanatory and can be achieved using a variety of both structured and unstructured questions, e.g. 'Could you tell me what you consider important about inflight service' to 'What did you think of the meal served on the flight?'

Both the above questions also satisfy the canon of specificity as they require the respondent to describe what *they* think is important. Range is determined by comparing the scope and detail of the respondents' answers with the actual content or dimensions of the subject being discussed as predetermined by the researcher, i.e. I have already defined the aspects of inflight service I believe to exist/consider important and will regard the interviews to meet the test if they cover the same issues. Finally, depth and personal context must be judged by the degree to which the interview secures the involvement of the respondent to the extent that they are revealing their true feelings rather than saying what they think the interviewer would like to hear or that which would cast them in a favourable light.

From the foregoing overview it is clear that the conduct of informal or unstructured interviews calls for considerable skills on the part of the interviewer. It follows that the user should inquire carefully into the background and experience of the interviewers used in work of this type so as to be able to form a judgement as to the quality of the data secured.

In recent years increasing use has been made of a variant of the one-to-one depth interview in which a *group* of persons are invited to discuss a topic. Here the moderator or interviewer can play a much less active role as the group will spontaneously generate ideas on its own and so reduce the likelihood of interviewer bias.

Group discussions[*]

A recurring theme of this book is that marketing decision makers are invariably confronted with time and budgetary constraints and so must select the most appropriate and effective research method to help them resolve the problems facing them. In this quest they will frequently have to choose between the apparently factual and objective data yielded by a quantitative survey and the more judgemental and subjective information generated by qualitative research. As a working rule of thumb, however, some qualitative research should always precede quantitative research when addressing a non-recurring problem where,

---

[*]This section draws heavily on an article, 'Group Discussions: A Misunderstood Technique' by Dr G.A. Fahad, a former colleague of Strathclyde University, which appeared in the *Journal of Marketing Management*, 1986, vol. 1, no. 3(3), pp. 315–27.

by definition, the decision maker has relatively little if any direct experience of the specific problem to be solved. In some cases this qualitative research will consist merely of a few unstructured or semi-structured individual interviews with a small number of persons believed to have some knowledge or insight relevant to the problem while in others the researcher will wish to develop a more detailed and in-depth insight into the problem of interest. Under the latter circumstances, group discussions may well prove the most satisfactory approach. What then is a group discussion?

Put simply a group discussion is a 'research technique designed to study the interaction of group membership on individual behaviour, with a free exchange of ideas, beliefs and emotions helping to form a general opinion about the subject' (*Macmillan Dictionary*, 1984). The origins of the method are to be found in the 'clinical laboratory' setting where many of the guidelines for its use were first developed. As a technique it is very flexible and comparatively easy to organise and execute which is in marked contrast with the administrative effort necessary to mount most sample surveys. Because of its clinical origins it is widely held that group discussions must be moderated by a clinical psychologist. While this may add somewhat to the perceived credibility of the technique, experience suggests that while such professional advice may be helpful in diagnosing some of the data, e.g. of a projective kind, group discussions may be run successfully by moderators without any particular formal qualifications provided they have experience and are skilled in moderating discussions.

Black and Champion (1976) have defined the key attributes of a group discussion as being:

1. Questions are asked and responses given verbally.
2. The interviewer rather than the respondent records the information elicited. (Most group discussions are tape recorded for later detailed analysis.)
3. The relationship between the interviewer and the respondent is structured in several specific ways, such as its transitory or temporary relationship where participants are often unknown to one another, etc.
4. There is considerable flexibility in the format the interview takes.

To these attributes Sampson (1978) has added the following characteristics.

1. The group varies in number but has anything between 8 to 12 individuals.
2. Individuals in the group are known to have knowledge about the topic or issues being discussed.
3. Respondents are encouraged to express their opinions and attitudes (freely) on issues being discussed.
4. The interviewer's duty is basically to guide the direction and depth of the discussions.

5. The underlying characteristic of the group situation is the need of the interviewer 'to learn about' the issues being discussed based on the respondent's own perspective.

As a methodology group discussions are adaptable to a wide range of situations amongst which Smith (1972) has listed the following:

1. For research concerned with motives, attitudes and opinions where social status and acceptance are involved.
2. For bringing out ideas in the dynamic group situation which cannot be elicited by other methods.
3. For attempting to answer the question 'why' in relation to behaviour.
4. Valuable in the preliminary or exploratory stage of a research project.
5. It enables a questionnaire to be constructed for piloting and pretesting, which should include all the possible lines of enquiry.
6. Useful for indicating the type of language people use when discussing the topic informally and ensures that in constructing a questionnaire, the wording of questions is meaningful.

Among other reasons cited in the general literature Kinnear and Taylor (1987) list the following:

1. To generate hypotheses that can be further tested quantitatively.
2. To provide overall background information on a product category.
3. To get impressions on new product concepts for which there is little information available.
4. To generate ideas for new creative concepts.
5. To interpret previously obtained quantitative results.

The last application is particularly important as it emphasises that qualitative research is an essential and inextricable element of the marketing research process necessary to help structure formal data collection and inform the interpretation of the data collected.

Advantages and disadvantages

From his comprehensive literature review Fahad identifies a large number of advantages which have been claimed for the group discussion technique. First, he cites Gorden (1969) who listed the following advantages:

1. It enables the researcher to obtain the desired information more quickly than, for example, a questionnaire.
2. It ensures that respondents understand the questions being asked.

3. Its flexible nature allows the interviewer to adjust his line of questioning.
4. Much more control can be exercised over the context within which questions are asked and answers given.
5. Information can be more readily checked for its validity on the basis of non-verbal cues by the respondent.

In addition to these advantages Fahad proposes ten others culled from a variety of sources as shown in Table 8.1.

TABLE 8.1   Advantages of group discussion

Synergism	Combined effect of the group produces a wider range of information, ideas, etc.
Snowballing	A comment by an individual often triggers a chain of responses from other respondents.
Stimulation	Respondents become more responsive after initial introduction and are more likely to express their attitudes and feelings as the general level of excitement increases.
Security	Most respondents find comfort in a group that shares their feelings and beliefs.
Spontaneity	As individuals are not required to answer specific questions, their responses are likely to be more spontaneous and less conventional.
Serendipity	The ethos of the group is likely to produce wider ideas and often when least expected.
Specialisation	Allows a more trained interviewer to be used and minimises the possibility of subjectivity.
Scientific scrutiny	Allows a closer scrutiny of the technique by allowing observers or by later playing back and analysing the recorded sessions.
Structure	Affords more flexibility in the topics that can be covered and in the depth in which these are treated.
Speed	Given that several individuals are being interviewed at the same time, this speeds up the process of collecting and analysing the data.

Of course, no technique is without its shortcomings and a number of disadvantages are associated with the group discussion technique. Fahad summarises these succinctly as:

1. Doubts about the validity of verbal responses particularly in relation to behaviour.
2. Interviewer variability means that the type and depth of information elicited can vary markedly.

3. In certain instances, respondents may have been recruited on the basis of a nominal fee, a present, etc., and this tends to affect responses provided.
4. Interviewers may exercise a high degree of freedom, often resulting in short-cuts, carelessness in recruiting respondents and so on.
5. Sample size is often too small or not representative and so limits the generalisability of the data obtained.
6. Interaction between participants often biases responses provided.
7. Self-appointed leaders in the group may influence the opinions of the rest.

However, many of these disadvantages may be minimised or even eliminated through professional practice (in recruitment, etc.) and skilled moderation. Certainly, the buyer of research would wish to satisfy himself on these points in both commissioning and evaluating the output of group discussions. Given these safeguards the benefits heavily outweigh the disadvantages.

Thus far the discussion has proceeded as if there were only one type of group discussion. In fact there are several each with its particular strengths and weaknesses. Fahad identifies three somewhat different approaches to classifying types of group discussion when he cites from Sampson (1978), Hartman and Hedblom (1979), and De-Almeida (1980).

Sampson (1978) suggests a three-way classification as follows:

1. *The group interview or discussion.* In this format, individuals are brought together under the direction of a group leader or moderator, who plays a more passive role than in the individual depth interview.
2. *Elicitation interview.* In this variant, the interviewer makes use of a battery of open-ended questions in the belief that the salient attitudes elicited may be more reliable measures of consumer behaviour.
3. *The repertory or Kelly grid technique.* In this format, stimuli are presented to respondents in the form of labels, written statements, drawings, etc., and responses sought to these.

By contrast, Hartman and Hedblom (1979) argue that classification can be made on the basis of structure, i.e.:

1. *Highly structured*: involves the use of a standardised set of questions determined prior to the interview.
2. *Open-ended*: this is uncontrolled, unstructured and entails very little guidance from the interviewer.
3. *Depth-interview*: involves an 'intimate', long-term conversation with respondents in which the interviewer is allowed to probe, expand and periodically summarise what he/she understands respondents to have said.

Based upon his own literature review De-Almeida (1980) came up with a four-way classification:

1. *Group discussions*: these tend to be mainly unstructured types of investigation of given topics, using small groups with basically non-directive moderation.
2. *Group interviewing*: in this format, questions are posed to a group rather than to a single individual, more or less using the same format as an interview with single individuals.
3. *Focused group interviewing*: individuals in the group are asked to base their responses on past subjective associations and emotions.
4. *Delphi group interviewing*: this format involves the group being asked to develop new ideas and insights based on knowledge of prior ones from other individuals, groups, or even from the same group.

While some observers regard the distinctions implied in the above classifications, as being inconsequential the evidence suggests that much of the reported dissatisfaction with group discussions as a technique is a direct consequence of the user failing to define precisely the kind of group discussion best suited to the needs of his problem.

However, choice of type of focus group is only one factor influencing the quality and value of the output from this method. Dickens (1982) identifies seven other factors likely to have a significant bearing on the success of a group discussion.

1. Preliminary planning
2. Respondent recruitment
3. Characteristics of the moderator
4. The venue
5. Format of the presentation
6. Management of the discussion
7. Analysis.

The value of preliminary planning is axiomatic in all research design and execution and will not be discussed further. Similarly, selecting respondents able to respond to the issues on which the discussion is to focus is self-evident. As to whom should perform this task there appears to be little if any difference between letting the moderator recruit his own group(s) or having an agent recruit respondents for him in accordance with some broad definition of the characteristics required, e.g. single parents between 25 and 40 from ABC1 socio-economic groups.

All agree that the overall success of the group discussion method depends very heavily upon the characteristics of the moderator and the literature provides copious advice on just what these characteristics might be. As Fahad comments 'The first-time user is often, however, left with the impression that a moderator is more an acrobat than an ordinary human being' – this in addition to being a paragon of all other virtues! We have already noted that the impression that all moderators should be trained clinical psychologists is erroneous — save for depth interviews exploring deeply-seated motivation the main requirement of a moderator is that they should be effective chairpersons — able to introduce the issues for discussion, to encourage participation from all the group members, to clarify ambiguities, to discourage a single person dominating the proceedings and knowing when to move the discussion forward when a topic has become exhausted, together with summaries of where the discussion has got to if appropriate.

The best advice on venues and format is that they should be appropriate to the topic and respondent mix. For example, our single parents would probably appreciate meeting in someone's home whereas a group of purchasing executives would prefer a more business-like environment. The single parents once introduced could probably talk all day about the problems they face when invited to do so while the purchasing executives would probably want a clearer definition of the purpose of the meeting, a broad agenda and a time limit.

Running the group discussion is a function of its purpose and the moderator's skills touched on above.

Analysis may be *systematic*, i.e. a factual summary of the content of the discussion using formal content analysis techniques on a recording of the interview, or *conceptual* in which the analyst identifies the key issues emerging from the discussion and, possibly, formulates these as hypotheses for subsequent testing. Most users will look for both kinds of analysis with the emphasis depending upon the original objectives in using group discussions in the first place.

While the subjective nature of group discussions is likely to ensure that its primary use is for exploratory research to gain insight into and understanding of attitudes, opinions and behaviour, with the possibility of subsequent quantitative research to establish the strength and direction of these factors, there are strong indications that the method may also be a valid basis for actual decisions. There is extensive support for this view including the analysis of Reynolds and Johnson (1978) who reported a 97 per cent level of agreement between the results from a group discussion approach and a survey on the same issue. Indeed, where the results differed the group discussion data matched more closely the reality of actual sales. Provided the manager clearly understands the advantages and shortcomings of the method it may well provide a relatively simple and cost effective aid to his decision making.

Interviewer guide

When addressing the issue of 'range' in unstructured interviews it was stated that one could judge this by judging the actual content of interviews with the researcher's prior expectations. Implicit in this statement is the belief that even in the most informal and unstructured interview one has some mental checklist to guide one through the interview. When committed to paper this checklist becomes the interview guide and enables the interviewer to make sure that he has indeed covered all the issues believed a priori to be important to the research. Table 8.2 is an example of an interview guide used by Baker and Hart (1989) when conducting exploratory research with 'potentates' and 'experts' to validate the conclusions drawn from their wide-ranging review of the secondary data on the subject of factors associated with competitive success.

TABLE 8.2   Interview guide

British industry and growth
- Definitions of growth and success in industries
- Prospects for British Industry
- Sunrise/sunset industries

Company performance
- Parameters of success
- Non-financial measures
- Specific companies

Attitudes to marketing
- Definitions of marketing
- Likert-type scale

Organisation of market in the company
- Inter-functional integration
- Responsibility for marketing; substance or trapping
- Organisational status of marketing
- Managerial background/marketing training

Corporate and marketing strategy
- Time horizon/strategic issues
- Formality of strategic planning; substance or trapping
- Strategies

Market research
- Information needs and sources
- Market research activities and uses
- Formality of market research; substance or trapping

Segmentation
- Typical customer versus groups of customers
- Product differentiation – proliferation of product ranges

The market mix
- Overall view of relative importance of mix factors
- Product quality – customer oriented versus absolute quality
- Product modification and NPD; market or technology driven?
- Service, selling, advertising and pricing

This kind of interview represents a further degree of formality beyond that of the interview guide which is simply a checklist or *aide-mémoire* to ensure comprehensive coverage of the topic. As its name suggests a standardised open-ended interview uses predetermined questions which are put in precisely the same format and sequence to every respondent. Table 8.3 presents the second stage interview schedule developed by Baker and Hart after their first round of preliminary and exploratory interviews.

The obvious advantage of this approach is that it is possible to make direct comparisons of the answers which will all be given in the same order. Against this is the problem that some respondents will be loquacious and others taciturn and that the meaning attached to their responses may vary considerably. However, the existence of a standardised set of questions makes it possible to use less well qualified interviewers as their role is simply to pose the questions and report accurately the answers. Here the skill requirement is centred on the *content analysis* of the responses.

TABLE 8.3 Semi-structured interview guide

British industry and growth
1. How do you think an industry's performance should be evaluated? Please give reasons for your answer.

   > PROBE: sales, profitability, employee numbers and prospects, export achievement, reputation, IR record, etc.

2. What is your opinion of the prospects for British manufacturing industry over the next 10 years?

   > PROBE: overall growth rates, profitability, employment, etc.

3. Which industries do you consider to be:
   (a) Sunrise industries (i.e. above average growth and profitability)
   (b) Sunset industries (i.e. Below average growth and profitability)
   (c) What do you consider to be the average growth and profitability in these industries?

Company performance
4. How do you think company performance should be evaluated? Please give your reasons for your answer.

> PROBE: innovativeness, reputation, among customers, public reputation, IR record, environmental responsibility, etc.

5. Do you think any non-financial measures of company performance should be incorporated into the study in hand?

> PROBE: Reasons for answer

6. Can you suggest any outstanding examples of companies with above and below average performance?

> PROBE: Contacts and possibility of introductions.

Attitudes to marketing
7. What is *your* definition of marketing?

Organisation of 'marketing' in the company
8. (a) Given your definition how do you think 'marketing' should be organised in a company?

> PROBE: Which functions are considered as the responsibility of marketing: sales, distribution/logistics, aftersales service, trade promotions, advertising, exporting, market research, product design, marketing staffing, marketing training, marketing planning, new product development, sales forecasting, pricing, packaging.
> NB. Usefulness of scale – full and sole responsibility – no responsibility.

(b) Which of the above functions (if any) do you think should be part of the marketing department?

> PROBE: Is the organisation and structure important at all?

(c) Do you think that the personnel in the above functions should be involved in any marketing activities?

> PROBE: How this might be measured?
> e.g. number of personnel in each
> department with marketing responsibility/
> number of marketing department personnel
> involved in each functional area.

9. In any company, how might you rank the importance of the following executives?

> PROBE: Production
> Finance/Accounting
> Sales
> Marketing
> R&D
> Personnel.

10. Do you consider that marketing as a department should be represented on the Board of Directors or Chief decision-making executive committee?

11. What is the function background of most managing directors and in your opinion, what should it be?

> PROBE: is this considered to be important?

12. Do you consider it important for a managing director to have worked in a variety of positions and/or industries?

> PROBE: reasons for answer.

13. Do you think that Marketing Training is an important aspect of a company's operation?

> PROBE: formal marketing training
> programme (in-house, external), length
> of 'marketing apprenticeship', breadth
> of training, integration with other
> functions. NB. Limited to marketing
> personnel, or company-wide.

Corporate and marketing strategy

14. What role and contribution has marketing to play in overall corporate planning strategy?

> PROBE: 'Company mission' and how this might be included in a structured questionnaire.

15. How would you define the time horizon of 'long-term' or strategic planning?

> PROBE: number of years, and how important. Substance or trapping.

16. What do you consider to be the issues relevant to strategic planning?

> PROBE: definition of product market, long-term investment, future sales volume, return on investment, cash flow/liquidity, forecasts of market size and share mergers and acquisitions, company image/reputation, forecasting technological change, other.

17. Do you consider processes and procedures for strategic planning to be important?

> PROBE: formal/informal meetings, written documents to guide planning, rules and roles; standardisation; centralisation. NB. Trappings and substance.

18. Do you feel that strategic plans should be:
    (a) written down?
    (b) accessible to others?

> PROBE: reasons.

19. Who do you feel should be involved in the strategic planning process?

> PROBE: level of personnel (hierarchical) and functional department.

20. Can you say which of the following strategies you consider to be most useful for achieving strategic objectives?

> PROBE: If respondent is industry-specific probe reasons for choice. If respondent is general clarify what the contextual influences on strategy might be.
> Check the following alternatives:
> (a) Increasing sales of current products in current markets.
> (b) Developing new markets for existing products.
> (c) Phasing out unprofitable products and markets.
> (d) Developing new products for existing markets.
> (e) Developing new products for new markets
> (f) Developing new products with higher value added/lower value added to serve new markets.

Market research
21. What do you consider to be a company's major information needs?

> PROBE: Market size, market share; market growth; future sales; competitive activity; customer requirements and preferences.

22. What do you consider to be the most useful sources of these types of information?

> PROBE: Secondary sources (government data, trade associations data, company records) customer surveys, distributor surveys, qualitative research, field experiments, in-house (laboratory) experiments, omnibus survey data.

23. In you view, which of the following marketing research activities are commonly undertaken (or commissioned) by companies?

> PROBE: industry research, motivation research, image research, advertising/ media research, pricing research, product competitive research, distribution research.

24. In your opinion, why might market research *not* be carried out (or commissioned) by companies?

25. What do you consider to be the main uses to which market research might be put?

> PROBE: sales forecasting and planning; identifying product opportunities; evaluating customers' reaction to a product; selecting channels of distribution; advertising planning estimating market potential.

26. Who is likely to be responsible for gathering and disseminating market research data in a company?

> PROBE: functional depts; in-house/ external. NB. Is this of any *real* importance. Substance or trapping.

27. How formalised is market research in companies?

> PROBE: Regularity of surveys; methodically carried out for specific purposes (e.g. NPD); use of MR techniques (are these a trapping?)

28. How would you rate the following measures as indicators of how thoroughly a company researches its market.
    (a) the existence of an MR department
    (b) the size of the department
    (c) the amount of money spent on MR.

Segmentation — (a) for industry — specific respondents only
29. In your opinion, do companies in the industry divide up the market into groups of relatively similar types of customer?

> PROBE: segmentation bases; geography, usage, customer size, purchase criteria.

30. In your view, how different are the products of companies in the industry and how do they differ?

> PROBE: quality, style, features, design, performance, price, delivery, services, reputation.

31. Has the overall number of products increased or decreased in the past 10 years?

32. What do you consider to be the most successful products and what accounts for their success?

Segmentation — (b) for a general expert
29. Do you think that markets should be divided into groups of relatively similar customers?

> PROBE: why

30. In your view, how do products of competing companies differ from one another?

> PROBE: why

31. Do you think there is a general trend to increase or decrease product ranges?

32. What factors do you think explain a product's success?

The marketing mix
33. In your opinion, what are the major factors in achieving competitiveness?

> PROBE: (for industry-specific respondents, probe for 1 industry only): product design, performance; range of products, aggressive marketing; increased manufacturing investment; after sales service and spare parts; price, delivery, guarantees and warranties, sales liaison and information, advertising, technological progressiveness, knowledge of the market.

34. In your opinion, what factors make up 'product quality'?

> PROBE: differentiation-number of products/choice; design; engineering and aesthetic; product performance — fitness for the task; quality of raw materials and components manufacturing/ technological progressiveness.

35. Do you think an absolute quality orientation and a marketing orientation for quality can be distinguished? If so, how?

36. In your industry, how often are products modified, and what form does the modification take?

> PROBE: style, features, variations, price, technology advancements, manufacturing/ raw material/component change.

37. In your view, what triggers product modification?

> PROBE: customer suggestion; technological progress, competitive activity; erosion of sales, general research for improvements.

38. In your opinion, at what rate are new products introduced into the market?

39. What do you think is the usual trigger for NPD?

> PROBE: customer suggestion; technological progress, competitive activity; erosion of sales, general research for improvements.

40. What do you consider to be the essence of successful NPD or modification?

> PROBE: good market analysis, product quality, product design, price, company image/reputation, wide distribution, good delivery and service; promotion, aggressive selling, product uniqueness, etc.

41. What do you consider to be the main causes of new product failure?

> PROBE: as above and also the aspect of 'over-engineering – absolute quality'.

42. In you opinion what are the hallmarks of "good service" and which do you consider to be of importance in achieving company objectives?

> PROBE: parts availability, guarantees and warranties, speed of service calls; delivery, availability, installation/demonstration/technical assistance, training operators, credit facilities, leasing, repair contracts.

43. What do you consider to be the role of personal selling?

44. What is important in the management of salespeople?

> PROBE: Selection of representatives; sales training; remuneration; control, etc. Probe *each* aspect separately.

45. What do you consider to be the role of advertising?

46. What do you consider to be important in the choice of media strategy?

(a)

> PROBE: Objectives; cost; competitive promotion; nature of the market, nature of the message.

(b) In your opinion, what is the most usual basis for choosing media strategy?

47. What do you consider to be the role of pricing?

48. In your opinion, what must be kept in mind when fixing prices?

> PROBE: The market, the competition, pricing objectives, profit, sales mix, sales volume.

49. What do you consider to be the most common methods of pricing setting?

Compiled by the author as part of a research project.

Semi-structured interviews

These represent the halfway house between the partly and fully structured interview and comprise a combination of standardised open *and* closed questions in a predetermined sequence to be followed exactly by the interviewer. Such questionnaires are widely used when sampling a population to ensure that one has the necessary factual information for determining its representativeness for ensuring that quotas have been filled, etc. but when the primary purpose is to get a feel for attitudes, opinions, etc. as a preliminary to developing a fully structured interview using a carefully prepared and tested questionnaire of the kind described in the previous chapter.

Structured interviews

The major difference between the structured and semi-structured interview is that in the former not only are the questions and structure predetermined but so also are the response categories. It should be appreciated that other than for fairly short and straightforward questionnaires very few interviews/ questionnaires which are regarded as 'structured' conform exactly to the definition. Most structured questionnaires will contain 'Others' and 'Write-in' opportunities where it would be counter productive or impossible to pre-identify and list all feasible responses, as well as the occasional open-ended question too. However, the main distinguishing feature of the structured interview is that it generates *reliable* data which is amenable to statistical analysis and which can be collected by trained interviewers with little or no knowledge of the research subject – something which is increasingly important the less structured the interview. That said accurate and consistent questionnaire completion is vital to ensure the data is valid and reliable. The following extract on questionnaire completion is taken from the *Fieldwork Guide* edited by Alison C. Scott of the Advertising Research Unit in the Department of Marketing at Strathclyde University and covers all the essential issues necessary to ensure the task is performed well.

Questionnaire completion

The results of a survey are based on the collection of data, which must be valid. This means that the interviewer must record the information given by the respondent in every interview with accuracy. In order to ensure that sufficient accuracy is achieved, the following points should be observed:

(1) General points to observe when asking questions

(a) *Each question should be asked exactly as it is written on the questionnaire.*
    The questions have been worded very carefully by the research worker in charge of the survey and piloted by experienced interviewers. Every interview is an exchange of communications between two individuals. Words are the essence of this communication. Some words may have quite different associations and if different words are used we shall have the wrong response.

    If we cannot be sure you have asked the questions in exactly the same way, we cannot compare results.

(b) *You should always read out the introductory phrase you are given on each survey in the exact words given to you at the top of the questionnaire.*

(c) *If you use a 'probe', which is really a supplementary question, you should use this in the exact words given to you for that type of probe.* (These probes are given later in this section.)

(d) *You should not explain any of the questions.*
The reason for this is that if you give your interpretation of the question, this may be different from that of another interviewer. So, in effect, you are asking a different question.

(e) *You should ask each and every question you are required to ask and in the order in which it is written.*
Often it may seem to you that the respondent has already given you the answer to a question by a comment she has made during the interview, or even, you may feel, in answer to a question which has already been asked. But you must still ask every question as you come to it, because the answer a person gives at one stage of the interview may be quite different from the one he/she gives at another.
    We very carefully arrange the questions in a certain order so that a train of thought is made. If you start rearranging the questions the train of thought is changed. Sometimes too, a question is repeated on purpose, as a sort of check question. If the respondent changes her mind about something or remembers something later on which she was trying to think of earlier, then you must not change the original answer you have recorded. Taking each question individually, the answer you get to a question at the time you ask it *is the correct answer.*

(f) *You should not put in any supplementary question on your own.*

(g) *You should always follow all the procedure given on the questionnaire for asking questions, showing cards, visual aids, scales etc.*
    (i)   We shall often ask you to handle a question in a certain way. There may be a procedure given to you about rotating the order of asking different sections of the question, or we may ask you to work through the sections in a certain way. This procedure should be followed meticulously. Otherwise you are doing the same as if you were to change the wording of the question – you are asking another question.
        Similarly, if there is a procedure for the respondent about what you want her to do – for example, explaining the meaning of a scale card, or choosing one of a series of statements – you should read out the appropriate instructions *exactly as written* on the questionnaire. These instructions can be easily identified as they always appear in block capitals.
        These procedures and instructions are *part of the question,* and are very carefully planned and worded by the research worker, who needs to be sure that every interview has been conducted in the same way, and that the same question has been asked in every case.

(ii) On many of the surveys you will be asked to show a *card*. On the card there may be a list of opinions from which you would like the respondent to choose one, or a list of opinions which you want the respondent to go through with you one by one, or a sort of thermometer scale on which you want the respondent to show you his opinion of something.

Remember that we always have a very good reason for asking you to show a card, and it is *not the same at all* if you do not show the card: you are in fact changing the question again.

(h) *'Don't know' responses.* If a respondent gives a 'Don't know' response to a question you should always try to elicit some kind of answer from him. At all times respondents should be aware that we are not testing their knowledge, merely interested in their opinions. A good way of dealing with this type of response is to say 'What do you think?' or 'We're interested in your opinions'. Try at all times to avoid recording a 'Don't know' response.

(2) Routing

These questions filter out respondents. On questionnaires there are usually some questions which do have to be asked of some respondents or if previous questions are answered in a particular way. In this case you skip the questions till you come to the question indicated in the routing column, e.g. if 'No' go to Q4, if 'Yes', ask Q3. You should pay particular attention to these routing instruction when going through the questionnaire at home, as you can create a very bad impression on the respondent if you fumble back and forth and ask unnecessary questions.

An example of a routed question is given below

Q19 Do you ever take an alcoholic drink?   (76)

	Yes	①
	No	2
IF 'YES' CONTINUE, IF 'NO' GO TO Q22	DK	3

Q20 Usually how often do you have a drink?   (77)
SHOW CARD 29

More than once a week	1
Regularly every week	②
2 or 3 times a month	3
About once a month	4
Only very occasionally	5
DK	6

Q21 Last time you had something to drink
what did you have?

PROBE FOR DETAILS OF WHAT WAS DRUNK

ASK Anything else?

	BEER/ LAGER (½ pints)	SPIRITS (single measures)	WINE/ SHERRY (glasses)	COCKTAILS (glasses)	
CODE NUMBER OF DRINKS OPPOSITE					(78)
No of drinks	2	1	....	....	(79)
					(80)

(3) Coding of answers

(a) *Precoded* In this type of question, we have anticipated all or most of the answers you are likely to get, and written these answers on the questionnaire opposite some 'code' numbers. All you have to do is put a circle round the appropriate code number. For example:

Q18 (a) On an average day, how many cigarettes/ (72)
cigars do you smoke?

ACTUAL NUMBER ...1 2... (cigarettes)	Less than 1 daily	1
	1–15	②
	16–20	3
	21 +	4
	None	5

(73)

ACTUAL NUMBER .... (cigars)	Less than 1 daily	1
	1–15	2
	16–20	3
	21 +	4
	None	⑤

(b) In an average week, how many ounces of (74)
cigarette/pipe tobacco do you smoke?

	Less than ½ oz daily	1
	½ – 1 oz	2
ACTUAL NUMBER .... (ounces of cigarette tobacco)	1 – 4 oz	3
	5 – 8 oz	4
	None	⑤
ACTUAL NUMBER .... (ounces of pipe tobacco)	Less than ½ oz daily	1
	½ – 1 oz	2
	1 – 4 oz	3
	5 – 8 oz	4
	None	⑤

There are several points to be remembered when you are recording pre-code answers:

(i) You should always record something for each question you are required to ask. If the answer is something like 'none' or 'never', and there is no code for this type of answer, write in 'none' or 'never'. If you have not filled in a code we cannot give you the benefit of the doubt; in other words, we will have to assume that you have not asked the question at all.

(ii) If the answers given do not seem to fit into any of the coded answers, do not force them into one of them. We would far rather you wrote out the answer in full, so that we can decide into which code it should go, than that you should code it wrongly. A 'golden rule' you should remember is *If in doubt, write it out*.

(iii) *Never* read out the answers to a pre-coded question unless you are instructed to do so. These answers are printed in to help you, not because we want the respondent to be forced to choose between them, or to know what the choices are. If we had wanted this we would have put the answers on a card for the respondent to look at and choose between.

The only exception to this is when you get a vague answer on timing and need to fit it into a specific category of the pre-codes. See later in this section — Prompt Probe (page 193).

(iv) Sometimes there is a code for 'others' for answers that cannot be put into the pre-codes. In this case you should write in the answer and code the 'others.' For example:

Q11 All the advertisements and leaflets we have been talking about were produced by the same people. Who do you think produced them?

....
WRITE IN

MULTICODE POSSIBLE

	(33)
SHEG	1
Another health education body	2
Other health bodies	3
The Government	4
Health Authority	5
Anti-smoking pressure group	6
Anti-drinking pressure group	7
Anti-drugs pressure group	8
Sports company	9
Magazine/newspaper publisher	0
Cigarette company	X
Drink company	V
	(36)
Drugs company	1
Other . . . . Schools	②
Don't know	3

(b)   *Open-ended*   An open-ended question is one where we cannot anticipate the answers and we want you to record exactly what was said as fully as possible.

In most open-ended questions you should record the answers verbatim, *in the exact words used by the respondent*. It does not matter if you think you can express what you know the respondent means much better than she can; we want you to take down, as if in dictation, her exact words. The reasons for this are two-fold. First, it is very interesting and useful for campaign development to know the exact words which people use to describe things. Second, you will not be tempted to record only that which you think is important (this leads to tremendous bias). Also, it is much easier for us to grade the exact shades of meaning in what a respondent says if you have given us her words.

Think of the following answer, and how important the words used are:

Q27   When you said there are things you can do to help to improve your health, what things did you have in mind?

PROBE FULLY, ASK ANY OTHERS?

Well, I don't know, some people   (30)

might say you should just give   (31)

up smoking but I think doing a   (32)

little exercise and watching what   (33)
you eat helps.

The answer is quite typical of the sort of thing you can expect. The respondent may not have thought about this subject before. Faced with the question she fluffs around a little, and she is really thinking aloud when she tells you what other people might think. But remember that the fact she is hesitant is interesting to us. If she had answered immediately and definitely, 'Give up smoking,' we would have known that the subject aroused pretty strong feelings.

Let us also consider the way this answer might have been recorded if the interviewer did not record everything. A really poor interviewer could probably cut the respondent off after the first sentence 'Well, I don't know,' recording 'don't know'.

The technique of verbatim reporting is something which comes with practice, but there are two hints we can give you:

— start writing immediately the respondent starts to speak;
— when she outstrips you, as she probably will unless she sees you writing and slows up (she often will), it is a good idea to repeat what she has said to you *as you write it*, which invariably has the effect of slowing her down to your pace.

(4)   Probing

Probing is a way of getting a respondent to:

— answer you in terms of the questions, or
— say more, or
— explain herself.

Probing, unless skilfully done, can introduce a great deal of bias. The interviewer is only human, and it is natural that she will probe more fully on points which appeal to her, or which she agrees with, or which she thinks are important. This is why we often do not think it is a good idea to let you know what we expect from a question: you may find yourself only recording what you think we want to know. It is impossible to gauge the importance of any point until the survey is finished. So always follow the probing procedures printed on the questionnaire faithfully.

There are *three main types of probe*, and these are described below:

A   BASIC PROBES — used to get the respondent to answer you in terms of the question.

The respondent, if she has misunderstood the question or does not know the answer, may do one of five things:

(a)   she may answer so far off the point that you can tell she has not grasped the meaning of what you are asking.
(b)   she may ask you what you mean.
(c)   she may ask you what your opinion is.
(d)   she may refuse to answer because she feel she does not know enough.
(e)   she may not answer you properly in terms of the card or scale which you are showing her.

Basic Probe (i) (Always used first, before other probes)
When the respondent answers so far off the point that you can tell she has not grasped the meaning of what you said, record the first answer she gives and then use basic probe (i), viz. *merely repeating the question,*

perhaps putting emphasis on different words. Repeat the question or part of the question slowly and clearly. You may think this makes you sound foolish but this is not so. The point is that a carefully piloted question can stand up to this treatment. You should, as an interviewer, be able to rely on your question to get the information you require.

Basic probe (i) is supposed to get you the answer you want, and should always be tried first, before you use any other probe.

e.g. You said you did get involved in sport/physical activity. Could you tell me the sorts of things that you are involved in?
A. I like watching football.
Q. Could you tell me the sorts of things that *you* are *involved* in?
A. Oh, I go swimming occasionally and long walks with the dog.

Basic Probe (ii) — 'What do you mean?'
This is used if the respondent asks you what you mean. This is, admittedly, a difficult one to parry, and you will probably only annoy her by repeating the question too many times. The way to deal with this is as follows: try repeating the question or part of the question, as in Basic Probe (i) and if the respondent still asks what you mean, say 'I would like to know what you understand by ...'.

e.g. Do you ever get involved in any sport/physical activity.
A. Are you counting walking?
Q. Any sport/physical activity.
A. I am not sure what you mean by physical activity.
Q. I would like to know what *you* understand by physical activity. Do you ever get involved in any sport/physical activity?
A. Oh well, I suppose I would count walking. In that case I do get involved in sport/physical activity.

If a respondent gives you an answer which you know to be incorrect, however preposterous it may seem to you, you must never correct her. It is most revealing to us if the respondent is in fact misinformed. Do not ever say something like, 'But you said before that you thought so-and-so', or 'had used so-and-so and now you've told me so-and-so'. Take each answer down as it comes, when it comes.

Basic Probe (iii) — 'What is your opinion?'
Another thing which happens often is when a respondent cannot make up her mind, and asks you for your opinion. Here you should throw the ball back into her court by saying, 'I would like to know what you think'. You should *never* express your own opinion. This would bias your respondent completely.

Basic Probe (iv) — 'What do you think?'
On some questions respondents may be asked to give an opinion on some subject to which she has not given much thought before. In this sort of case you often find a respondent reluctant to answer. She may say something like, 'I can't tell you, as I say I've never really thought about it before'. In this case you should repeat the question, emphasising the word 'think', and then if she still says she does not know, use the following probe question:

'Would you tell me what you think, from what you have heard or seen about ...?'

and, as a last resort: 'Would you make a guess?'

These last probes are only to be used if all else fails. Do try repeating the question or part of the question (Basic Probe (i)). You should usually be able to get an answer from this. If not, go on to use Basic Probe (v).

Basic Probe (v) — Getting the respondent to answer in terms of a show card.
If you are asking the respondent to choose one of a series of statements or opinions on a card, you must be sure that she answers by using one of the words on the card. If she does not you must draw her attention back to the card by using the basic probe, 'Would you tell me which of these words or phrases on *this card* comes closest to what you think?', or 'Would you show me on this card?'

e.g. I have a card here with some statements on it. (READ OUT CARD) I would like you to tell me which of them applies to eating salt? (VERY GOOD, QUITE GOOD, NEITHER GOOD NOR BAD, QUITE BAD, VERY BAD.)
A. I think eating salt is all right in moderation.
Q. Would you tell me which of the phrases on this card comes closest to what you think?
A. Oh, 'NEITHER GOOD NOR BAD' I would say.

B   PROBES FOR OPEN-ENDED QUESTIONS — to get people to say more. There are three kinds of probes used here:
(a) *Continuing probe* The next important probe to master, and possibly the most difficult, is the continuing probe. Briefly, what we are trying to do is to get people to say as much as possible, without leading them in any way. Ideally, no probe except this and the basic probe, should be used.

(i) The first continuing probe may not sound to you like a probe at all, but simply the normal thing you would do in any interview.

It involves looking expectantly at the respondent with your pen posed over the paper, as if she were about to say more.

(ii) You may also repeat the last words of what she has just said, in exactly the same words as she has used. If you change the words, you may introduce bias.

(iii) You can say 'mm' or 'yes' in an anticipatory manner.

Written down, these 'continuing' probes sound very strange, but once you have practised them for a time you will find they come quite easily and naturally. It is essentially a conversational probe. You should look upon all interviews as a conversation between you and the respondent. Always draw her out sympathetically, without giving any opinions of your own.

(b) *What else/Any other probe* This is the final probe used on open-ended questions.

The way you ask this is as follows:

'What else can you tell me about . . . ?' inserting the appropriate question, and recording fully any further information you are given. Never ask 'anything else?' as this usually elicits the answer 'no'. Rather ask a positive question — 'What else?' — because, although it might not be as socially acceptable, it produces results.

e.g. Could you tell me the sorts of sports/physical activity that you are involved in?
PROBE FULLY

A. I take exercise three times a week.
Q. Exercise?
A. Yes, swimming, walking, that sort of thing.
Q. Mm?
A. That's all really.
Q. Any other kinds of physical activity you do?
A. I do a lot of gardening I suppose
Q. Mm?
A. That's all.

(c) *Explanatory probe* This is used to get people to explain themselves (only to be used if instructed).

On an open-ended question, when the respondent has said as much as she can, there may still be some points which are incomplete, or incomprehensible. If this happens, do not interrupt the respondent as she is speaking to you, as you may interrupt her train of thought. Wait until she has stopped speaking after all the continuing probes, and *then* use one of the following two probes:

(i)   If the respondent's answer is ambiguous, incomprehensible, or incomplete then you should repeat exactly the words she has said, and then ask:

either   – 'What do you mean by that?'
or   – 'In what way was it ...?'
or   – 'What makes you say that?'

(ii) e.g.   When you said there are things you can do to help improve your health, what things did you have in mind?
PROBE FULLY, ASK ANY OTHERS?

A.   Have a good diet.
Q.   What do you mean by diet?
A.   Eating the right kinds of food.
Q.   Mm?
A.   Like fruit and vegetables and brown bread.
Q.   What makes you say that?
A.   They've got lots of fibre in them.
Q.   Mm?
A.   Isn't that enough? I can't think of anything more to say.

This is the sort of thing people often say. In open ended questions, you should record verbatim even these 'finishing up' statements, so that we know you have got absolutely all you can from that person. If you use a 'continuing' probe and get no response, you should *always* record that you have used probe.

C   SPECIFIC PROBES – used to get the exact information you want.
(a)   *Amplifying probe* On some questions, especially precoded ones, you may not get exactly the information you require. For instance, if you were asking someone about physical activity, and she told you she did 'exercise', you might want to know what sort of exercise. In this case you would *not* prompt her by asking her something like 'Would that be running, aerobics, swimming?' This would be prompting, putting your own interpretation of a word into the respondent's mind, instead of letting her give you her interpretation. You should deal with this question in this way. Ask 'What kind of/sort of ...?' *Do not* use any other phrase except those.

(b) *Playback specific probe* This probe is used mainly on questions of frequency or time. If the answer given is not given to you in the terms you want, you 'play back' what the respondent has said to you.

e.g. How often these days do you take an alcoholic drink (if at all)?

    A. Only on special occasions.
        (Here the interviewer should not interpret the answer herself – after all your idea of what constitutes a 'special occasion' may be quite different from that of another person.)
    Q. How often is that?
    A. How often do special occasions occur?

(c) *Prompt probe* This probe is only to be used if all else fails, and it must *only be used in questions of frequency or time* – 'How long ago?' or 'When did you?' It is sometimes very difficult to get an accurate answer to these questions without using the prompt probe, in which you offer a series of pairs of alternatives to the respondent.

This prompt probe is the only exception to the rule that you must never prompt – i.e. put something into the mind of the respondent that is perhaps not there – and should be used with great restraint, and only as it is written above.

The way to proceed with this sort of probe is as follows:

Look at your questionnaire and find which is the least frequent or the longest ago and taking that, ask one of these questions:

(1) *On frequency* – 'Would it be once in...or more often than that?' and work down to the right answer.
(2) *On questions of 'how long?'* – 'Would it be within the last ... or longer ago than that?' and work down until you get the right answer.

e.g. When did you last take an alcoholic drink?

A. Ages ago.
Q. Would it be within the last 12 months or longer ago than that?
A. Oh, within the last year.
Q. Would it be within the last 6 months or longer ago than that?
A. Oh, within the last 6 months.
Q. Would it be within the last month or longer ago than that?
A. No, it is longer ago than a month.

SUMMARY OF PROBES

(a) Probes to get respondent to answer in terms of the question

Basic probes:

(i)	When she answers off the point	Repeat the question or part of the question
(ii)	When she asks what you mean	Basic probe (i) first and then 'I would like to know what you understand by...?'
(iii)	When she asks what you think	Basic probe (i) first and then 'I would like to know what *you* think. We are interested in your views.'
(iv)	'Last ditch' probes if respondent will not answer because she feels she does not know enough	Basic probe (i) first and then 'Would you tell me what you think, from what you've heard or seen?' then 'Would you make a guess?'
(v)	Basic probes on showing a card	Basic probe (i) first and then 'Which of the words/phrases/brands on this card come closest to what you mean?' 'Would you show me on the card?'

(b) Probes to make people say more

Continuing probes:

(i) Looking expectantly
(ii) Saying 'mm' or 'yes'
(iii) Repeating the last words of what respondent has said in an anticipatory manner

What else probes

Explanatory probes:

(i) What did you mean by that?
(ii) In what way was it...?
(iii) What makes you say that?

(c) Probes to get specific information

   (i) Amplifying probe   What sort of/kind of . . . ?
  (ii) Playback probe   Playback what respondent has said in order to get *specific* answer required
(iii) Prompt probe   How long ago? or When did you?

HOW TO INDICATE PROBES

Write (P) beside each comment where you have asked the respondent for more.

e.g. What sort of things can you do to improve your health?

> Everything in moderation (P) cut down drinking and smoking (P) don't eat too many fatty foods (P) a little exercise (P) nothing else

You carry on probing till the respondent has nothing more to say and then end with '(P) nothing else' to indicate that you did try to probe further but the respondent had nothing more to say. This is called probing to a negative.

(5)   Show cards

These are cards showing lists of words or phrases. They are used to prompt answers to certain questions, e.g. what advertising is respondent aware of. They also help to make the respondent define his attitude to some element of a campaign. Make sure cards are shown and that the respondent reads the card properly, and if necessary wait until he fetches his glasses! Explain that here is a list of items we would like him to consider, and he is to choose one or two, depending on the instructions. If he does not appear to understand the card or perhaps cannot read, read out the items and make a note on the questionnaire of what you have done.

When there is more than one show card attached to each other, you must take the cards back before the next question to prevent the respondent leafing through. Reading the cards prematurely can be fatal to some types of questions.

Here are three important points about card showing:

  (i) Unless the respondent is blind or says he cannot read, you must *always* show the card. If you cannot show the card for these reasons, then you must record this on the questionnaire.

(ii) When you show the card, you should read out the words on it *before* you ask the questions. Many people read carelessly or incorrectly; there is much more semi-illiteracy in the country than you might think.

(iii) If you are asking the respondent to choose one of a number of statements or opinions on a card, you should be sure that he answers you exactly in terms of one of the words on the card.

ARU questionnaires indicate which show card should be used with each question thus, e.g. 'SHOW CARD 12.' Photographs, pictures, leaflets, booklets, posters, stickers, etc., are referred to as VISUAL AIDS with an approximate number. The system of numbers used for both show cards and visual aids runs consecutively, so 1, 2 and 3 might be show cards; 4, 5 and 6 visual aids, and 7, 8 and 9 show cards.

(6)   Scales

We often need to know how significant a respondent perceives a given concept to be. Commercial Market Research companies often need to know how a respondent rates a brand or product, either against other brands or against other products, or with regard to specific attributes required from that kind of product. In this case we use some form of scale, of which there are three main types:

(a) *Verbal scale* Here the degrees of the scale are expressed in the form of words, for example:

How well do you think the advertisements we have been talking about manage to get across the point that being healthy is not just a matter of giving up smoking and drinking? Choose a phrase from this card which best describes your answer.

> Very well
> Reasonably well
> Not really well
> Not at all well

(b) *Marks* This type of scale tends not to be used by the ARU, although other companies use it more commonly. In this case the respondent is asked to award marks, usually out of 10, to an advertisement or brand for a specific attribute, e.g. how many marks out of 10 would you give the *Daily Mirror* for being a newspaper that gives you all the health news you want?

(c) *Semantic differential scales* These scales, as used by the ARU, consist of five or six alternative responses to a statement. The responses at either end of the scale are more or less opposite in meaning. There are usually about 10–12 statements per question (see example below).

Q31 Here is a list of things that other people have said may be good for health. READ OUT WHOLE LIST
How important do you think each of them is for health?
SHOW CARD 35, READ OUT EACH STATEMENT INDIVIDUALLY AND OBTAIN RESPONSE
ROTATE START

	Very important	Quite important	Not very important	Not at all important	DK	
Giving up smoking	①	2	3	4	5	(56)
Eating more fibre	6	⑦	8	9	0	
Drinking less alcohol	1	②	3	4	5	(57)
Losing weight	6	7	⑧	9	0	
Eating less sugar	1	②	3	4	5	(58)
Taking exercise	6	⑦	8	9	0	
Getting the doctor's advice on how to stay healthy	1	2	③	4	5	(59)
Relaxing/getting plenty of sleep	6	7	⑧	9	0	
Eating less salt	1	②	3	4	5	(60)
Using medicines	6	7	8	⑨	0	
Eating less fatty foods	1	2	③	4	5	(61)

The respondent chooses her response from a show card. The interviewer circles the code number which applies to the respondent's reply.

We use this type of scale because, if *administered properly*, they give us information that we cannot easily obtain in any other way.

Sometimes these scales will consist of five or seven boxes placed between two words or phrases. The words at either end of the boxes are more or less opposite in meaning. There are usually about 20 or so scales set out on a page. At the top of the page is a *concept*, which the respondent is being asked to rate. Usually, the concept will be a brand of some product field, but sometimes it may be the respondent's own opinion of herself, or a company, or just about anything.

Where this 'empty box' type scale is used, respondents are required to tick the scales as quickly as they can, and if they do put down their first, objective opinions, the results will be some measure of their subconscious motivations and attitudes.

You can appreciate that clients find such information extremely useful to improve their products and advertising.

The only alternative technique to obtain this kind of psychological information is 'depth' interviewing. Such methods are difficult to carry out on a large scale and tend to give somewhat misleading results if the samples of respondents involved are small.

The proper administration of semantic differential scales is a more advanced skill than simple interviewing techniques. The interviewer must be aware of the purpose of the technique, and must strive to create the proper milieu, or 'psychological atmosphere'.

The most important thing to get across to the respondent is that we do not want a slow, considered opinion. Their first impression is the thing we are after.

Some people are naturally cautious and will be slow. Others may try to ponder over the 'correct' answer in a misguided attempt to be as helpful as possible. If it is explained properly, the speed element of the administration of the scales can by conveyed to most respondents. Interviewers will have to experiment a bit to find the best way of dealing with people who go too slowly.

On average, about four seconds per scale should be allowed as a reasonable speed. Some respondents will be much faster, but others will try to drag on beyond this point.

If much more than four seconds per scale is being taken, the respondent is getting bored and the information being obtained is actually of less value. If possible, the interviewer should interject to try to speed things up.

(7)   Tick start

On some questions it is not possible to rotate the actual statements or lists of products, and then the researcher asks the interviewer to rotate the order and TICK START. In this case the interviewer ticks the statement she starts with.

On the first interview she would tick the first statement. On the next interview, she ticks the second statement, reading out the statements starting from the second statement and ending with the first one and so on. In most cases it is possible for the interviewer to tick the appropriate statements at home before doing the interviews, as it is sometimes difficult to remember in the middle of an interview which statement was ticked at the last one, e.g.

Q28 Now I'm going to read out a list of things people do.
READ OUT WHOLE LIST
Could you tell me how good or bad you think they are for your health, giving your answer from this card.
SHOW CARD 35, READ OUT EACH STATEMENT INDIVIDUALLY
AND OBTAIN RESPONSE
ROTATE START, TICK START

		Very bad	Quite bad	Neither good nor bad	Quite good	Very good	DK	
1	Go to the pub for an occasional drink	1	2	3	4	5	6	(35)
2	Eat high fibre food	7	8	9	0	X	V	
✓3	Take gentle exercise once or twice a week	1	2	3	4	5	6	(36)
4	Smoke cigarettes occasionally	7	8	9	0	X	V	
5	Eat sugary food	1	2	3	4	5	6	(37)
6	Run in marathons regularly	7	8	9	0	X	V	
7	Eat fatty food	1	2	3	4	5	6	(38)
8	Spend most evenings in the pub	7	8	9	0		X	V
9	Drink a lot of milk	1	2	3	4	5	6	(39)
10	Smoke heavily	7	8	9	0	X	V	
11	Eat salt	1	2	3	4	5	6	(40)

(8)   Summary of points on the interview

Important points to remember when asking questions:
(a) Each question should be asked exactly as it is written on the questionnaire. Do not add words to try and soften the question. The questionnaires have been carefully worded, to make sure that all

interviewers have asked the same question in the same way. In order that we can compare results, you must be very scrupulous about this ruling.

(b) You should always read the introductory phrase given at the beginning of each survey as it is written.

(c) Each and every question should be asked in the order in which it is written on the questionnaire. This ensures that no questions are omitted. Bear in mind that the questionnaire has to follow a certain pattern and that we sometimes ask the same question again on purpose, as a sort of check. If you are routed past a question, put a line through it to show it was not asked. Never leave a question completely blank.

(d) The respondent may change her mind in the course of the interview because of something you have been discussing. You should not change an answer previously given, even if the respondent contradicts herself, or asks you to change the question. The ruling is that whatever the respondent answers at the time of being asked the question is the correct answer to that question. Make a note on the questionnaire if she has changed her mind.

(e) You should never explain the question. If the respondent does not understand, repeat the question. If she still does not understand, make a note of this on the questionnaire and go on to the next question. Never change the wording or ask a supplementary question, except one of the standard probe questions.

(f) Write legibly and always in blue or black biro. All answers must be recorded at the time of the interview.

(g) There must be an answer recorded for every applicable question on the questionnaire. Unless you explain why there is no answer recorded at any question, the questionnaire is incomplete and we cannot use it. The questionnaire will be returned to you.

(h) Make a note beside any question where odd circumstances prevented you from asking the question as instructed, e.g. respondent was blind, and you read out from show card etc.

(i) Cross out a wrongly recorded code with two diagonal lines, e.g. ⫽ Never cross it out with an X, as this causes confusion.

(j) Where you have been given a vague answer, do not make a guess. If you are not sure what to code, throw the question back at the respondent until you get a definite answer.

(k) Instructions in capital letters are addressed to you and should not be read out to the respondent. Only where the writing is in ordinary small letters do you read this out to the respondent.

(l) Record replies accurately and swiftly. Control the interview by asking questions at a speed to suit the respondent. If you are too slow they get irritated, if too fast they will not understand.

(m) Give adequate thanks to the respondent for their co-operation when the interview is concluded.

Interviewer selection and control

From the above discussion of questionnaire completion it should be clear that the role of the interviewer is critical to the effective administration of a questionnaire. No matter how much effort has been put into the structuring and design of a questionnaire poor administration can invalidate all the data collected and render the survey useless. It follows that interviewers must be *professionally* qualified for the task in hand.

As we have seen the level and kind of qualification will depend very much upon the type of interview. For in-depth, informal and unstructured interviews one requires a person with knowledge of the subject matter, interpretative skills and judgement as the scope and content of the interview and the explanation of this will depend entirely upon the interviewer. Conversely, in the case of semi-structured or structured interviews using a questionnaire the interviewer will not require specific knowledge or interpretative skills but they will require personal skills in initiating and conducting the interview if one is to secure the desired information from the intended respondents. Because of these demands, and the fact that few organisations undertake a sufficient volume of field research to keep professional interviewers fully employed, specialist divisions or firms have developed to undertake field interviewing on a sub-contract basis.

In the *Consumer Market Research Handbook* John F. Drakeford and Valerie Farbridge deal with the subject 'Interviewing and field control' in considerable detail. Much of this is more relevant to the professional practitioner than the user but in concluding their chapter they offer the following checklist for buyers.

Research planning and design:

(a) Is the right degree of emphasis placed upon the interviewing phase of a project, compared with the other phases through which the project has to go?
(b) How are the questionnaires, recording forms, diaries or inventories laid out, and by whom are they designed?
(c) Has the designer any interviewing experience, and has he or she at any stage piloted the questionnaire?
(d) Are instructions to interviewers comprehensive; and who drafted them?
(e) Are the sampling procedures to be used in the project feasible in the field?
(f) How are the interviewers instructed on these sampling procedures and under what circumstances, if any, are they allowed to deviate from instructions?
(g) What checks are imposed to ensure that a sampling plan is followed?

Field Control

(a) How is the field management at head office organised in general and in relation to the implementation of a particular project?
(b) How much contact is there between head office staff and the supervisors and interviewers?
(c) What documentation exists as a control on contact rates, interviewing rates, etc?
(d) How is supervision in the field organised and how are queries that arise in the field dealt with?
(e) What is the ratio between supervisors and interviewers and what responsibilities have the supervisors for maintaining adequate interviewer standards?
(f) What procedures are followed in briefing interviewers, either personally by post or telephone?
(g) How well are these procedures supported by written material of a general kind (e.g. interviewer manual) or of a kind specific to the survey (e.g. instructions, call-sheets, etc.)?

The interviewers

(a) What is the composition of the field force and how has it been built up?
(b) How are the interviewers initially selected?
(c) How are they trained, either at formal training sessions or in the field?
(d) How frequently are the interviewers seen by head office staff and supervisors?
(e) Are they aware of the nature and depth of the quality control procedures conducted?
(f) What are their terms of employment and how are they paid?
(g) How regularly do the interviewers work for the organization?
(h) To what extent do they work also for other field forces?
(i) What methods of identification are carried?

Quality control

(a) What checks are imposed on interviewers while work is in the field and how are the problems and queries resolved?
(b) How often and at what level are supervisor spot checks, postal checks, revisits to respondents conducted as further control measures?
(c) What are the check-editing procedures once work has been returned to head office and how are queries and suspect interviewing dealt with?
(d) Has the organisation been able to build up a data bank on individual interviewer performance; if so, what does this data bank comprise?

Source: John F. Drakeford and Valerie Farbridge, 'Interviewing and Field Control', in *Consumer Market Research Handbook*.

As a further check the buyer might also ask to see the kind of fieldwork guide issued to interviewers and check its scope and clarity against the extract on questionnaire completion given above.

Telephone surveys

Earlier in the chapter reference was made to the fact that many more households in the UK now have access to a telephone (84 per cent in 1988 up from 77 per cent in 1983) so that its use is becoming increasingly commonplace in consumer research. (It has always been used extensively in industrial and organisational research.) In this section we examine some of the key aspects of the telephone survey method.

In the introduction to one of the few specialist books on the topic (*Survey Research by Telephone*, vol. 150, Sage Library of Social Research, Sage Publications, 1983), James H. Frey comments that the significant shift to the use of the telephone can be attributed to the 'rising costs and declining response rates experienced by the face-to-face survey' reinforced by improved telephone technology, research procedures and the 'nearly complete accessibility of any population via the telephone'. That said, the telephone is not appropriate to all kinds of survey and its use should be restricted to those situations where it offers significant advantages over other interviewing methods in light of the usual time and budgetary constraints. Frey offers a very useful table comparing mail, face-to-face and telephone survey methods and this is reproduced as Table 8.4.

TABLE 8.4   Relative advantages and disadvantages of survey methods

	Personal	*Telephone*	*Mail*
Bias (from interviewer)	3	2	1
Control over collection	2	1	3
Depth of questioning	1	2	3
Economy	3	1	2
Follow up ability	2	1	3
Hard to recall data	2	3	1
Rapport with respondent	1	2	3
Sampling completeness	1	2	3
Speed of obtaining response	2	1	3
Versatility	1	3	2

Source: James H. Frey (1983) *Survey Research by Telephone*, Sage library of Social Research, vol. 150 (Sage Publication).

The use of telephone surveys has also grown in popularity with the introduction of Computer-Assisted Telephone Interviewing (CATI). CATI has become the generic name for a number of proprietary systems developed by commercial firms and academic institutions each of which has specialist features that makes it particularly suited for a given kind of survey problem. However, all systems share the common feature that interviewing is undertaken using a CRT terminal. Frey describes the process as follows:

> The interview is actually controlled by preprogrammed machine processes. Thus, in effect, the respondent talks to the computer through the interviewer. CATI directs the flow of each interview with exactly the right question — one question at a time. Preprogrammed editing instructions work to ensure that the responses are valid and consistent with answers to previous questions. If an interviewer keys in an inappropriate response (for example, not included in response categories), an error message automatically appears on the screen and corrective measures can be implemented immediately. When the correct response is entered the computer determines which question should be asked next. The next question will not appear until the previous question has been answered with an appropriate response category. At the end of the interview, all respondents' replies are automatically and instantaneously entered into the computer memory.

The ability to check for consistency and validity, to ensure precise and correct administration, to drop questions once sufficient data has been collected and so shorten succeeding interviews, and to create a database in one step in real time are all significant advantages of CATI. Unfortunately, the increase in telephone selling and in direct mail are resulting in respondent resistance and the problems of securing participation in surveys of all kinds are likely to become increasingly acute in the 1990s. (Reference to packaged software available to devise and execute CATI is contained in Chapter 12).

Mail surveys

While documented evidence is hard to come by, many researchers believe that the data secured from a properly designed and executed mail survey is as good as that which may be obtained from face-to-face personal interviews and/or telephone surveys with the in-built checks described above.

The obvious and major advantage of the mail survey is that every firm and household in the country can be reached for the same basic cost with the result that mail surveys are estimated to cost one third as much as a personally administered questionnaire (see Lindsay Brook, 'Postal Survey Procedures', Chapter 7 in *Survey Research Practice*, Gerald Hoinville and Roger Jowell, Heinemann Educational Books, 1978). Postal surveys also have the advantage that they are completed at the respondents' convenience so that participation may occur which would have been impossible or rejected if initiated by a personal approach or telephone call. This facility also allows the respondents to reflect on their answers, check records or consult with others if appropriate.

As with most things, however, the particular strengths of the mail survey are also regarded as weaknesses by critics of the methodology. Perhaps the strongest criticism raised is that of respondent self-selection, i.e. only those willing to go to the bother of completing the questionnaire will make a return. Given that in many postal surveys the return is 20 per cent or less it is understandable that one should be concerned as to whether the respondents are in fact representative of the sample which itself was designed to be representative of the target population. Users of research should probe deeply on this issue. Most published reports contain the claim that 'an examination of the respondents' characteristics revealed no significant differences from the characteristics of the sample'. Fair enough, but ask for the comparative information to satisfy yourself that this is indeed the case. Better still, ask for a sample of the non-respondents to be interviewed face-to-face or by telephone to see if their responses are in line with the 'volunteer' respondents.

Of course, the real problem is to secure better response rates in the first instance and there are a number of techniques to help achieve this. Perhaps the most successful technique is the careful identification and selection of respondents in the first place. By choosing persons for whom the issues are salient and addressing the survey to them personally very high levels of response may be achieved. While there is possibly a 'halo' effect around academic institutions, which make extensive use of mail survey for reasons of economy, the author has supervised numerous surveys with response rates of 50 per cent or better involving chief executives and directors of major firms. Most textbooks offer extensive advice on techniques for increasing response rates from the use of adhesive postage stamps (how many chief executives open their own mail?) through the use of incentives to follow-up letters or telephone requests (see Brook, 'Postal Survey Procedures', for example). As with other technical matters the users best defence is to select a reputable and experienced practitioner and to ask them to justify the use of a particular technique or method.

Drop and collect surveys

While comparatively little has been written about this technique it is likely to become more popular in future because it combines the low cost of the mail or telephone survey with an element of personal involvement which encourages respondent participation. In a recent article in *Marketing Intelligence and Planning* (vol. 5, no. 1, 'Drop and Collect Surveys: A Neglected Research Technique'), Stephen Brown reviews the method and reports a simple experiment to demonstrate its effectiveness.

As Brown explains:

> The drop and collect technique involves the hand delivery and subsequent recovery of self-completion questionnaires though several other variants exist. These include hand delivery and postal return and postal delivery and personal pick-up. By combining the strengths and avoiding the weaknesses of face-to-face and postal surveys, drop and collect provides a fast, cheap and reliable research tool. The speed stems from the fact that the questionnaire is completed in the respondent's own time not the interviewer's. Comparisons are obviously difficult, but Walker estimates that one agent can deliver approximately 100 questionnaires per working day. This incidence of contact is not far short of that achieved in telephone surveys and, depending on the circumstances, considerably more than that attained by personal interviewing.

A significant advantage of personal collection is that it encourages both high response rates and timely completion with up to 70 per cent of questionnaires being available at the agreed collection time. Because of this high response rate it has been estimated that 'in terms of cost per completed questionnaire drop and collect surveys [is] ... on average ... 20–40 per cent less expensive than postal surveys and around half the cost of face-to-face interviews' (Brown, 'Drop and Collect Surveys'). In part the lower cost than personal interviews is because one can use relatively unskilled 'delivery agents' in place of trained interviewers and because the actual personal contact time is much less. However, response rates of up to 90 per cent almost match those achieved by face-to-face interviews, are equivalent to the best telephone survey returns and are considerably in excess of the response to mail surveys.

In addition, as Brown comments, because respondents can complete the questionnaire in their own time it is possible to use longer and more detailed questionnaires than in most face-to-face or telephone surveys. Also, when collecting the completed questionnaires the collection agent can check that they have been completed correctly, clarify any points as required by the respondent as well as ask supplementary questions if desired. But, because the interaction between agent and respondent is limited the possibility of interviewer bias is greatly reduced.

A third factor in favour of the technique, cited by Brown, is its reliability because of the control it gives over the sample selection process. On delivery the agent can ensure that the questionnaire is given to the intended respondent and, in the case of non-response, establish reasons for this – e.g. unable to contact, doesn't satisfy the sample criteria (e.g. non-user), unwilling, etc.

As one would expect the technique also has a number of weaknesses. In common with all self-completion questionnaires there is a bias towards literate respondents, there is no guarantee that the claimed respondent actually completed the questionnaire (although personal delivery and collection helps minimise this risk), and the personal nature of the method requires one to depend on highly clustered samples compared with mail or telephone surveys (but not with face-to-face interviews).

On balance, however, the advantages outweigh the disadvantages and Brown reports the design and implementation of an experiment to determine its effectiveness amongst retailers in Lisburn, Northern Ireland. The experiment confirmed the advantages of speed, low cost and high response rates and also showed that the nature of the covering letter, questionnaire length and sex of the delivery agent had little effect on the overall response rate.

Summary

In this chapter we have examined a wide range of issues involved in the collection of data through various kinds of interview. The uses and advantages/disadvantages of the various approaches have been looked at in some detail as have the issues to be taken into account when administering questionnaires. While it is unlikely that many readers will actually be responsible for administering structured questionnaires, an appreciation of what is involved will enable the user to ask meaningful questions on the subject and assess how well the fieldwork has been executed on his behalf.

In Chapter 9 we will review some of the methods and techniques used to interpret the data gathered by the various methods discussed here.

References

Baker, Michael J. and Hart, Susan J. (1989) *Marketing and Competitive Success* (Oxford: Philip Allen).

Baker, Michael J. (1984) *Macmillan Dictionary of Marketing and Advertising* (London: Macmillan).

Black, J.A. and Champion, D.J. (1986) *Methods and Issues in Social Research* (New York: John Wiley).

De-Almeida, P.M. (1980) 'A Review of Focus Group Methodology', *European Research*, 8 (3) pp. 114–20.

Dickens, J. (1982) 'The Fresh Cream Cakes Market: The Use of Qualitative Research as part of a Consumer Research Program', in U. Bradley (ed.), *Applied Marketing and Social Research* (New York: Van Nostrand Reinhold) pp. 4–43.

Gorden, R.L. (1969) *Interviewing: Strategy, Techniques, and Tactics* (Homewood, Ill.: Dorsey Press).

Hartman, J. and Hedbolm, J.H. (1979) *Methods for the Social Sciences: A Handbook for Students and Non-Specialists* (Westport, Conn: Greenwood Press).

Kinnear, T.C. and Taylor, J.R. (1987) *Marketing Research: An Applied Approach* (New York: McGraw-Hill).

Madge, John (1953) *The Tools of Social Sciences* (London: Longman, Green).

Merton, R.L. and Kendall, P.L. (1946) 'The Focussed Interview', *American Journal of Sociology*, 51, pp. 541–57.

Reynolds, F.K. and Johnson, D.K. (1978) 'Validity of Focus Group Findings', *Journal of Advertising Research*, vol. 18 (3) pp. 21–4.

Roethlisberger, F.J. and Dickson, W.J. (1939) *Management and the Worker* (Cambridge, Harvard University Press).

Sampson, P. (1978) 'Qualitative Research and Motivation Research', in R.M. Worcester and J. Downham (eds), *Consumer Market Research Handbook*, 2nd edn (New York: Van Nostrand Reinhold).

Smith, D.M. (1972) *Interviewing in Market and Social Research* (London: Routledge & Kegan Paul).

Data interpretation

Introduction

In earlier chapters we have emphasised strongly that the purpose of research is to shed light on areas of uncertainty in order to enable the decision-maker to arrive at an optimum decision within the inevitable constraints of time and money. To this end we have examined at some length the need to define problems in a clear and unambiguous way, to communicate this problem definition accurately to those responsible for attempting to solve it, and to the development of a research design best suited to the collection of the necessary data. Implicit to the whole process is the assumption that the researcher has considered carefully the analytical techniques and methods appropriate to the interpretation of the data once it has been collected. Thus, while it is convenient for the logical development of a textbook to examine procedures for analysing data at this juncture, *in reality* consideration of this matter should emerge at an early stage in the problem-solving process.

Where complete data is available one is entitled to make substantive statements about the relationships between variables revealed by the data, e.g. the relationship between income and purchase behaviour. In the great majority of cases, however, it will be neither feasible nor possible to collect complete data and it will be necessary to make do with partial data collected by means of a survey. In these circumstances one will be able to draw inferences concerning the relationship between variables but will be uncertain of the confidence which one may place upon these inferences unless some satisfactory technique exists which allows us to make meaningful pronouncements on the matter which are verifiable by and acceptable to other researchers. Fortunately, statistical techniques provide this capability and the purpose of this chapter is to review the methods and procedures available. The point we are seeking to make here is that knowledge of these methods and procedures should guide and inform the formulation of hypotheses and the design of the research through which the data is to be collected. Accordingly, in this chapter we will look first at the issue of confidence and statistical significance. This consideration leads naturally to a discussion of the salient differences between descriptive and inferential statistics.

In the case of descriptive statistics we shall look at plotting, tabulation and averaging. For inferential statistics the main topics will be cross tabulation, correlation, differentiation and pattern analysis. We conclude the chapter with a review of the main multivariate methods of analysis which have gained widespread acceptance in the analysis of complex marketing data in recent years.

Data interpretation

While marketing is a comparatively new discipline it has the advantage that it can draw upon many other disciplines in advancing its own interpretation of the nature of exchange relationships. In doing so, however, it is bound by the principles and conventions of the social sciences on which it is founded and some knowledge of these principles and conventions is essential if one is to draw meaningful conclusions from the information generated by marketing research. But this is not the place for an exploration of the philosophical foundations of the nature of truth and the discussion will be confined to a selective and somewhat simplistic review of some key ideas and concepts.

If marketing is concerned with the study of 'mutually satisfying exchange relationships' then our primary concern must be with the question of how individuals and organisations make such decisions. A cursory review of a number of the longer established social sciences — economics, psychology, anthropology, sociology, social psychology, etc. — quickly reveals that each adopts its own particular perspective and thus draws a rather different interpretation as to the nature of exchange relationships. John Madge (1953) in his excellent analysis *The Tools of Social Science* (Longman) addresses this problem when he observes that the underlying theories which underpin the economics of the superpowers of the USA and USSR are derived from the same base but that Pierce and James took a quite different view from that propounded by Marx and Engels. Madge suggests that Karl Mannheim has helped both to explain this apparent contradiction and develop a more constructive approach through his 'sociology of knowledge' in which:

He renounces the abstract concept of objective knowledge, but shows that in given circumstances it is possible to arrive at reliable decisions in factual disputes. These decisions are limited by the observers' incomplete perspective, *but when members of a group have aims in common, they will also tend to reach agreement on questions of fact.* [emphasis added.]

In other words our interpretation of the 'facts' or 'reality' is a product of our beliefs, experiences and knowledge all of which are the product of our background and upbringing. Armed with this insight it is clear that while disagreement may arise because the parties have access to different information it is just as likely to arise because they place a different interpretation upon the same information. This possibility is to be seen daily in case discussions in Business Schools where all the participants start with the same information as recorded in the case study but come to quite different conclusions as to its interpretation and as to the most appropriate course of action to solve the problem described. Thus, if one has studied economics it is likely that the desire to impose order and structure through quantification will encourage one to suppress subjectivity and so regard the unit of analysis − people − as homogeneous. Conversely, the behavioural scientist, in spite of John Donne's observation that 'No man is an island', will regard the individual as the unit of analysis and start from a belief in heterogeneity. Given the start point and orientation of economists and behavioural scientists both groups can survive amicably by agreeing to disagree but this does not help the marketer with his pragmatic interest in groupings of people which are less than the total demand for a given product or service. To develop a marketing mix to meet the particular needs of a market segment we need an explanation of group behaviour which incorporates elements of both disciplinary approaches.

While we are the product of our experience, and it is unlikely that we will be exposed to a blinding revelation such as Saul on the road to Damascus which will totally change our *perception* of the world, if we are aware of the possibility of alternative interpretations then we will have a significant competitive advantage over those who will not admit to such a possibility. Thus marketers should recognise that their's is a synthetic discipline which seeks to pull together concepts and ideas from a variety of other disciplines in an attempt to develop a *holistic* interpretation of exchange behaviour in just the same way as a doctor draws on both the physical and social sciences in developing an understanding of health as a concept. It follows that knowledge and understanding of the key concepts 'borrowed' from other disciplines is a prerequisite to the analysis of marketing problems and the interpretation of information pertaining to them. In addition one needs an understanding of the methods employed by social scientists in gathering and interpreting data and it is this topic which we shall address in this chapter. Specifically, data analysis using descriptive and inferential statistics.

Marketing research is rarely if ever undertaken out of sheer curiosity. Its initiation is purposive and usually directed to 'reducing the areas of uncertainty surrounding business decisions'. In turn business decisions are concerned with future courses of action with the result that most marketing research is an attempt to understand current behaviour better as the basis for predicting future behaviour. As pointed out in the introduction to this chapter it is inevitable that subjectivity will influence the whole process. Indeed, it is doubtful if there can be such a thing as value-free social research. That said it is vital that in collecting and interpreting data one should seek to do so *objectively* in terms of the prevailing conventions designed to satisfy the needs of accuracy, validity and reliability.

While prediction is a basic goal of social science research all are agreed that this is much more difficult than is the case in the physical sciences. As Madge (1953) points out this may be the result of two interpretations:

> Some people conclude that human and social behaviour is not wholly subject to determining factors, but that every individual has some capacity of choice which enables him to vary his conduct in partial independence of the forces operating upon him. Others believe that, although human behaviour is fully determined by circumstances, these circumstances in all their ramifications are so numerous and so unknowable that we can never hope to predict how any individual or any group will respond to a given situation.

But, for operational purposes, we can ignore the metaphysical arguments concerning free will or determinism. What is needed is that 'the principle of causality be applied to social phenomena'. (Durkheim (1938) − quoted by Madge). In other words we undertake research to determine if there is a causal relationship between antecedent and consequent events of a kind which will enable us to make predictive statements about their future occurrence. For example, if we observe that a 10 per cent change in price is accompanied by a proportionate increase or decrease in demand on every occasion that such a change is made then it is reasonable to infer that it is the change in price which causes the change in demand. Of course, the problem for the marketer is that it is very difficult if not impossible to emulate the physical scientist and seek to establish the causal relationship between changes in the marketing mix and buyer behaviour owing to his inability to control all the other factors likely to influence the outcome. (See section on Experimentation, pp. 81–2.) Of course, it is not all plain sailing for the physical scientist either as the controversy over Pons and Fleischmann's 'discovery' of cold fusion in 1989 clearly shows. At the time of writing opinion is polarised between chemists who accept the possibility and physicists who do not but all are agreed that Pons and Fleischmann did not follow the accepted protocol of the scientific method nor did they publicise their findings according to normal conventions.

The basic problem in marketing (as in other social sciences) is highlighted by the debate over qualitative versus quantitative research. As we have seen (pp. 32–4) qualitative research provides insight and a richness of information but lacks the conviction and credibility which are associated with quantification. Ideally, the marketing researcher should use both approaches − qualitative research to inform him of the nature and parameters of the problem and quantitative research to derive empirical generalisations which may be used to determine future courses of action. Madge (1953) endorses this view when he writes:

While, however, it is proper to guard against the misuse of quantification, it cannot be implied that there is very much choice in the matter if we aim at empirical generalisation. At their very least, statistical techniques expose the principal assumptions underlying the generalisations arrived at and provide some stable measure of the degree of confidence with which it is reasonable to accept them. The statistical method gives precision and system to the more or less unconscious inductive processes constantly used in everyday life. When a man attempts to generalise from his own unrepresentative selection of data, and perhaps even openly rejects statistical method you may at best regard his generalisation as a brilliant and illuminating piece of guess work. He may have lighted on an inspired hypothesis, but he has certainly proved nothing.

It is in this spirit that we now review the methods and procedures which will be encountered most often in the analysis of marketing data.

Confidence limits and statistical significance

When Lord Kelvin observed that unless you can measure a thing you know nothing about it he was expressing not merely a scientific opinion but a common aspect of human nature. Numbers, of course, are a language and a very powerful one in that through them one can communicate highly complex ideas in a very succinct way. But, as with Arabic and Chinese, unless the intended receiver of the communication can speak the language there will be no understanding. It is ironic, therefore, that in many aspects of marketing one is invited to quantify the existence or otherwise of a relationship but then has to resort to a verbal interpretation in order to communicate the meaning of the quantification to those who asked for the quantification in the first place. However, as our earlier discussion of qualitative versus quantitative research revealed, quantified data carries more conviction with most decision makers and they will ask for such quantification even though they cannot interpret the numbers generated by such research.

This belief in the credibility of numbers is not wholly misplaced for, provided the data is accurate, valid and reliable, then an understanding of the language of statistics will enable us to make quite precise statements about the interpretation which may be placed upon it which will conform exactly with the interpretation made by any other other statistically literate person. It follows that while the user of research findings need not be wholly fluent in the language of statistics he should have a sufficient familiarity with it to understand the basics and know when to call upon the service of an interpreter to explain nuances beyond his own comprehension. In this context the nature of confidence and significance are particularly important.

Technically, confidence limits and statistical significance are two sides of the same coin. This will become clearer when we look at particular statistical techniques later in this chapter but it will be helpful here to consider briefly their role in data analysis. In the first chapter of this book we defined the aim of marketing research as being 'to reduce the areas of uncertainty surrounding business decisions'. It follows that having conducted a piece of research one would like to know how much confidence can be placed in the results. In other words how likely is it that the outcome indicated by the research results will be the correct one? The answer to this question will almost invariably be expressed in probabilistic terms such as 'It's ten to one/a hundred to one against this happening' or 'It's 95%/99% certain that the real outcome will be the same as the test result'. The first pair of statements are of the kind which 'ordinary' people use when making statements about the likelihood of an outcome and usually represent a subjective probability. The second pair of statements are of the kind which a statistician would make based upon the sampling of a population and so are objective probabilities. However, the first statements are also statements of significance while the latter two are statements of confidence. Both measures are derived from the concept of the continuous or *normal distribution* which itself is a convenient substitute for the *binomial distribution*. (These distributions are described in the Technical Appendix to Chapter 6.)

It will be recalled that the normal distribution defines the relative frequency or probability with which given values occur. For example, suppose that we are interested in monitoring the retail price of a particular washing machine then sampling of a variety of outlets in different locations yields 100 observations which range from £180 to £220. If the prices are distributed normally then we can use the parameters of the normal distribution (the mean and standard deviation) to predict that 90 per cent of the prices will be in the range £189–£211, 95 per cent of the prices £187–£213 and 99 per cent in the range £183–£217. These are confidence levels. (If you are unsure how the price ranges were derived refer to pages 121–3 which gives the parameters of the normal distribution.)

When it comes to reporting significance then the parameters are used rather differently and, by convention, one would only report that an observation was 'significant' if it was more than 1.96 standard deviations from the mean. In our washing machine example 95 per cent of all cases lie within ± 1.96 standard deviations of the mean – only if the price was less than £189 or greater than £211 would it be regarded as statistically significant. In other words *observations are regarded as significant if they are unusual*. By the same convention an observation is said to be *highly significant* if its likelihood of occurrence is less than one in 100 which means that it will be at least ± 2.58 standard deviations from the mean which applies to prices of less than £183 or greater than £217. In this example both exceptionally high and low prices were considered in determining whether they were significant or not on the grounds that the manufacturer would probably want to explore further what factors, e.g. town centre or out of town outlet, were associated with them. Accordingly, a two tailed test of significance was applied. But if the manufacturer was only concerned that discounting by some of his customers was undercutting other outlets because his product was being used as a loss leader he may only have been concerned with prices below a certain limit and applied a one-tailed test of significance. We return to this issue later in the chapter.

In sum, a confidence level will indicate the likelihood that an observed relationship will occur with a given frequency on future occasions so that the decision maker can decide what level of confidence is acceptable to him on the basis for taking future courses of action. By contrast the occurrence of statistically significant findings signals something out of the ordinary which may merit further investigation and analysis. Once again it is up to the decision maker to decide at what level of occurrence he would wish to have exceptions drawn to his attention — $p < 0.05$, $p < 0.01$, $p < 0.001$, etc.

Having established this distinction it will be useful now to look at the nature of descriptive statistics before moving on to the more sophisticated area of statistical inference.

Descriptive statistics

With increased access to computers and the development of more and more sophisticated data analysis software there has been a growing tendency in recent years to neglect the use of basic descriptive statistics in favour of 'more powerful' techniques. Without in any way wishing to diminish the value of these new techniques this author would wish to affirm the value of descriptive statistics both in their own right and as a precedent to more technically sophisticated methods and procedures. Further, and as a broad generalisation, it is probably true to say that the more obvious and robust relationships on which action decisions may be based will often emerge from an evaluation of the basic data. By contrast relationships which can only be detected through the use of complex and sophisticated procedures are most often useful in formulating further hypotheses for detailed and focused analysis rather than making action oriented decisions.

Given a body of data the first task is to structure and organise this in a manner which will make it amenable to further analysis. Tabulation and plotting are invariably the first steps in this process.

Where data has been collected using a properly designed test instrument of the kind discussed in Chapter 7 then the *tabulation* of information should be largely a formality of summarising the responses to the questions asked. For example, a furniture manufacturer is interested in determining what kind of furniture respondents have purchased within the past five years. Having determined that a purchase has been made within this period he asks:

'Could you tell me what kind of furniture you have bought in the last 5 years' and provides the following listing for the interviewer.

Lounge suite   _____
Dining-room suite   _____
Bedroom suite   _____
Fitted kitchen   _____
Bed   _____
Table   _____
Chair(s)   _____
Settee/Sofa   _____
Wardrobe   _____
Dressing Table   _____
Others (write in) ....   _____

....   _____

....   _____

Once coded this information can be transferred direct on to the database and it is a simple matter to print out the number of mentions of each kind of furniture and convert these into a percentage of the total respondents to the survey as in Table 9.1.

TABLE 9.1   Furniture purchases in the past five years

Type of furniture	No. mentioning	%
Lounge suite	311	67.6%
Dining-room suite	104	22.6
Bedroom suite	127	27.6
Fitted kitchen	54	11.7
Bed	222	48.3
Table	85	18.5
Chair(s)	116	25.2
Settee/sofa	82	17.8
Wardrobe	35	7.6
Dressing table	109	23.7
Others (e.g. video cabinet, coffee table, chest of drawers)	449	97.6
Total respondents	460	100

A table of this kind summarises 'what' has occurred. While one may draw some broad conclusions from it concerning the relative popularity of different kinds of furniture further analysis would obviously be desirable. For example, is furniture purchase correlated with age and/or income? Methods for answering such questions will be addressed later in the chapter.

In Table 9.1 the data is presented in exactly the same order as the alternatives were listed on the questionnaire. While perfectly understandable in this format the impact of the table would be improved if one were to restate it in terms of rank order according to the number of mentions as in Table 9.2.

TABLE 9.2   Furniture purchases in the past five years (rank order)

Type of furniture	No. mentioning	%
Others (e.g. Video cabinet, coffee table, chest of drawers)	449	97.6
Lounge suite	311	67.6
Bed	222	48.3
Bedroom suite	127	27.6
Chair(s)	116	25.2
Dressing table	109	23.7
Dining room suite	104	22.6
Table	85	18.5
Settee/sofa	82	17.8
Fitted kitchen	54	11.7
Wardrobe	35	7.6
Total respondents	460	100

In turn this data would have even greater impact if presented as a bar chart as shown in Figure 9.1.

Plotting data in this manner greatly enhances the readability of a report as one gets an immediate visual impression of the size and relative importance of the data classes being reported. The ability to plot data as bar charts, graphs or pictograms is a feature of most basic computer-based analysis programmes and can literally be achieved at the 'touch of a button'. Given such a capability the analyst can easily afford to try more than one approach to see which form of presentation has the most impact. Figure 9.2 reproduces the output of a typical presentation package (Harvard Presentation Graphics) for a simple data set.

However, although tabulation and plotting will provide some 'feel' for the data they are relatively crude in terms of what they can communicate and more sophisticated methods are called for if one is to derive the full benefit from a

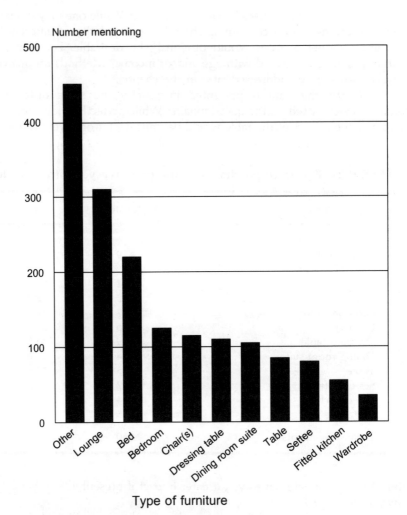

Figure 9.1   **Figure 9.1   Furniture purchases in the past 5 years**

database. Selltiz *et al.* (1959) suggest that given a database the analyst will typically want to do one or another, or several of the following things:

1. To characterise what is 'typical' in the group.
2. To indicate how widely individuals in the group vary.
3. To show other aspects of how the individuals are distributed with respect to the variable being measured.
4. To show the relation of the different variables in the data to one another.
5. To describe the differences between two or more groups of individuals.

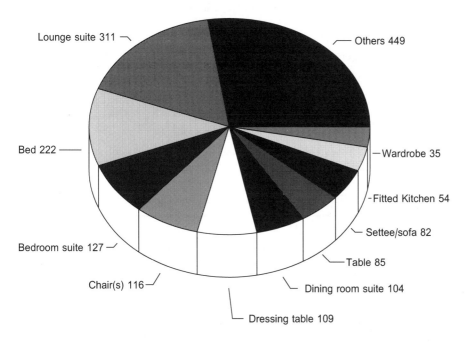

Figure 9.2   Furniture purchases in the past 5 years (rank order)

To accomplish these tasks the analyst has access to a number of basic tools which for convenience may be classified as *univariate, bivariate* and *multivariate* analysis. As the names suggest univariate analysis is concerned with only one variable, bivariate analysis deals with pairs of variables, while multivariate analysis can deal with three or more variables simultaneously. In general, and as Selltiz *et al.*'s (1959) list implies it is usual to progress from description and analysis of a single variable, to an examination of relationships between pairs of variables and finally to the much more complex task of exploring relationships between three or more variables at once.

Descriptive statistics are of particular value in describing databases containing a large number of values. Selection of the appropriate statistic(s) will depend upon the nature of the data to be analysed; specifically, is it nominal, ordinal, interval or ratio in character? It will be recalled that in Chapter 7 when discussing the nature of scales the basic differences are that:

(a) Nominal data is the weakest kind in that the number assigned serves only to identify the subject, e.g. library classifications.

(b) Ordinal scales seek to impose more structure on objects by rank ordering them in terms of some property which they possess such as height or weight.

(c) Interval scales have greater power in that it is assumed that the distance between numbers is known and constant so that one can draw conclusions about the meaning of differences between numbers.

(d) Ratio scales are the most powerful and possess all the properties of nominal, ordinal and interval scales and also permit absolute comparison between objects.

Given that one knows the type of data then one can easily select the most appropriate statistics as shown in Table 9.3 taken from Alreck and Settle (1985).

TABLE 9.3   Tool selection for descriptive statistics

Scale type	Average	Spread	Shape
Nominal	Mode		
Ordinal	Median Mode	Range Maximum Minimum	
Interval	Mean Median Mode	Standard deviation Range Maximum Minimum	Skewness Kurtosis
Ratio	Mean Median Mode	Standard deviation Range Maximum Minimum	Skewness Kurtosis

Source: Pamela L. Alreck and Robert B. Settle, *The Survey Research Handbook* (Homewood, Ill.: Richard D. Irwin, 1985).

Descriptive statistics serve two basic purposes, they provide a measure of central tendency and of dispersion. In everyday speech we refer often to 'the average' in the sense of 'the typical or normal amount, quality, degree, etc.'. (*Collins Concise English Dictionary*) in other words it is used to convey the idea of the most common or frequently occurring event. However, while the 'average' — be it expressed as the mean, median or mode — may be the most typical value, in and of itself it provides only limited insight into a database unless we also possess some knowledge of the dispersion or spread of data about this most typical value. Such information is provided by statistics such as the range, standard deviation and shape of the distribution itself (kurtosis, skewness). A brief description of these various measures will help clarify the point.

As indicated in Table 9.3, three 'averages' are in common use – the mode, the median and the mean. Of the three the mode is the weakest in that it simply defines the category which appears most frequently – in the furniture purchase survey referred to earlier. 'Others' were mentioned by 98 per cent of the respondents and so this is the mode for this particular distribution and tells us that the most likely purchase is likely to be a smaller piece of occasional furniture outside the range in which the manufacturer was primarily interested. Such information may be particularly valuable as a strategic insight in that it might encourage the manufacturer to make some of these smaller items as a means of keeping his brand name in front of consumers so that they will recognise it when making the larger but less frequent purchase of say a lounge suite. However, in many distributions several categories may occur with equal frequency giving rise to multiple modes and difficulty in interpretation.

When data is ordinal, interval or ratio the analyst will also be able to refer to the median as a measure of central tendency. The median is literally the middle case in a data set organised in terms of the 'value' of the object being measured. Thus in Table 9.2 there are 11 categories rank ordered in terms of number of mentions so the median category is dressing tables with five other types of furniture each receiving more or less mentions. Perhaps its most important characteristic is that it is unaffected by extremes although, in the context of the furniture data, this is largely irrelevant!

The third commonly used measure of central tendency is the arithmetic mean which is computed by adding up the sum of the values and dividing this by the number of categories. For example, in the furniture case the total number of responses from the 460 respondents was 1694 so we could recalculate Table 9.2 on the basis of number of mentions with the result given in Table 9.4.

TABLE 9.4   Furniture purchases in the past five years

Type of furniture	No. of mentions	% of all mentions
Others	449	26.5
Lounge suite	311	18.4
Bed	222	13.1
Bedroom suite	127	7.5
Chair(s)	116	6.8
Dressing table	109	6.4
Dining-room suite	104	6.1
Table	85	5.0
Settee/sofa	82	4.8
Fitted kitchen	54	3.2
Wardrobe	35	2.1
Total	1694	100

The arithmetic mean for the number of mentions is $\overline{X} = 1694/460 = 368$. Obviously the mean is heavily influenced by the high scores for Others, lounge suites and beds with the 'others' exercising a particularly strong effect. To summarise the distribution of values around the measures of central tendency we need to compute a number of other measures of dispersion. For nominal data measures of dispersion are inappropriate but for all other categories of data our understanding will be considerably enhanced if we know the *range* of values. The range is calculated simply by taking away the lowest (minimum) value from the highest (maximum) value. In our survey of furniture purchases the range is:

$$449 - 35 = 414$$

If we compare these data – maximum, minimum and range – with the mean we will begin to get some feel for the overall distribution of values. This understanding will be greatly enhanced if we also calculate the *variability* or spread of the observations around the mean. The most frequently used statistic for this purpose is the *standard deviation*. It will be recalled from the discussion of the characteristics of the normal distribution as the basis for sampling (Appendix to Chapter 6) that the standard deviation is in fact the square root of the variance and provides a single value of the spread of data about the mean in the same units as the mean. Clearly, the smaller the standard deviation the more tightly the observations are clustered around the mean and vice versa.

All distributions do not assume the shape of the normal distribution and two measures are used to describe how much the actual distribution departs from the normal. These statistics are *skewness* and *kurtosis*. As the term suggests skewness is the degree to which the distribution is biased towards one or other side of the mean. In the normal distribution data are distributed symmetrically around the mean and the skewness is zero. In a skewed distribution the distribution of observations is asymmetrical. Where the distribution is skewed to the left as in Figure 9.3(a) then the coefficient of skewness will be positive and when to the right, as in Figure 9.3(b), it will be negative.

The importance of calculating the coefficient of skewness is that it helps interpret the value of the standard deviation as a measure of the spread of the

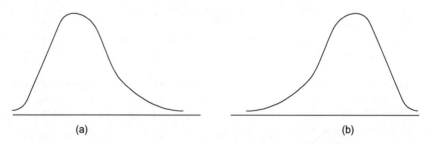

(a)   (b)

Figure 9.3   (a) Positive skewness (b) negative skewness

distribution, i.e. if it is zero we can assume a normal distribution and proceed accordingly. Otherwise, depending upon the sign and size of the coefficient, we would recognise that the distribution was asymmetrical.

Kurtosis measures whether a distribution is more (positive) or less (negative) peaked than a normal distribution.

Most of the measure touched on here — variance, standard deviation, skewness and kurtosis — are laborious to compute manually but we can produce them on command using packages such as SPSSX. Given their value in helping to interpret a database they should be provided routinely in any formal data presentation.

Descriptive statistics are concerned with just that — the description of variables in a data set. Because we look at one variable at a time, such as the high street price of a washing machine or the frequency of purchase of different items of furniture and, useful and informative as such *univariate* analysis is, the description of what is provides only limited understanding as to why it is so. To determine why things are as they are we need to examine the relationship *between* variables and it is to this topic which we now turn.

Inferential statistics

Univariate or *marginal* analysis is an essential first step in data interpretation and will give the researcher a good feel for his database. But, as noted, it is usually the relationship between variables which is of primary interest as it is these which may enable one to infer why things occur in a particular way. The conditional 'may enable' in the previous sentence is essential for the mere fact that two events are associated or correlated does not necessarily mean that they are causally related. Indeed the relationship between two events may be entirely spurious as is the case with the thesis that amputation causes deafness, a proposition which a professor attempted to prove to his students as follows. First, he placed a flea on the laboratory bench and clapped his hands. The flea jumped. Next he cut off the flea's legs and clapped his hands again. The flea did not move, prompting the professor to declare triumphantly that it was clear amputation causes total deafness in fleas!

Real world examples of the drawing of incorrect inferences abound. Recently, a report appeared in which it was claimed that Germans eat twice as many bananas as the British. This conclusion was based on the responses to the question 'How often do you eat a banana?' As neither Britain nor Germany produce bananas it is a relatively simple matter to determine their consumption of this fruit by dividing recorded imports by the populations of the countries — an analysis which reveals that Britons and Germans consume nearly the same average volume per capita. The report is both true and false depending upon how one measures consumption. Most marketers would infer that a statement stating someone did something twice as often meant they consumed twice as much. In this case, however, it is clear that the average 'German' banana is half the size of its 'British' counterpart so that actual consumption in volume/price terms is virtually the same. The finding does point to different sources of supply (e.g. the Canaries (small) versus Colombia (large)) but not to the major differences in consumption behaviour which could have been inferred from the first statement.

The two examples given above are by way of a caveat as to the interpretation of the inferential statistics to be reviewed in the next few pages. The purpose of inferential statistics is to facilitate comparison of two or more variables and to determine the strength of any relationship and the likelihood, especially when it is based on sample data, that it is representative, i.e. that a replication of the study/analysis would yield the same result.

Having reviewed the marginal or nominal data through univariate analysis the next step in the process is to seek to establish whether there is any association between pairs of variables through bivariate analysis. The first step in this process is usually to distinguish between dependent and independent variables. A *dependent variable* is one which, as the name suggests, is affected by another *independent variable*. In other words, when one defines a dependent variable it is hypothesised that changes in it will be caused by changes in the independent variable(s) with which it is associated. Suppose, for example, that one hypothesises that the speed of adoption of an innovation is a function of Everett Rogers's five characteristics of relative advantage, complexity, compatibility, communicability and divisibility then the five characteristics (which would need to be defined with some precision for purposes of data collection) are independent variables in that it is anticipated that a change in any one of them will result in some change in the speed of take up of the innovation. It is necessary for the researcher to hypothesise the existence and direction of causality, e.g. the more complex an innovation the more slowly it will be adopted, in order to be able to select which of the various measures of association will be most appropriate.

In some circumstances, however, the researcher may have no preconceived ideas or hypotheses about causality. In such cases it is not necessary to specify whether a variable is dependent or independent but fewer statistical techniques are available for analysing the data. In deciding which technique to use Alreck and Settle (1985) provide the very useful summary table reproduced as Table 9.5. In order to use the table one must be able to determine whether variables are categorised or continuous and which is to be treated as the independent variable and which the dependent variable. It will be recalled that categorised or 'discrete' data consists of data which is classified into separate or discrete categories. In other words it is nominal data in which the categories are not related to one another. By contrast, and as the name implies, continuous data is any form of numerical data that is arrayed or distributed on some continuum.

While continuous data may be presented in categories in order to summarise it more effectively, e.g. age groups, income bands, the underlying distribution is continuous and it is this which matters. It will also be recalled that categorical data results from the use of nominal scales whereas continuous data may be derived from ordinal, ratio and interval scales. Having defined the variables in this way it is a simple matter to select the most appropriate statistical measure(s) from the table.

TABLE 9.5   Statistical measures of association

		INDEPENDENT	
		Categorical	*Continuous*
D E P E N D E N T	Categorical	Cross-tabulation (contingency) [Chi-square]	Discriminant analysis [F ratio]
	Continuous	Analysis of variance [F ratio] Paired T-test [Value of *t*]	Regression analysis [F ratio] Correlation analysis [Probability of *r*]

Source: Pamela L. Alreck and Robert B. Settle, *The Survey Research Handbook* (Homewood, Ill.: Richard D. Irwin, 1985).

Cross-tabulation

Of the methods cited cross-tabulation is the most common and widely used. The reason is not hard to find – both variables may be categorised and it does not matter which is classed as dependent and which independent. Thus if we are in doubt as to whether our data is continuous or not we can still use cross tabulation to determine the presence and degree of association between any pair of variables we choose to analyse. For this reason it is commonplace to compute the cross tabulations for all the possible combinations of the key variables in a survey. (Given the power and speed of modern computers one should be wary of comparing everything with everything when one is likely to be overwhelmed by a mountain of print-out. One of the reasons for marginal analysis is to select those variables whose distribution looks promising for further analysis and to reject those which lack this property.)

Probably the best way to explain cross tabulation is through an actual example. Several years ago (1983), when interest first began to develop in the potential market for multichannel cable TV, the author was involved in a survey into the likely reaction to such a service in the West of Scotland. The following description was given to respondents:

> For a basic monthly subscription charge, you can get access to over 20 separate channels. These channels will include all the normal BBC and ITV channels, the new satellite ITV and BBC television, and also channels with full length feature films, sport, news and local community programmes. Such a service could cost about £14 per month.

A total of 985 responses were received to the questionnaire Table 9.6 gives two examples of cross tabulations in which intention to subscribe is compared with the age and social class of the respondents. Look at the table relating age to intention. This table comprises two *rows* – non-intenders and intenders and five *columns* – representing age groupings – giving a total of ten *cells*. Each cell contains three *values* the first of which is the actual number of persons/ respondents who satisfied the age and intention criteria for that cell. The second value is the column percentage and the third is the row percentage which may be compared with the total values provided. Thus the top left hand cell in the table tells us that 47 respondents aged between 16 and 24 said they did *not* intend to subscribe to the service which was equivalent to 59.5 per cent of all respondents in the age group and 5 per cent of the total sample. So what does the table as a whole tell us? The key values to look at are the distribution of column percentages in each cell compared with the row total. For the sample as a whole 681 respondents said they did not intend to subscribe representing 72.3 per cent of all respondents, i.e. 261 or 27.7 per cent said they would subscribe to the new service. Now look at the column percentages for each age band from which it is immediately apparent that the younger the respondent the more likely it is that they will subscribe to the new service.

If you would like to see if you understand this look at the table comparing intention with social class and write down your interpretation of it. Then turn to the end of the chapter to see how your analysis compares with the author's.

In undertaking cross-tabulation analysis it is important to keep the number of categories within reasonable proportions otherwise it becomes very difficult to interpret and can also result in cells with very low frequencies or values, e.g. a cross-tabulation of age (five categories) and social class (seven categories) would give a table with 35 cells. It is important to ensure that the cell frequencies satisfy a minimum *expected* value as otherwise it will not be possible to calculate the chi-square statistic which is used to measure the significance of

TABLE 9.6 Intentions to subscribe to cable TV

Cross tabulation of intention to subscribe to TV by age group of respondents

Count Col. % Total %	16 – 24 years	25 – 34 years	35 – 44 years	45 – 54 years	55 years and over	Row Total
Non-intenders	47 59.5 5.0	152 62.6 16.1	169 72.8 17.9	111 70.3 11.8	202 87.8 21.4	681 72.3
Intenders	32 40.5 3.4	91 37.4 9.7	63 27.2 6.7	47 29.7 5.0	28 12.2 3.0	261 27.7
Column Total	79 8.4	243 25.8	232 24.6	158 16.8	230 24.4	942 100.0

Cross tabulation of intention to subscribe to cable TV by social class of respondents

Count Col. % Total %	Social Class A	Social Class B	Social Class C1	Social Class C2	Social Class D	Social Class E	Unemployed	Row Total
Non-intenders	7 58.3 0.8	125 74.4 13.9	116 67.4 12.9	164 67.8 18.2	98 67.6 10.9	93 90.3 10.3	47 78.3 5.2	650 72.1
Intenders	5 41.7 0.6	43 25.6 4.8	56 32.6 6.2	78 32.2 8.6	47 32.4 5.2	10 9.7 1.1	13 21.7 1.4	252 27.9
Column Total	12 1.3	168 18.6	172 19.1	242 26.8	145 16.1	103 11.4	60 6.7	902 100.0

the reported distribution against the likelihood that it could have occurred by chance even if there were no differences in the sample from which the sample was drawn.

As Alreck and Settle (1985) explain, computer programs will calculate chi-square statistics 'regardless of whether or not the expected cell frequencies are of adequate size' with the result that if the expected values are below the required minimum the statistic generated will be invalid. Thus the researcher must check the cell frequency to ensure it meets the minimum expected size requirement of five cases. The important point here as Alreck and Settle underline is that it is the *expected* not the *actual* cell frequency which counts and this cannot be determined by inspection alone but must be calculated, i.e. you could have a cell frequency of 0 and it would not affect the chi-square statistic so long as the expected frequency was 5 or more. To determine the expected value of the cell with the smallest frequency one must find the smallest row total, divide it by the total for the table and multiply it by the smallest column total. Thus in the table comparing intentions with age the cell to examine is 'Intenders' aged 16 to 24. The relevant numbers are $261/942 \times 79 = 21.88$. The smallest cell value is 28 for 'Intenders' 55 years and over which is above this so the chi-square statistic for this table would be valid. You might like to try your hand on the intention by social class table to see if this is also acceptable or whether it might be necessary to recode the data in order to achieve larger cell frequencies, e.g. by combining the A and B categories. The answer is at the end of the chapter.

As noted above, given the distribution of responses yielded by our survey what we need to know is whether these reflect genuine differences in the population or whether the same distribution could have arisen purely by chance, i.e. sampling error. To compare observed and expected values one needs to calculate the chi-squared (x^2) statistic. A description of this statistic and the procedure for calculating it will be found in any basic statistics textbook and most marketing research texts with an emphasis upon techniques and so need not detain us here. What the user needs to know is how to *interpret* the statistic.

Basically, the larger the chi-square value the greater the relationship between the variables to which it relates. However, the size of x^2 is also a function of the size of the distribution itself so that the larger the number of items in a distribution the larger x^2 is likely to be. In order to allow for this one must establish the number of ways in which the two sets of data — expected and observed — may vary. This is known as the *degrees of freedom* and is usually provided by most statistical analysis programmes. If not, for contingency tables it is simply calculated by multiplying the number of rows minus 1 times the number of columns minus 1. Hence, for our intentions data the degrees of freedom or d.f. are 4 for age and 6 for social class. The reason we need this information is that the chi-square distribution varies according to the number of degrees of freedom and in order to establish the significance of our x^2 value we will need to refer to the appropriate table of values (to be found in most statistics books). However, most computer packages will provide a probability value which will indicate the likelihood that the observed values could have occurred by chance. In the case of our two tables the values are:

Intentions by age $x^2 = 46.0424$ d.f. 4 prob $= 0.0000$
Intentions by social class $x^2 = 25.2367$ d.f. 6 prob $= 0.0003$

As we have observed, the great advantage of cross-tabulation or contingency tables is that we can use them to compare both categorical and continuous data and need have no prior hypotheses about relationships between variables, i.e. which are dependent and which independent. (In practice one would establish a null hypothesis so as to be able to confirm or infirm it.) Much can be learned from such analysis but this can be greatly increased if one or both of the variables represents continuous data. Where this is so a number of other techniques are available as indicated in Table 9.5. A brief description of these techniques follows.

Analysis of variance (ANOVA)

As Table 9.5 indicates the appropriate technique to use when the independent variable is categorical and the dependent variable is continuous is analysis of variance or ANOVA. Analysis of variance is measured using the F-test with the objective of determining whether there is one or more significant differences among the sample groups represented in the table. The statistic is derived by examining the significance of the difference between means by comparing the variability of values both within and between groups.

As with chi-squared and student-*t* (which is a special case for measuring variance when only two distributions are involved) the F-test is a standard test included in most computer programs and so easily obtained 'on command'. However, its use is only appropriate where the samples all have similar distributions, where the dependent variable data have been derived from an interval or ratio scale (not ordinal) and from *different* respondents. Provided the data satisfies these requirements the F-test will generate values which indicate whether or not significant differences exist, the degrees of freedom present in the table and the probability associated with the measurement. (Where the program does not provide d.f. and p. these may be obtained from tables for F in the same way as for x^2.)

Correlation

Correlation analysis is a technique for measuring the strengths of the linear relationship between two variables. If observations of the relationship were plotted graphically on a scattergram then we might find the following patterns.

Correlation is measured by the statistic r and may have values ranging from $+1$, meaning a perfect positive correlation, and -1, meaning a perfect negative correlation, with the value O meaning that there is no correlation between the two variables at all.

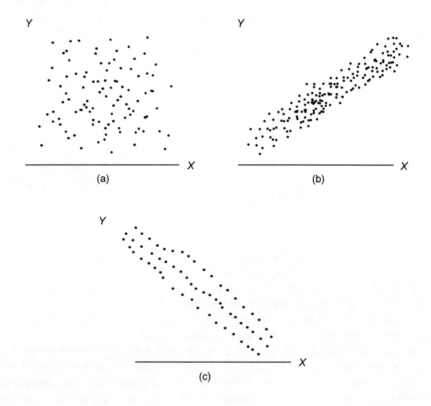

Figure 9.4 **(a) No correlation, (b) high positive correlation, (c) high negative correlation**

As our summary Table 9.5 shows correlation analysis is appropriate where both variables are continuous, e.g. sales and advertising expenditures. However, one does not need to specify which variable is dependent and which independent. By the same token one cannot use correlation to *prove* causation although given results may provide evidence to support such an inference. For example, in the case of the sales–advertising relationship if the firm fixes its advertising budget as a percentage of sales then advertising spend would go up and down with sales but sales would be regarded as the independent variable and advertising spend as the dependent variable. Conversely, if one varies the advertising spend and detects a parallel movement in sales up and down it would seem reasonable to infer that advertising expenditures have an effect on sales i.e. advertising spend is independent and sales are dependent upon them. This would be shown by a positive correlation – the higher the value the stronger the relationship.

Negative correlations indicate that an inverse relationship exists so that an increase in one variable – say, immunisation against diphtheria – results in a decrease in the other – the number of reported cases of the disease.

While high values of r indicate a strong relationship, low values may give a misleading impression of the strength of the association between the two variables. This is so because r does not represent the proportion of a perfect (± 1) relationship which the two variables share. To establish this one must compute the *square* of the correlation coefficient to yield R^2 which is known as the *coefficient of determination*. Thus values of r and R^2 would be as follows:

$r = 0.10$ R^2 0.01
$r = 0.20$ R^2 0.04
$r = 0.30$ R^2 0.09
$r = 0.40$ R^2 0.16
$r = 0.50$ R^2 0.25
$r = 0.60$ R^2 0.36
$r = 0.70$ R^2 0.49
$r = 0.80$ R^2 0.64
$r = 0.90$ R^2 0.81
$r = 1.00$ R^2 1.00

Thus a correlation of 0.5 means that only 25 per cent of the variance between two items is shared between them and even a 'high' correlation of 0.7 indicates that less than half the observed variance is shared by the two variables concerned.

As with other tests described earlier the significance of a correlation coefficient will usually be produced automatically by computer analysis programs but, if not, it can be determined by reference to statistical tables.

Finally, it should be noted that there are two main types of correlation analysis: the Pearson product – moment correlation (Product–Moment or PM) which is appropriate for interval or ratio scaled data, and Spearman's rank correlation which may be used for interval or scaled data but is mainly used for ranked or ordinal data.

Regression analysis

Regression and correlation are closely related concepts. As we have seen correlation analysis measures the degree of association between two or more variables. By contrast *regression* analysis examines the nature of statistical dependence between a dependent variable and one or more independent variables. According to Claycamp (1974):

> The basic measures produced by regression techniques are of two types:
>
> 1. The parameter values of a mathematical model – called a regression equation – that can be used to calculate expected values of the dependent variable as a function of specific independent variable values.
> 2. Measures of the deviations, or variance, between the original and expected values of the dependent variable.
>
> Correlation techniques, on the other hand, produce standardised summary statistics to measure the goodness-of-fit of the regression equation to the data as well as to analyse the relative strength of statistical relationships among alternative combinations of variables.

When there is a single independent variable the technique is referred to as *simple* or *linear* regression; where there is more than one independent variable it becomes *multiple* regression. Like correlation analysis, regression analysis produces a summary statistic r^2 (r-square) which measures the proportion of variance in the dependent variable that is explained by the independent variable(s).

To compute a regression equation it is necessary for both the dependent and independent variables to be derived from interval or ratio scales. Normally the relationship between the variables should be linear but it is possible to convert curvilinear relationships to linear ones where desired as is often the case when one wishes to predict from observed data, e.g. when forecasting.

Discriminant analysis

Discriminant analysis is the last technique proposed in Table 9.5 from which it can be seen that it is appropriate where the dependent variable is represented by categorical data and the independent variable(s) by continuous data. However, as Alreck and Settle (1985) point out 'If the researcher wishes to measure the relationship between two variables *that need not or cannot* be identified as independent and dependent, analysis of variance is recommended,

. . .' (my emphasis). Quite simply this is because Anova programmes are much more commonplace than discriminant analysis ones and are easier to understand. If, however, one wishes to predict the category of a dependent variable when it is not known, but the value of the independent variable is, then one must use discriminant analysis. Users presented with a discriminant analysis should invite the analyst to explain its use, and the justification for preferring it, in the context of the database to be analysed.

Multivariate analysis

In Chapter 1 we claimed that the problems facing marketing managers are difficult to resolve because they contain many variables interacting dynamically with one another, often simultaneously. As a consequence it is rarely possible to undertake experiments of the kind familiar to scientists in which one varies one factor while holding all others constant in order to determine what effect such variation may have. In the preceding sections we have reviewed techniques appropriate to the analysis of a single factor (univariate) and to the interaction of two factors (bivariate analysis). In this section we will look briefly at some of the techniques available to the analyst concerned with more than two variables – multivariate analysis – which, given the complexity of most marketing problems, have become increasingly popular in recent years particularly because of the enormous increase in computing power which is now readily available.

Some years ago Hooley (1980) wrote a paper in which he referred to multivariate analysis as 'the academic's playground but the manager's minefield'. The allusion is apt – the mathematical complexity underlying most multivariate techniques is high but much of the output appears convincingly simple. The result is that the non-statistician is likely to be persuaded that powerful techniques which can apparently reduce a large and dense matrix into a simple summary statistic, plot or diagram must be right.

We can only reiterate the caveats introduced at the beginning of the chapter:

(a) Before setting out to collect any data you should have clear objectives as to precisely what it is you wish to discover or clarify;
(b) Data analysis should proceed methodically from marginal analysis to univariate analysis and then bivariate analysis by which time you should have a good understanding of the relationships within the data set.

As Ehrenberg (1963) has argued, when discussing the uses of factor analysis, a perceptive analyst is probably able to derive as much information from looking at a correlation matrix as can be derived by using such a matrix as an input to a factor analysis. That said, multivariate techniques represent an important device in the marketing researcher's tool kit and can be of great value when applied to the correct problems.

The paper referred to earlier by Graham Hooley was in fact the introduction to a special edition of the *European Journal of Marketing* (vol. 14, no. 7, 1980), 'A Guide to the Use of Quantitative Techniques in Marketing', which remains one of the most 'user-friendly' overviews of the topic available to the non-mathematician. It will be referred to extensively in the following pages!

Hooley (1980) follows Heenan and Adelman (1976) when he classifies multivariate techniques as falling into two broad categories – predictive and descriptive. Among the best known and most widely used predictive techniques are multiple regression, principal components analysis, multiple discriminant analysis, conjoint analysis and automatic interaction detection (AID). In the descriptive category factor analysis, cluster analysis and multidimensional scaling have now become commonplace. A brief discussion of each of these is given below.

Multiple regression

As the name implies multiple regression involves analysis of the relationship between a dependent variable and two or more independent variables. This technique was described briefly in the preceding section.

Principal components analysis (PCA)

Cliff Holmes in the *Consumer Market Research Handbook* (1986) introduces PCA with the following explanation:

> In the statistical analysis of relationships between variables it is often important that the variables are uncorrelated (orthogonal) with one another. This is particularly true in multiple regression techniques and in the interpretation of factors in factor analysis. The method of principal components analysis is a technique for obtaining new 'artificial' variables which are uncorrelated with one another.

If one were to visualise one's observations plotted in a three-dimensional space then a principal components analysis proceeds by selecting those grouped around the longest axis plotted through the centre of the plot and represents the component or factor which accounts for the highest amount of the total variance in the data set. The second component is then derived by selecting the next longest axis orthogonal, i.e. at right angles, to the first, and so on. While there are as many components as there are variables most analysts will content themselves with selecting only the first few which account for the majority of the variance and discard the remainder as individually they explain relatively little of the total variance.

Holmes discounts PCA as having much practical use in interpreting marketing data (although he cites examples of its use in selecting test market locations, classification of towns, and the stratification of local authority areas for sampling purposes) but stresses its value as an input to factor analysis.

Multiple discriminant analysis (MDA)

Rob Lawson (in Hooley (1980)) defines MDA as:

> a technique employed to discover the characteristics that distinguish the members of one group from another, so that given a set of characteristics for a new individual, the group to which he should be assigned can be predicted. MDA was originally developed in the botanical sciences as a way of discovering distinguishing features of generic plant groups, on the basis of criteria such as leaf size and type, so that new species could be subsequently classified.
>
> In marketing the technique is perhaps most useful as a method for identifying the characteristics that discriminate between market segments – the segments are defined prior to the analysis based on whatever criteria are of interest to the particular study.

For example, if one wishes to segment the market on the basis of usage one would categorise the population as say heavy, medium, light and non-users and then use MDA to determine how independent factors such as age, income and occupation vary according to these categories as the basis for developing the most appropriate marketing mixes to exploit the maximum potential from the market.

Lawson explains that 'MDA works by providing maximum separation between the groups. This is obtained by maximising the difference between the means of the groups in relation to the standard deviation within the groups'. As such MDA proceeds in much the same ways as multiple regresssion analysis. Lawson provides both a worked example and an analysis of Evans's (1959) classic use of discriminant analysis to try and predict car purchase for those wishing to explore the technique in greater detail.

Conjoint measurement (CM)

According to Hooley (1980): 'conjoint measurement seeks to identify the relative importance of each product attribute in creating an overall desirability for the product. This information can then be used to suggest ways of improving the product or even new product possibilities. Similarly, the information can be used to estimate how respondents would trade-off one attribute against another in approaching an "ideal" brand or product.'

Antilla *et al.* provide a useful review of the method together with a detailed analysis of its application in the Finnish market for colour televisions in the Hooley monograph. In their view a particular advantage of CM 'over the more traditional multivariate marketing research methods lies in its ability to take into account the trade-off phenomenon and to provide operative information on the utilities the decision-maker relates to product attributes'. In the TV example six attributes are used – price, brand name, size, colour reproduction, guarantee and design – with 4, 3, 3, 3, 2 and 2 'levels' or categories respectively. This yields 431 possible alternative combinations to which the conjoint analysis yields answers to the four key questions identified by Wind *et al.* (1978) namely:

1. What is the utility of each attribute level?
2. How important for the buyer is each attribute?
3. What kind of trade-offs can be made between attributes?
4. How do answers to the above questions vary across respondents and can they be segmented in a meaningful way?

However, as Antilla *et al.* explain 432 combinations of attributes would make ranking an impossible task and a key skill of the analyst wishing to use the technique is to reduce the number of combinations to feasible proportions. As with all multivariate techniques the mathematics are off-putting to the less numerate but the value of the output is readily apparent in Table 9.7 reproduced from Antilla *et al.*'s study.

TABLE 9.7   Relative attribute importance for three utility segments

Attribute	Price sensitive segment N = 59 (%)	Quality prone segment N = 71 (%)	Design-size conscious segment N = 35 (%)
Price	44	9	5
Tube size	15	12	24
Brand name	14	24	12
Colour reproduction	20	38	25
Guarantee	5	16	4
Design	2	1	30

As the authors explain:

> The results clearly indicate the differences in relative attribute importance between segments. Although colour reproduction is an important factor for all groups (also shown by the high relative importance for the entire sample), the quality-prone segment would be characterised by its strong willingness to trade-off price against colour reproduction (i.e. to pay more for better colour-reproducing sets). This group is also much more sensitive to changes in attributes considered to be related to quality such as guarantee and brand name. A characteristic of the second segment is the extreme importance of price relative to the other attributes. A preference for modern design and small-tube-size television sets is common among the third segment.

Clearly, analysis of this kind provides valuable pointers to the marketing decision maker plotting strategy and planning the marketing mix. Unless one is qualified to discuss the technical aspects of the method perhaps the safest test of its suitability is to ask the common-sense question, 'Are the respondents being asked to make realistic comparisons?'. If they are, and the researcher(s) is reputable and has prior experience of using the technique, then the method offers obvious benefits to managers wishing to segment markets and develop differentiated marketing mixes.

The automatic interaction detector (AID)

Although AID is 'not strictly a multivariate technique (as the independent variables are not examined simultaneously)' (Hooley, 1980) it is usually considered as one. AID is often used as a preliminary to cluster analysis (see below) and represents an intermediate step between it and cross-tabulation and so is of particular value when seeking to reduce large databases to manageable proportions. It was developed for this purpose by Sonquist and Morgan (1964) and represents a development of the 'Belson sort' which was first proposed in 1959.

In the Hooley monograph Cliff Holmes describes the technique as follows:

> The technique is essentially very similar to that of Dr. Belson. It divides a sample through a series of binary splits across a set of independent variables which produce the greatest discrimination in the dependent variable. The computation steps are:
>
> 1. Take each candidate variable, one at a time and split into all possible dichotomies.
> 2. For each dichotomy calculate the between sums of squares (BSS) and select that split which maximises BSS.
> 3. Next the dependent variable is split into two categories on the one independent variable which explains the maximum amount of variance.
> 4. Repeat step (3) treating each of the two new groups independently.

While this may sound complicated the procedure yields an easily understandable 'tree' diagram of the kind shown in Figure 9.5.

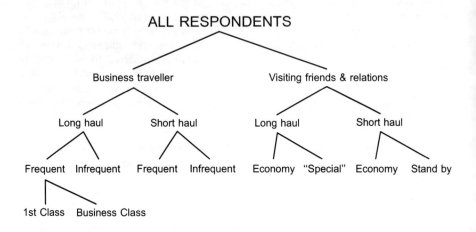

Figure 9.5   Aid analysis of airline usage decisions

As with all techniques AID has its strengths and limitations. As noted above it is particularly useful as an exploratory device for detecting patterns within large data sets but against this must be set its potential to generate spurious results particularly because it does not distinguish correlated variables.

Factor analysis

Essentially, factor analysis is ' . . . a statistical technique which can analyse the relationship between any number of variables and produce a set of "factors" each factor being a composite of some cluster of the original variables' (Harvard University Computation Center, 1967). Because of its ability to reduce very large and complex databases into a smaller set of explanatory factors, and its easy availability in programs such as SPSSX, factor analysis is a widely used analytical technique. However, a great deal depends upon the interpretative skill of the analyst and one must be wary not to be 'seduced' by the simple descriptive labels used to identify factors which are obviously a composite of several complex and interacting variables. An example will help establish the point.

In a major survey of the principal factors underlying design success in international markets Ughanwa and Baker (1989) identified 34 contributory elements. A factor analysis reduced these to 11 principal components which between them explained 75.5 per cent of the variance in the data. Table 9.8 indicates the original factors and Table 9.9 gives the output of the factor analysis. The interpretation of these factors was as follows:

1. *Managerial and technical synergy and proficiency.* This dimension describes the managerial and technical orientation that underpins the design success in international markets. The managerial functions include: management of design/ innovation, looking far into the future and making relevant long-term plans, giving support (financial, expertise, moral, etc.) to economically viable projects, setting clear and achievable objectives, reviewing and evaluating products in line with customer needs/wants and changes in the environment as well as introducing modern techniques to enhance the effectiveness of new products.

   Technically, products are expected to perform well in operation and be easy to use. Often, this involves the application of new technology to improve the quality of new products, and in this context, to enhance the functional performance and ease of use of new products, both of which are unique selling points (USP).

2. *Aesthetic/ergonomic, and communication synergy.* Factor 2 draws attention to the aesthetic, ergonomic, and communication advantages that account for the design success in international (export) markets. The aesthetic features include: style/ fashion and attractive appearance/shape, whilst 'easy to use', 'operator comfort', 'flexibility and adaptability in use', etc., exemplify ergonomic features. Aesthetic and ergonomic features can substantially influence the sale of one product over another. As discussed elsewhere, bulldozers, tractors, etc., are now produced in glittering colours, even though the manufacturers know, as we do, that these implements will soon soil in use and may never be clean. However, to increase awareness of sales, new products should be advertised and promoted.

3. *Performance in use.* Factor 3 describes the performance in use dimension. Customers/users expect products to be easy to use and maintain. In some products, flexibility and adaptability in use (e.g. mains/battery radio) and technical sophistication (e.g. remote-control TV) constitute important buying influences. A farmer may prefer to purchase a technically sophisticated agricultural machine that can combine two or more functions (e.g. planting and harvesting crops) rather than one with only one function.

   However, not all customers or users are skilled in or have time for carrying out repairs or routine maintenance of products in use. Therefore, there is the need to provide adequate after-sales service, particularly for sophisticated products. Thus, firms that have the capability of incorporating these various customer requirements in their new-product designs are likely to be more competitive than those who have not.

4. *Marketing knowledge and proficiency.* The fourth factor, which explains 5.5 per cent of the variance points to a marketing orientation as an important dimension underlying design success in world markets. It stresses that a firm with adequate knowledge of the market — a factor that may be brought about by carrying out a deep study of the market — often makes extensive use of ideas derived from the market when designing and developing new products. Close interaction with

Table 9.8   Factors underlying design success in international markets

Factors determining the competitiveness of firms in manufactured exports

1. Top management support.
2. Had clear objectives.
3. Effective management of design and innovation.
4. Closer interaction between R & D, production and marketing.
5. Made extensive use of ideas derived from the market.
6. Made extensive use of ideas derived from technology.
7. Readiness to carry out in-depth research before entering new markets.
8. Readiness to adopt modern techniques (e.g. CAD, CAM, automation, etc.).
9. Readiness to look far into the future.
10. Willingness to enter into collaborative arrangements
11. Government support

Factors determining the successful design and development of the award-winning products

12. Was directed by an individual with outstanding authority and power (top person).
13. Interacted closely with customers/users in design and development stages.
14. Had higher technological content than rival product offerings.
15. Made continuous product reviews during and after product design and development in the light of changes in the environment.
16. Made more use of new and improved manufacturing techniques.
17. Designer(s) saw product through to commercialisation.
18. Product designed and developed by a team of qualified engineering and industrial designers.

Factors influencing the sale of award-winners' products against their rival offerings in international markets

19. Performance in operation.
20. Reliability.
21. Sale price.
22. Efficient delivery.
23. Quality of after-sales service.
24. Technical sophistication.
25. Durability.
26. Easy to use.
27. Safe to use.
28. Easy to maintain.
29. Parts availability.
30. Attractive appearance/shape.
31. Flexibility and adaptability in use.
32. Advertising and promotion.
33. Operator comfort.
34. Style/fashion.

TABLE 9.9 Major factors underlying design success in international markets

Factor name (% variance explained)	Variables loading on factor	Type of variable	Variable loadings
1. Managerial and technical synergy and proficiency (24.4%)	Effective management of design and innovation	Management	0.790
	Readiness to look far into the future	Management	0.764
	Top management support	Management	0.753
	Had clear objectives	Management	0.745
	Had higher technological content that rival product offerings	Commercial entity	0.716
	Closer co-operation between R&D, production, and marketing	Project	0.688
	Readiness to adopt modern techniques (e.g. CAD, CAM, automation, etc.	Project	0.604
	Easy to use	Ergonomic	0.441
	Performance in operation	Technical	0.436
	Made extensive use of ideas derived from technology	Technology push	0.390
	Made continuous product reviews during and after product design and development in the light of changes in the environment	Project	0.372
2. Aesthetic/ergonomic, and Communication synergy (10.1%)	Easy to use	Ergonomic	0.395
	Style/fashion	Aesthetic	0.823
	Attractive appearance/shape	Aesthetic	0.771
	Advertising and promotion	Marketing	0.721
	Operator comfort	Ergonomic	0.703
	Flexibility and adaptability in use	Ergonomic	0.426
	Durability	Technical	0.363
3. Performance in use (7.6%)	Had clear objectives	Management	0.313
	Easy to use	Ergonomic	0.366
	Easy to maintain	Ergonomic	0.805

Table 9.9 *cont.*

Factor name (% variance explained)	Variables loading on factor	Type of variable	Variable loadings
	Parts availability	Ergonomic	0.735
	Flexibility and adaptability in use	Ergonomic	0.480
	Quality of after-sales service	Marketing	0.378
	Technical sophistication	Technical	0.426
4. Market knowledge and Proficiency (5.5%)	Made extensive use of ideas derived from the market	Need-pull	0.849
	Interacted closely with customers/users in design and development stages	Project	0.807
	Readiness to carry out in-depth research before entering new markets	Marketing	0.586
	Designer(s) saw the product through to commercialisation	Commercial entity	0.309
5. New product development synergy and proficiency (5.4%)	Readiness to adopt modern techniques (e.g. CAD/CAM, robotisation, etc.)	Project	0.459
	Readiness to carry out in-depth research before entering new markets	Marketing	0.396
	Made more use of new and improved manufacturing techniques	Project	0.790
	Efficient delivery	Marketing	0.688
	Quality of after-sale service	Marketing	0.622
	Made extensive use of ideas derived from technology	Technology push	0.386
	Designer(s) saw the product through to commercialisation	Commercial entity	0.314
6. Product uniqueness/ superiority (4.9%)	Performance in operation	Technical	0.405
	Quality of after-sales service	Marketing	0.303
	Safe to use	Ergonomic	0.737
	Durability	Technical	0.613
	Made extensive use of ideas derived from technology	Technology push	0.567
	Reliability	Technical	0.566
	Technical sophistication	Technical	0.495

Factor name (% variance explained)	Variables loading on factor	Type of variable	Variable loadings
7. Commercial production synergy (4.5%)	Product designed and developed by a team of qualified engineering and industrial designers	Project	0.808
	Made continuous product reviews during and after product design and development in the light of changes in the environment	Project	0.624
	Designer(s) saw the product through to commercialisation	Commercial entity	0.565
8. Design/manufacture, management synergy and proficiency (3.6%)	Top management support	Management	0.330
	Closer co-operation between R&D, production and marketing	Project	0.327
	Easy to use	Ergonomic	0.329
	Technical sophistication	Technical	0.315
	Designer(s) saw the product through to commercialisation	Commercial entity	0.368
	The design and development of the award-winning product was directed by an individual with outstanding authority and power (top person)	Project	0.794
9. Collaboration and research magnitude (3.5%)	Readiness to carry out in-depth research before entering new markets	Marketing	0.373
	Willingness to enter into collaborative arrangements	Management	0.835
10. Government effort (3.1%)	Government support	Government	0.900
11. Flexibility/adaptability advantage (3.0%)	Flexibility and adaptability in use	Ergonomic	0.420
	Sale price	Commercial entity	0.846

customers/users is also a particular characteristic in marketing knowledge orientation. It enables firms to ensure that the new ideas derived from the market are built into new products in accordance with customer/user specifications.

Further, marketing knowledge is enhanced through the firm's encouragement of its designer(s) to see new-product design through to commercialisation. The rationale is to get feedback on the product performance upon which the existing products may be improved/modified or new ones designed.

In sum, a firm with adequate knowledge of the market tends to identify and understand clearly the specific needs of the market and is thus, better able to satisfy them (i.e. to provide better value for money).

5. *New-product development synergy and proficiency*. Factor 5 describes the company and its proficiency in new-product development. The readiness of firms to find out exactly what the market's needs and wants are, before designing and developing new products; adopt modern techniques (e.g. CAD/CAM); and/or make more use of new and improved manufacturing techniques complemented by efficient delivery and effective after-sales service, all combine to create commercially successful manufactured products.

6. *Product uniqueness/superiority*. A product that performs well in operation, is durable, reliable, safe to use, technically sophisticated, and supported by an adequate after-sales facility is truly unique or superior; and is likely to be more competitive than its rival offerings.

7. *Commercial production synergy*. Design success in international markets is more likely to be achieved when a product is designed and developed by a team of relevant professionals (e.g. engineering designers and industrial designers), rather than by a single individual. It is an old adage that two heads are better than one. In other words, a team of qualified people working on a design project is more likely to produce a synergistic $(2+2=5$ effect) than that executed by one person.

None the less, to maximize this effect, the product must be continuously reviewed and evaluated in line with the market requirements to ensure that the product incorporates the prevailing needs of customers/users. Thus the successful commercialisation of new products appears to depend on the extent to which adequate market information/feedback is obtained to enable designers to create products that people would want to buy.

8. *Design/manufacture management synergy and proficiency*. The design and manufacture of commercially successful products is enhanced when it is supported and directed from the top by someone with enthusiasm, outstanding authority and power. As alluded to earlier, the management tends to encourage designers of products to interact with users aimed at soliciting on-the-spot comments about the overall performance of products while in use. The user records of the good and bad aspects of the product performance are noted and subsequently used to improve the existing products or make new ones to satisfy customers/users in a better way.

9. *Collaboration and research magnitude*. Factor 9 explains 3.5 per cent of the variance, and addresses the collaborative and research orientation. Design success in international markets is stimulated and triggered by the extent to which firms are willing to collaborate with 'outsiders' (users, universities/colleges, competitors, etc.) in design projects. Such collaborative arrangements often inject new

innovative ideas into design projects that, in turn, help to create acceptable and competitive products. Examples include collaborative design project arrangements between Austin Rover (UK) and Honda (Japan); Bedford (UK) and Pontiac (USA); Vauxhall (UK) and Suzuki (Japan).

Nevertheless, the success of collaborative design projects appears to depend on the extent to which the market needs have been clearly identified and understood. In other words, the success or failure of new products largely depends on the extent to which firms carry out in-depth research of markets to find out what the specific user needs/wants and tastes/preferences are, before designing and developing new products.

10. *Government effort.* The role of government in the marketplace can be of considerable importance to the success of firms in manufacturing products. Many firms, particularly small firms, cannot compete in some product areas – 'high-tech' sector, for example – either because they have no technical expertise or have expertise but not sufficient funds to support design projects or undertake research aimed at discovering new uses, modifying existing products, or designing new ones. In both respects, the government can be of immense help by providing support (financial and/or expertise) that will enable these companies to develop their potentials and expand. The UK government, for example, operates a 'funded consultancy scheme' whereby firms are provided with a range of consultancy services on design projects, free of charge. Under the Funded Consultancy Scheme – administered on behalf of the Department of Trade and Industry by The Design Council – the Government helps pay for the consultant design work needed to develop a new product or improve an existing one. The scheme has a dual purpose. First, is to help British companies, in the short term, to get well-designed products on the market quickly. Second, is to persuade companies, in the longer term, through their own practical experience, that investment in design pays off – in fuller order books and healthier profits. By 1984 'more than 1,700 firms have already taken advantage of the scheme, which is available for most kinds of product-related design in most kinds of company'.

11. *Flexibility/adaptability advantage.* A product that is flexible and adaptable in use is more likely to generate sales than one without these qualities. In sum, firms who are able to build flexibility and adaptability into their new products are likely to be more competitive in international markets than those who do not possess this capability.

Although this is a somewhat extended example it shows the kind of information the user should expect to receive from the researcher as a basis for informing decisions on future strategy.

Cluster analysis

This technique is described in some detail in *Marketing Strategy and Management* in the chapter on marketing segmentation. Rather than re-invent the wheel, and for the sake of convenience, that description is reproduced here.

The marketer's interest in segmentation is a particular example of a general problem faced by analysts and decision-makers in virtually all areas of activity, namely: 'Given a sample of N objects or individuals, each of which is measured on each of p variables, devise a classification scheme for grouping the objects into g classes. The number of classes and the characteristics of the classes to be determined.' (Everitt, p. 1.)

Everitt continues:

These techniques have been variously referred to as techniques of *cluster analysis, Q-analysis, typology, grouping, clumping, classification, numerical taxonomy* and *unsupervised pattern recognition*. The variety of the nomenclature may be due to the importance of the methods in such diverse fields as psychology, zoology, biology, botany, sociology, artificial intelligence and information retrieval.

In addition to the many fields of study in which different approaches to clustering have been developed, it is also important to recognise that such methods can be used for a number of different purposes. Thus Everitt cites Ball's (1971) list of seven possible uses of clustering techniques as follows:

   (i)   Find a true typology
  (ii) Model fitting
 (iii) Prediction based on groups
 (iv) Hypothesis testing
  (v) Data exploration
 (vi) Hypothesis generating
(vii) Data reduction

In market segmentation studies each of these different objectives may be appropriate.
Ideally clusters should be self-evident and capable of identification simply by reviewing a set of data and distinguishing natural groupings within it e.g. classifying people as male or female. However, for most purposes decision-makers require a much finer discrimination than is possible using the two or three dimensions, which is the maximum which most of us can conceptualise simultaneously. Because of this need for greater sophistication there has been a proliferation of techniques, which Everitt classes into five types:

Hierarchical
Optimisation − partitioning
Density or mode-seeking
Clumping
Others

Hierarchical clustering techniques may be either *agglomerative* or *divisive* in nature. Under the former procedure one would start from the stance of the behavioural scientist in our earlier description of approaches to market segmentation and regard each individual as a potential market in his or her own right. In most cases such an assumption would be unrealistic in economic terms so one would begin to combine individuals into groups. Conversely, the economists' undifferentiated demand schedule would be the logical starting-point for a divisive approach to segmentation. Everitt observes: 'Both types of hierarchical technique may be viewed as attempts to find the most efficient step in some defined sense, at each stage in the progressive subdivision or synthesis of the population.

Partitioning techniques differ from hierarchical techniques in that they allow for adjustment of the original clusters, created on the basis of a predetermined criterion, through a process of reallocation. Thus, if one's *a priori* expectations as to the optimum way to segment a market leads to groupings which look less than ideal or do not perform as expected one can relocate individuals until an optimum segmentation is achieved.

Density search techniques are, as the name suggests, methods which seek to emulate the human observer's ability to distinguish clusters of high density surrounded by spaces with a lower density.

The fourth main type of technique, *clumping*, is seen as necessary where overlapping clusters are desirable. The case cited by Everitt is language where, because words tend to have several meanings, they may belong in several places. Finally, there is a number of other techniques such as 'Q' factor analysis, latent structure analysis, etc., which do not conform to any of the previous categories. These techniques, and many more from the other categories, are described at some length in Chapter 2 of Everitt's book.

The existence of so many different clustering techniques is itself evidence of the fact that there is no clear 'best' method and that one can anticipate arguments for and against any given approach. Everitt provides a useful summary of problems associated with cluster analysis *per se* and then in the context of the five-fold analysis discussed above. General problems include those of the precise definition of a cluster, the choice of variables, the measurement of similarity and distance and deciding the number of clusters present. These are technical matters beyond the scope of a book of this kind, but Everitt points out that there are various intuitively reasonable ways for validating clusters, namely:

Firstly, several clustering techniques, based on different assumptions, could be used on the same set of data, and only clusters produced by all or by the majority of methods accepted. Secondly, the data could be randomly divided into two and each half clustered independently. Membership assignment in the partitioned samples should be similar to that of the entire sample, if the clusters are stable. A third method of establishing the underlying stability of groups produced by a clustering program is to make predictions about the effort which the omission of some of the variables would have on the group structure and then to check that the predictions are verified.

The final word should also be given to Everitt, who reinforces the adage that any interpretation of data is only as good as the person making it when he comments that:

Cluster-analysis is potentially a very useful technique, but it requires care in its application, because of the many associated problems. In many of the applications of the methods that have been reported in the literature the authors have either ignored or been unaware of these problems, and consequently few results of lasting value can be pointed to. Hopefully future users of these techniques will adopt a more cautious approach, and in addition remember that, along with most other statistical techniques, classification procedures are essentially descriptive techniques for multivariate data, and *solutions given should lend to a proper re-examination of the data matrix rather than a mere acceptance of the clusters produced.* [my emphasis]

John Saunders provides an extended discussion of the method in Hooley (1980) as does Holmes in the *Consumer Market Research Handbook* under the heading 'Numerical Taxonomy'.

Multidimensional scaling (MDS)

Derived from a set of techniques developed originally in the field of mathematical psychology MDS has now been applied extensively in the marketing domain. According to Hooley (1980):

> While MDS techniques can operate on a variety of different types of data they have a common set of objectives:
>
> To produce a representation of the relationships between objects (in the marketing context usually brands) and/or between variables (often product attributes), and/or between evaluators of the objects or variables (respondents).
>
> The relationships discovered are used to build a picture of brand images in the minds of the respondents and an indication of individual respondents' product requirements. In essence MDS techniques seek to represent these relationships in a spatial configuration or model so that the relationships between brands and variables can be used for product positioning purposes (see, for example, Doyle, 1975) and the locations of respondents' product requirements can be used as a basis for market segmentation (see, for example, Johnson, 1971).

Hooley describes a variety of algorithms which have been developed to address different kinds of problem and provides an analysis of the UK market for king-sized cigarettes to illustrate their application. His conclusion, which applies to the output of most multivariate analysis, is that:

> While MDS has yet to be fully accepted by marketing management as a definitive, strategic management tool, it has gained wide acceptance as an exploratory tool to enable a feel for a market to be developed. Findings and suggestions are then further investigated using some of the more familiar, tried and tested techniques. It is probably in this latter, exploratory role, that the major value of MDS will be realised.

Conclusion

We can do no better here than imitate Hooley who cites Sheth's (1977) seven commandments to the researcher:

1. *Do not be technique-oriented.* Focus the problem on the needs of management, then select the appropriate analytical tool – not vice versa.
2. *Consider multivariate models as information for management.* Any model produced from multivariate techniques is an aid to managerial decision making and not a substitute for managerial judgment.
3. *Do not substitute multivariate methods for researcher skill and imagination.* Use common sense to evaluate the results of multivariate analyses. Do not rely on statistical measures of robustness alone.
4. *Develop communication skill.* Learn how to communicate findings to management in a non-technical way wherever possible. Adoption of findings as information inputs to decisions depends on management feeling confident about how that information was derived.
5. *Avoid making statistical inferences about the parameters of multivariate models.* Beware of generalisations to populations where the nature of a sample is unclear.
6. *Guard against the danger of making inferences about market realities when such inferences may be due to the peculiarities of the method.* Do not take results at face value. Even where high levels of statistical significance can be attached to findings ensure that results have a sound theoretical and common sense basis. Where possible use split samples to validate models developed on fresh data.
7. *Exploit the complementary relationship between descriptive and predictive methods.* Do not use techniques in isolation where other techniques may add to the information obtained, or further validate findings. Often techniques can helpfully be used in sequence.

Most important we must remember that the techniques are not a panacea in themselves. This has been neatly put by Young (1973):

> The danger we must always avoid is becoming peddlers of techniques in search of problems rather than problem solvers in search of techniques.

The primary consideration of any study must be the basic problems that it sets out to solve. This will lead to a search for specific types of information rather than a preference for particular analysis techniques. The various techniques available do, however, form a comprehensive set of tools to aid the interpretation and presentation of that information.

Answers to Questions (pp. 227–8)

The interpretation of part 2 of Table 9.6 ('Intentions to subscribe to Cable TV by social class of respondents') is that intention is influenced by both income and usage dimensions of social class. Thus social classes C1, C2, D and the unemployed (heavy users) have stronger intentions to subscribe than class B (light users). In the case of class A high incomes increase the intention to subscribe for a light user category whereas low incomes debar class E (heavy users of TV).

The chi square statistic for the table would be valid as the calculation is $252/902 \times 12 = 3.35$ and the smallest cell value of 5 exceeds this.

References

Alreck, Pamela L. and Settle, Robert N. (1985) *The Survey Research Handbook* (Homewood, Ill.: Richard D. Irwin).

Antilla, Mai, Van Den Heuvel, Rob and Moller, Kristian, 'Conjoint Measurement for Marketing Management', *European Journal of Marketing*, 14, 7.

Claycamp, Henry J. (1974) 'Correlation and Regression Methods' in *Handbook of Marketing Research*, ed. Robert Ferber (New York: McGraw-Hill).

Durkheim, Emile (1895) *The Rules of Sociological Method*.

Evans, F.B. (1959) 'Psychological and Objective Factors in the Prediction of Brand Choice: Ford verses Chevrolet', *Journal of Business*, vol. 32, no. 4, October, pp. 340–369.

Ehrenberg A.S.C. 'Some Queries to Factor Analysis', *The Statistician*, vol. 13, 4, 1963.

Everitt, Brian (1974) *Cluster Analysis* (London: Heinemann).

Harvard University Computation Centre (1967).

Heenan, D.A. and Adelman, R.B. (1975) 'Quantitative Techniques of Today's Decision Makers', *Harvard Business Review*, July–August.

Holmes, C. (1986) 'Multivariate Analysis of Market Research Data', ch. 13 in *Consumer Market Research Handbook*, 3rd edn, ed. Worcester, R. and Downham, J. (New York: McGraw-Hill).

Hooley, Graham (1980) 'A Guide to the Use of Quantitative Techniques in Marketing', *European Journal of Marketing*, 14, 7.

Madge, J. (1953) *Tools of Social Science* (Lara: Longman, Green).

Selltiz, Claire, Marie Jahoda, Morton Deutsch, Stuart W. Cook (1959) *Research Methods in Social Relations*, rev. one-volume edn (New York: Holt, Rinehart & Winston).

Sheth, J.N. (1977) *Multivariate Methods for Market and Survey Research* (Chicago, American Marketing Association).

Sonquist, J.A. and Morgan, J.M. (1964) *The Detection of Interaction Effects*, Monograph 35 (Survey Research Centre, University of Michigan).

Ughanwa, D.O. and M.J. Baker (1989) *The Role of Design in International Competitiveness* (London: Routledge).

Wind, Y. and Grashof, J.F. and Goldhar, J.D. (1978) 'Market-Based Guidelines for Design of Industrial Products', *Journal of Marketing*, vol. 42, July, pp. 27–37.

Young, S. (1973) 'Pitfalls Down the Primrose Path of Attitude Segmentation', *European Research*, November, pp. 157–73.

CHAPTER 10

Report presentation

Introduction

A recurring theme of this book has been that research for marketing should be a continuous process designed to inform the decision-maker of what has happened, what is happening and what is likely to happen in the marketing domain relevant to the firm's survival and prosperity. The tangible output of this process is the MIS or marketing information system which contains the output of the firm's research effort together with the output of syndicated or specific research commissioned from external agencies and third parties. However, our analysis has also shown that the term 'marketing research' is often used in a much narrower and specific way to describe particular and limited pieces of research designed to address a distinct problem or issue that cannot be fully answered by reference to the MIS. In recognition of this the structure of the book has followed the classical approach to *ad hoc* marketing research from problem recognition through problem specification to research design, data collection analysis and interpretation. It now remains to examine the output of this process – the research report.

The importance of the report, written and oral, is self-evident for it is the means through which the researcher must communicate his findings to those who initiated the process in the first place by defining a problem to which they were seeking an answer. It is also the means through which one may inform others of a present or potential problem which demands their attention and, possibly, action. Two concepts familiar to students of marketing underline the importance and difficulty of effective communication – Schramm's model of communication and the concept of the hierarchy of effects.

Schramm's basic model is described in *Marketing* (4th edn, 1985) and points out that communication involves a minimum of three basic elements – sender, message and receiver. However, in order to communicate effectively the sender must encode his message in a manner which is meaningful to and understandable by the intended receiver and then transmit the message through a medium to which the intended receiver has access and to which he is paying attention. Attention or awareness is the first step in so-called hierarchy-of-effects models such as those proposed by Lavidge and Steiner (see *Marketing*, pp. 274–5). These models emphasise that if one is to initiate action on the part of another then it is necessary to move them from unawareness, to awareness, to interest, to desire and to action. The problem, of course, lies in securing and holding the audience's attention for long enough to influence their attitudes and behaviour.

It has been estimated that the average individual is exposed to approximately 1500 advertising messages a day but only consciously recognises six of these. Clearly, if one were to recognise all the messages and only give them 15 seconds' attention each it would occupy six and a quarter hours of one's day. Fortunately, our subconscious and the phenomenon of selective perception ensure that only a fraction of the information available to us actually triggers our attention and invites us to consider whether we wish to consider the new information any further. Written and oral reports, especially when related to one's work, are likely to clear the first hurdle and capture one's attention – whether they can retain and stimulate it is another matter. It is for this reason that report presentation is of such vital importance.

According to Gallagher (1969) reports comprise two essential and inextricably linked elements – content and form. The content of a report is proscribed by the key steps in the research process which may be summarised as:

1. Stating the problem.
2. Defining the scope.
3. Planning the research.
4. Collecting the information.
5. Analysing the information.
6. Forming the conclusions.

while the form determines how this information will be presented to the intended audience and normally comprises four steps:

1. Organising the report.
2. Preparing the first draft.
3. Editing the draft.
4. Publishing the report.

In this chapter we shall examine each of these steps in some detail.

Report content

John Mitchell in his small book *How to Write Reports* (Fontana, 1974) defines a report as 'a written statement of the facts of a situation, project, process or test; how these facts were ascertained; their significance, the conclusions that have been drawn from them; the recommendations that are being made'. He goes on to suggest that:

The storage and analysis of information in reports is essential to the functioning of modern industry and undoubtedly plays a part in its expansion. Reports are needed to:

a) record work done, whether conclusive or not;
b) assess a situation;
c) test the validity of information;
d) avoid repeating work already done;
e) circulate new ideas;
f) provide means of cross-fertilisation of ideas;
g) indicate a course of action to be taken as a result of work done;
h) keep others, especially management, informed of work done and of progress made.

Marketing research reports fulfil all these needs but, in the majority of cases, will address areas (a), (b), (g) and (h) and provide a concise summary of the analysis of a specific problem. In the case of a specific research task undertaken for a client by a professional agency the Market Research Society guidelines require that the report should cover the following areas:

Reporting

C.10 By the time a survey is completed the agency shall have provided the client with:
A copy of the questionnaire (or, in the case of multi-client surveys, the relevant part of a questionnaire) or similar document.
Any relevant extract from interviewers' instructions.
Relevant details of:
(a) its objectives;
(b) its universe — actual if different from intended;
(c) size and nature of sample — achieved and intended;
(d) any weighting methods used;
(e) where relevant, weighted and unweighted bases (clearly distinguished) for all major conventional tables;
(f) where relevant, statement of response rates and discussion of any possible bias due to non-response;
(g) method(s) by which information was collected;
(h) general nature of any informant incentives offered;

    (i) dates and times of day when, and main locations where, fieldwork was done;

    (j) fieldforce(s) involved at any stage;

    (k) sub-contractors used for major parts of the research;

    (l) in qualitative work – method of recruitment;

    (m) in desk research – sources used.

C.11 When presenting results members shall endeavour to make a clear distinction between the results themselves and their own interpretation of the data and recommendations.

Similar lists are to be found in most major textbooks and serve to remind the writer that in developing a report he should constantly remind himself what is the object of the exercise – namely, to communicate effectively with an identified audience. To do so one must keep the audience's information needs constantly at the front of one's mind, eliminating anything which will not serve this objective – whatever its intrinsic interest to the researcher/author – and concentrate on the essentials. To achieve this it is generally agreed that a systematic approach is of crucial importance. Britt (1971) recognises that one may address report writing in a number of ways, e.g. in some reports the conclusions will be presented first and in others last but, in all cases, it will be necessary to cover the following five areas which are virtually identical to the six content areas proposed by Gallagher, namely:

1. *Problem*: This is a concise statement of the specific question or questions asked and the reasons for asking them.
2. *Method*: An explanation of the design of your research is needed – for instance, your sample, control methods, and techniques of measurement.
3. *Results*: You need to present enough data to justify your conclusions, but not necessarily every last bit of data.
4. *Discussion*: Your discussion of your results, perhaps including comparisons with other studies, should be relevant to the original problem.
5. *Conclusions*: Your conclusions are not the same as your results; instead they 'flow from' the results. And so-called negative conclusions are just as important to report as positive conclusions. The main consideration is the application of the findings to the problem at hand, the one that was set forth at the beginning of the report.

The need to define the problem precisely was discussed at considerable length in Chapter 2 for, in the absence of an agreed problem definition, it is unlikely that the researcher will come up with a solution that meets his clients' needs. Some years ago the Training Department of the Carborundum Company Limited produced a short series of booklets (12 pp. long) on a variety of management topics including report writing. In this booklet it was emphasised that, 'success or failure of the report depends upon the author being perfectly clear about the objective of the study before going any further'. To ensure this clear *Terms of Reference* are required which, as a minimum 'should state the kind of information required, the degree of urgency and – whenever possible – the boundaries of the enquiry'. Three examples which meet these criteria are:

Please let me have a Summary Report on the advisability of establishing a Sales Office in Northern Scotland. I suggest we discuss your findings at the Sales Conference in March.

Please submit a Summary Report as soon as possible indicating whether or not labour turnover within our Manchester factory compares favourably with other firms (a) in the Manchester area, and (b) throughout the country.

Please investigate current operating conditions in the Assembly Division in relation to:

(a) Labour relations*
(b) Line and staff co-ordination
(c) The delegation of duties and responsibilities
(d) Liaison with other Divisions in personnel matters*

*Including (or excluding) wages and working conditions.

A SUMMARY and DETAILED report is required before March 31st next.

Each of the above examples provides a clear indication of what is required – the objective of the report – but is capable of considerable refinement in terms of the precise *scope* of the work to be done to achieve the proposed objective. Dissatisfaction with a report invariably results from a failure to define the scope of a project/report sufficiently closely. If management is unclear as to exactly what it wants to know then it is unreasonable to blame the researcher if his efforts fall short of this, particularly when this judgement is usually made with the benefit of hindsight and on the basis of better but incomplete information provided by the unsatisfactory report. While the responsibility for defining the scope of a project ultimately must rest with the person commissioning a piece of research, the researcher cannot absolve himself of all blame. As noted when discussing problem definition, it is up to the researcher to agree the detailed terms of reference with the 'client' as these form the basis of the 'contract' between them (literally when commissioning an external agency) and form the benchmark against which the report will be assessed. Such agreement is also necessary as the basis for determining the level of detail required, the time needed to achieve this and the budgetary implications.

Introduction

The Problem Statement/Terms of Reference may be stated separately in order to give them emphasis but, usually, will be contained as an element of the *Introduction* to a report. Given that the purpose of an introduction is to inform readers as to the factors which gave rise to the need for the report in the first place, what issues it is to address and the sequence and manner in which they are to be addressed, the nature and length of the introduction will depend very much upon the audience's needs. Where the report is a response to a clear-cut request from a particular individual or group little time need be spent on preliminaries. Conversely, where a report has been prepared for an ill defined and/or poorly informed audience the writer will need to provide much more detail of the background to provide context and perspective to the report itself.

In drafting an introduction it is often as necessary to spell out what is not covered or has been excluded as it is to describe the actual content. Failure to do so will expose the researcher to questions as to 'Why didn't you . . .?' when such problems were probably considered but discarded for very good reasons. Thus the purpose of the introduction is to capture the reader's interest, define the background to the issue and the precise problem(s) to be addressed, on whose behalf, and the way in which the report itself is to be developed.

Method

The second major element of a report following the introduction is a description of how the researcher addressed the problem to be solved. Here again the cardinal rule is to consider first and foremost just what the audience's needs are. Senior managers are unlikely to be excited by extended discussions of how a sampling frame was constructed, a questionnaire designed or bias minimised. On the other hand this is the very information which other professional researchers will wish to scrutinise in order to help them decide what value they can place upon the research findings. Of course both needs can be satisfied by providing only a limited description in the main body of the report and supplementing this with technical appendices for the benefit of other professional researchers. (See the Technical Appendix to Chapter 6 as an example.)

Results

The main problem with results is that usually one has too many and so has to be highly selective in determining those which are most *relevant* to the problem being addressed. The question of relevance is a difficult one and depends upon a thorough understanding of the information needs of the audience backed by experience and judgement. In *Marketing and Competitive Success* (Prentice-Hall, 1989) Baker and Hart report the findings of a major survey and provide a good example of the trade-offs which must be made in reporting results.

Project MACS was designed to address criticisms levelled against a number of earlier studies which had examined the existence and nature of factors associated with above average business performance such as those reported in *In Search of Excellence, The Winning Streak* and similar managerial best sellers. Based upon an exhaustive review of the literature a comprehensive list of critical success factors was compiled and data collected from a matched sample of above average and below average performers in six industries – three 'sunrise' (above average growth) and three 'sunset' (stable or declining growth). The completed questionnaires yielded a mass of data which was analysed using the SPSS programme (Statistical Package for the Social Sciences) and generated over 3600 tables. In reviewing the output the researchers were guided closely by the rules of data interpretation discussed in Chapter 9. Given the findings of earlier researchers, surprisingly few analyses of the relationship between the independent variable 'success' and the dependent variables – the critical success factors – showed a statistically significant association. In the event the researchers decided to report only 38 relationships (including what was seen as the most surprising result of all – the use or rather lack of use made of marketing research) and of these 13 were not statistically significant. In presenting these selected findings in written and oral reports to groups of academics and managers the overall reaction has been that the chosen data is sufficient to support the conclusion drawn that as the functions and activities considered to be critical success factors are to be found in both more and less successful firms then it is the quality of implementation which differentiates between them.

The physical presentation of results is also vitally important with graphical and pictorial representations communicating much more effectively than a series of detailed tables with accompanying commentary. An excellent example of this contention is provided in Figure 10.1(a) and (b) which summarises the responses to a battery of questions put to incoming students as to their expectations on a variety of issues related to postgraduate programmes in the Strathclyde Business School. Reported separately as a series of tables this information occupied 17 pages in the first draft report. These tables were consigned to an appendix for the benefit of decision makers responsible for specific parts of the school's programme, while the 'profile' illustrated in Figure 10.1 was used to inform the School's Board of Management of the findings. Given the wide range of graphics packages available on PCs no researcher now has an excuse for not presenting their data in easily assimilable form as shown in Figure 10.2.

Discussion

While the discussion was identified as a discrete element in Gallagher's review of a report's contents more often than not this will be integrated with the presentation of the findings or results. Purists argue that the narrative which is included to aid interpretation of the results is a commentary and should be

Statement	MCom	MSc	MBA	Total
a) Improved knowledge	4.785	4.782	4.888	4.825
b) Obtain PG degree	4.121	4.391	4.25	4.274
c) Move into a higher degree	3.25	2.676	2.436	2.759
d) Prepare for new career	4.052	4.594	4.042	4.258
e) Formulate long-term plans	4.35	4.289	4.472	4.375
f) Identify career interests	3.794	3.782	3.828	3.803
g) Improve knowledge/skills for present career	4.421	4.716	4.436	4.514
h) Increase chances for raise/promotion	3.540	3.616	4.071	3.790
i) Increase organisational mobility	3.621	3.666	4.041	3.806
j) Actively involve in student life	3.707	3.260	2.819	3.197
k) Increase cultural/ social participation	3.487	3.463	2.916	3.252
l) Meet people	3.75	3.710	3.876	3.787
m) Increase self-confidence	4.536	3.840	4.082	4.087
n) Improve leadership skills	4.268	3.739	4.333	4.093
o) Improve ability to get along with others	4.225	3.507	3.859	3.75
p) Learn skills that will improve daily life	4.048	3.217	3.527	3.527
q) Develop ability to be independent	4.560	3.840	3.722	3.921
Summated Means	68.515	65.288	65.571	65.996

Figure 10.1(a)   Data for profile and summation analysis of the student motivations

distinguished from the discussion in which the reporter is seeking to synthesise the various ideas contained in the results in relation to one another. This distinction has merit in that it focuses attention on the need to provide a summary of the findings. A particularly important element of the discussion is the statement of limitations associated with the findings. As noted earlier it is far better that the researcher admit these and explain why they may compromise or qualify the results (but not dismiss them) rather than be 'caught out' by someone seeking to question or discredit the report as a whole.

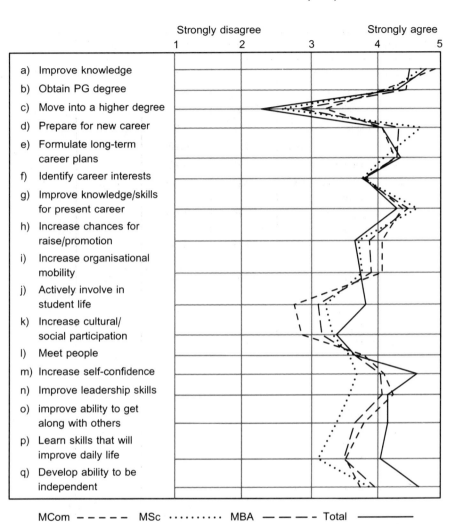

| | Strongly disagree | | | Strongly agree |
| | 1 | 2 | 3 | 4 | 5 |

a) Improve knowledge
b) Obtain PG degree
c) Move into a higher degree
d) Prepare for new career
e) Formulate long-term
     career plans
f) Identify career interests
g) Improve knowledge/skills
     for present career
h) Increase chances for
     raise/promotion
i) Increase organisational
     mobility
j) Actively involve in
     student life
k) Increase cultural/
     social participation
l) Meet people
m) Increase self-confidence
n) Improve leadership skills
o) improve ability to get
     along with others
p) Learn skills that will
     improve daily life
q) Develop ability to be
     independent

MCom – – – – –   MSc · · · · · · · · · ·   MBA – — – – -   Total ———————

Figure 10.1(b)   Goals of postgraduate study in management

Conclusions

The conclusions should address the questions posed in the terms of reference which, in turn, have become the objectives of the research. In drawing conclusions one must have due regard for the issues reviewed in Chapters 8

Summated means

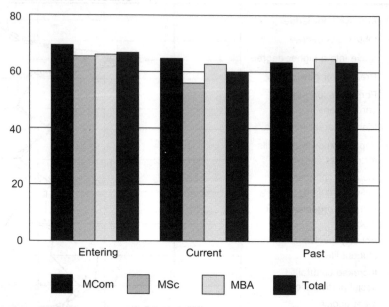

Means

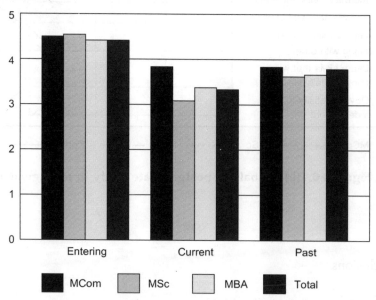

Figure 10.2   Comparison of summated means

and 9 which dealt with data analysis and data interpretation and carefully distinguish between fact and opinion. Where appropriate the researcher should also be prepared to offer recommendations as to the courses of action which flow from the conclusions.

Organisation of the written report

We have already noted that while the presentation of a report may be varied, e.g. the conclusions and recommendations presented first, there is general agreement that a written report should contain all of the following:

1. *Title page(s)*. This should communicate as concisely as possible the subject matter of the report in the title itself, the author's name, the date of presentation, classification data and, possibly, key words. Classification data will depend upon whether the report is an internal document or a formal publication. If an internal document it may have a project or reference number as well as an indication of who may have access to it. If a published document then a variety of publishing data including key words will be found (see the preliminaries to this book).

2. *Abstract or executive summary*. An abstract is usually a very concise statement describing the core content of the report and not exceeding one page in length (see Research Theses in University libraries). By contrast an executive summary may run to several pages and cover the objectives, findings, conclusions and recommendations – in other words the key information which may be all that senior managers may consider in coming to a decision of what action to take. It follows that the Executive Summary may be the only opportunity the researcher has to have any influence on events and he must use it accordingly.

3. *Contents list*. The table of contents is a vital guide to the reader – it reveals the structure of the report and indicates where the issues addressed by it are to be found.

4. *Introduction*. This has already been discussed above. Potter (1974) suggests it should include:

   a) Terms of reference;
   b) a short history of the case or subject;
   c) reasons for writing the report or for conducting the investigation;
   d) who called for the report;

e) the scope of the report;
f) the limitations of the report;
g) the way the subject is to be treated;
h) any special considerations that apply to it.

5. *Methodology*
6. *Results or Findings*
7. *Discussions and Limitations*
8. *Conclusions*
9. *Recommendations*
10. *Appendices*

Mitchell (1974) proposes that the rule governing the inclusion of material in an appendix is that it comprises:

> that which the reader does not need to study in order to understand the report, but which he may turn to if he wishes to examine in detail the supporting evidence. It includes:
>
> a) statistical tables;
> b) detailed results of experiments;
> c) series of graphs;
> d) summaries of results obtained elsewhere;
> e) correspondence;
> f) lengthy quotations from outside authorities;
> g) maps, charts and diagrams.

To this end the marketing researcher would add details of the sampling methodology, data collection methods, analytical measures used, etc.

11. *Bibliography.* The bibliography should list all the secondary sources consulted by the researcher and serves the dual purpose of enabling the reader to check or follow up sources of particular interest, while also indicating the scope of the secondary research undertaken.

12. *Glossary.* Not all reports require a glossary but they are particularly useful when the report deals with a subject with which the audience has had little prior experience or contains a number of technical terms which need to be defined precisely.

13. *Index.* Only found in long and complex reports where multiple references occur to the same objects.

Presentation of the written report

While the organisation and structure of a report will have an important influence on its impact ultimately this depends greatly upon the actual writing and presentation of the document. As has been noted at several places in this chapter the acid test is whether the intended audience will be able to understand the report. In determining this Gallagher (1969) suggests that the writer-editor should ask the following questions:

- Does the report tell the complete story?
- Are the conclusions substantiated?
- Is the proper emphasis given to each topic?
- Is all the information pertinent?
- Is the information accurate?
- Is the material presented clearly and logically?
- Are all special terms defined?
- Would a table, graph, schematic, or photograph eliminate the need for considerable textual discussion?
- Does any material in the body of the report interfere with orderly presentation and easy assimilation of key ideas and therefore perhaps belong more appropriately in the appendix?
- Is the report easy to read?

Gallagher devotes over 100 pages of advice as to how the writer can ensure that his report matches the standards implied by these questions. Similar advice is to be found in numerous other books and articles on report writing and emphasises strongly the correct use of language, the need for clarity and accuracy. Much of the advice given closely resembles that touched upon when discussing the design and wording of questionnaires in Chapter 8. However, detailed examination of this topic is not the province of this book and readers should consult sources such as Gallagher, Mitchell or Gower for valuable advice and guidance on effective written presentation.

Increasingly report writers are required to make an oral report of their findings in which case the written document is frequently regarded as supporting material for possible reference, assuming the audience has been sufficiently impressed by the presentation to consider it worth the effort. As most teachers know to their cost the attention span of an audience is decidedly limited and few lessons or lectures can sustain this for more than 60 minutes at a time and this tends to set the upper limit for an oral presentation. Faced with such a limit the oral report will have little scope for detail and will depend heavily upon audio-visual aids (overhead projector transparencies, 35 mm slides, video, flipcharts, etc.) to communicate the essence of the report. Scripting and rehearsal are vital.

Evaluating research reports

An understanding of how to prepare a report will undoubtedly assist in interpreting the reports written by others. However, there are many more readers of reports than there are writers and editors and to conclude this chapter it will be helpful to provide some guidelines for evaluating research reports. The US Advertising Research Foundation has developed such guidelines and Tull and Hawkins (1987) summarise them as follows:

Reading research reports

Substantially more people read research reports than write them. Managers need to develop skill in reading research reports (and listening to research presentations) in order to evaluate the usefulness of the research results. The Advertising Research Foundation has developed a set of guidelines that managers can follow to evaluate research reports.* A brief summary follows.

Origin – What is behind the research. The report should contain a clear statement of why the research was conducted, who sponsored it, and who conducted it. Key questions:

- Does the report identify the organisations (divisions, departments) that requested the research?
- Does it contain a statement of purpose that clearly states what the research was to accomplish?
- Are the organisations that defined and conducted the research identified?

Design – The concept and the plan. The research approach, the sample, and the analysis should be described clearly and they should be appropriate for the purpose of the study. Key questions:

- Is there a complete non-technical description of the research design?
- Is the design consistent with the purpose for which the research was conducted?
- Does any aspect of the design, including the measuring instrument(s), induce any bias (particularly bias in favour of the sponsor)?
- Does the design control for patterns of sequence or timing or other external factors which might prejudice the results?
- Are the respondents capable of answering the questions raised?
- Is there a precise statement of the populations the research is to represent?
- Does the sampling frame fairly represent the population?

---

*Public Affairs Council, *Guide for the Public Use of Market and Opinion Research* (New York: Advertising Research Foundation, 1981).

- Does the report specify the type of sample used and describe the method of sample selection?
- Does the report describe how the data are analysed?
- Are copies of the questionnaire, field and sampling instructions, and other materials available in the appendix or on file?

Execution – Collecting and handling the information. Data should be carefully collected by competent people using forms and methods appropriate for the task. Key questions:

- Does the report describe the data-collection procedures including 'quality control' procedures?
- Does the report specify the proportion of the selected sample from which information was collected?
- Were those who collected the data treated in a manner that would minimise any bias they might introduce?

Stability – Sample size and reliability. The sample size should be reported and it should be large enough to yield stable results. Key questions:

- Is the sample large enough to provide stable findings?
- Are sampling error limits shown (if applicable)?
- Is the calculation of sampling error, or the lack of such a calculation, explained?
- Does the treatment of sampling error make clear that it does not include nonsampling error?
- For the major findings, are the reported error tolerances based on direct analysis of the variability of the collected data?

Applicability – Generalising the findings. The research report should clearly indicate the boundaries which limit the findings. Key questions:

- Does the report specify when the data were collected?
- Does the report state clearly whether its results apply beyond the direct source of the data?
- It is clear which groups, if any, are underrepresented in the data?
- If the research has limited applications, is there a statement describing who or what it represents and the times and conditions under which it applied?

Meaning – Interpretations and conclusions. All assumptions and judgements involved in reaching any findings, conclusions or recommendations should be clearly specified. Key questions:

- Are the measurements described in simple and direct language?
- Does the use of the measurements make sense?
- Are the actual findings clearly differentiated from any interpretation of the findings?
- Has rigourous objectivity and candid reporting been used in interpreting research findings as evidence of causation or as predictive of future behaviour?

Candour – Open reporting and disclosure. The research report should be an honest, complete description of the research process and outcome. Key questions:

- Is there a full and forthright disclosure of how the research was done?
- Have all the potentially relevant findings been presented?

As a user of a research project, you need to know what the results of the study are and how accurate they are likely to be. The Advertising Research Foundation guidelines can assist you in this evaluation.

References

Britt, S.H. (1971) 'The Writing of Readable Research Reports', *Journal of Marketing Research*, May.

Gallagher, William J. (1969) *Report Writing for Management* (Reading, Mass.: Addison-Wesley).

Potter, Jenny (1974) *Introduction to the Findings of the 'Consumer Concerns Survey'* (National Consumer Council).

Tull, Donald S. and Hawkins, Del I. (1987) *Marketing Research*, 4th edn (New York: Macmillan).

CHAPTER 11

Syndicated market research services

Introduction

From Chapter 4, 'What do we know', it became clear that the marketing manager has an abundance of secondary sources of information at his disposal. It was also clear that these sources should be fully consulted before embarking upon the costly exercise of primary research. By the same token, the marketing manager should always explore the availability of proprietary market research, collected by a professional research organisation, for sale openly or under contract to multiple clients, with a common interest in the subject area, before setting out to commission or undertake primary research on his or her own. In this chapter, we examine the 'syndicated' market research services available to him or her.

Syndicated market research

Syndicated research is 'research, often based on samples or panels, in which all or part of the same results are supplied to different users' (Baker, 1984).

Many marketing research companies, aware of potential clients' need for information and clients' concern over the high cost of marketing research, conduct research into specific industries, usually on an on-going basis. Syndicated research can be initiated either by the marketing research agency or by a client.

A marketing research agency will commission syndicated research if it uncovers a shortage of published information on a particular industry. The agency will normally circulate a research proposal for a study into the area to companies in the industry inviting them to take part in the research. Clients can normally request information for their own private use, for example, on competitors' activities, at a price. The project will proceed when the agency knows there is enough demand to cover the research costs.

If a company wishes to commission syndicated research, it is normally because it wishes to divide the cost of the project. A client will approach an agency, and a proposal is drawn up from the client's briefing. This briefing is then sent to a number of companies within the industry to invite them to participate in research, without the client's identity being revealed. The research is undertaken, again, when demand is high enough.

In each case, whether client or agency initiated, everyone who takes part in the research programme will receive the same basic report, with minor modifications, when, for example, the client has requested specific questions. There is usually little difference in the price of each report. Costs of reports vary a great deal, depending on the cost of the research undertaken and the expected demand for the report. As noted earlier (Chapter 4) when discussing the expected value of information, decision-makers in business should be aware of the value of information, in the same way that they appear to place a value on advertising. However, there often appears to be a relatively low appreciation of the skill, time and effort required to execute a project which could result in millions of pounds being made or saved, compared with the equivalent inputs required to produce an advertising campaign. A review of some of the types of reports that exist in the UK and the costs involved are given in this chapter to provide some idea of the cost and the scope of these services.

Kinnear and Taylor (1987) classified syndicated data sources into five major categories, these being:

1. *Consumer data* – this research focuses on consumer behaviour, both in the types of products they buy and the circumstances of the purchase. Attitudes, opinions, life-styles and consumption patterns may be explored.
2. *Retail data* – this research requires the assistance of retail outlets for information on sales of products by range, brand and competing products. Normally there is no large degree of overlap between agencies that conduct this type of research, perhaps to avoid duplication of effort on the part of the major retailers involved.
3. *Wholesale data* – this data is usually obtained through warehouses and is used to estimate sales at retail level.

    Some services are so detailed that information on the movement of brands in 425 product categories on a monthly basis are available so that clients can analyse trends at whatever level is appropriate to them.
4. *Industrial data* – Unfortunately, syndicated information on industrial goods is more difficult to collect and therefore, there are not too many sources

available to the industrial marketing manager. Kinnear and Taylor recommend Dun and Bradstreet's *Market Identifiers*; *Fortune* magazine's *Input/Output Matrix* and McGraw-Hill's *Dodge Reports*.

5. *Advertising evaluation data* – This data is of most value to marketing managers responsible for high advertising expenditures, especially in consumer goods markets. Clients can expect information on the effectiveness of advertising campaigns of both their own and of competitors; competitors' advertising spend and the media mix competitors' use.

Some of these services merit wider discussion, and we shall go on to discuss trade research, panel research and omnibus surveys.

Trade research

'Trade research is a collective term for a series of specially developed techniques serving the needs and objectives of marketing management at the various stages of the distribution network' (Pymont and Welch, 1986). In other words, it is used to provide marketing management with feed back on the success or failure of marketing mix decisions they have made and to assist them in making better decisions in future. Trade research covers areas like the best channels of distribution to use for particular products; channel behaviour; feedback on promotional campaigns – either your own or competitors; pricing decisions; and if the company has the 'correct' product mix. Pymont and Welch (1986) classified trade research into five areas:

1. Retail and wholesale audits
2. Invoice analysis
3. Distribution checks
4. *Ad hoc* research
5. Point of sale research

Retail and wholesale audits

Many manufacturers use syndicated research services offered by specialist market research agencies such as Nielsen and Retail Audits – although some choose the option of conducting their own in-house audits. The choice for an individual company is usually a trade-off between the high cost of conducting the research and a tailor-made research report which answers to its specific requirements.

Retail audits can help marketing management at both the tactical and strategic decision-making level.

At the tactical decision-making level, management can evaluate the success of recent promotional campaigns they have conducted, and base future campaigns on those which have had the most positive effect on the market. This will also help management avoid repeating those campaigns which have clearly not worked well. Another value of retail audits at this level is the 'ability to read quickly and to act upon, competitive successes and failures' (Pymont and Welch, 1986).

At the strategic decision-making level, management can observe the long-term trends of market activity and base their future predictions of the company's performance *vis-à-vis* competitor's, with some degree of accuracy. Information on the performance of 'individual brands, brands of a certain type, formulation or price range (may) indicate a need for the company to review its product mix, its pricing policy, where it should concentrate its promotional expenditure etc.' (Pymont and Welch, 1986).

Trade research is conducted through a panel of sample shops who have agreed to take part in the retail audit. This co-operation is usually based on the confidentiality of individual shop's sales being maintained, and some form of compensation for the inconvenience caused — either in the form of monetary payment or in terms of being given the reports when they are complete. The sample shops are visited by auditors at predetermined intervals who count the stock and record the details of the paperwork concerned with the deliveries of stock to the shop. The shop's sales are calculated using the following formula:

Opening stocks + deliveries − closing stock = sales

This process is not as easy as it sounds, as many managers will appreciate when their *financial* audits are taking place each year. The process is conducted with a great deal of care to ensure accuracy of sales. For this reason, any details regarding the quantity of individual brands, the positioning of brands within the store, delivery notes and any additional material which will be of relevance, such as promotional campaigns, are gathered in order to build the pattern of trading for that particular store. This process will become a great deal easier with many stores converting to EPOS — Electronic Point of Sale. The auditing process will be more accurate in future, and results will be more quickly available (Pymont and Welch, 1986).

When the audit information reaches the processing centre it undergoes a further series of accuracy checks. At this point, any of the 'additional data' collected, such as promotional campaigns will help explain any unusual sales activity in the area. When the checks are complete, the figures for stocks held, deliveries made, and sales of individual products for all the sample shops are totalled. The data are then 'grossed up' or increased to reflect the universe level of sales. Pymont and Welch (1986) go on further to describe the process:

the process of totalling is common to both small and large 'national' audits, except that in the latter case the shops are first sorted into cells (shop type within area) and then totalled. For each cell, the value of the universe is known and the expansion is simply:

$$\frac{\text{Universe}}{\text{Sample}} \times \text{sales (or stock or deliveries)}$$

By adding the expanded cell data, area totals and shop type totals are obtained and thus a representation of the national market is constructed.

The presentation of data can be given in many different formats, depending upon how the project is analysed. Pymont and Welch (1986) identified the following types of presentation which a client may either expect or request from the market research agency running the project: consumer sales, retailer deliveries, retail stock, stock cover, average stocks and average sales per shop handling, average price paid by consumers, distribution and showings (i.e. display material). These tables may be further analysed by region, manufacturer's sales divisions, shop type, size of shop or membership of a voluntary organisation. In this way, a 'total and composite picture of the retail trade is obtained' (Pymont and Welch, 1986). Further tabulations are available upon request – and at a fee – which can make the project more relevant to the company's needs. These options should be discussed fully with the client service executive in charge of the project, before the analysis is undertaken, as the cost of analysing back data specially for a client is too expensive for it to be considered worthwhile.

The client should also be aware of the sampling technique used by the agency. In the main, samples fall into two categories – those which represent a particular trade or shop and those which can reflect the distribution characteristics of a product class. This second type of sample uses a combination of store types to make up the panel, in order to give as representative a picture as possible of the number and type of outlets selling the product. Key areas the marketing manager should consider with respect to the sampling technique used by the market research agency are:

1. The representativeness of the sample – not all of the major companies (which represent a substantial proportion of the universe) are willing to take part in the audit, and this affects estimates of turnover. The marketing manager should look for 'minimum/maximum estimates with some indication of "best guess"' (Pymont and Welch, 1986).
2. When the data are collected, care must be taken when a shop type index is used as the basis of the sample. Sales volume does not necessarily correlate with the number of stores of a specific shop type. For example, the *number* of independent grocers far exceeds the number of high street multiples in the UK, but the *sales volume* they generate is far less than the multiples generate. This would mean this type of sample would be biased, and

would not reflect the real trends in sales activity. Pymont and Welch (1986) recommend the sample should be chosen according to sales volume whilst ensuring an adequate number of stores are used.

3. If the proposed sample is to reflect the sales of a product class, the sample must reflect the 'total sales volume of the product only in each shop type, and within each to contain sufficient of the various organisations to give approximately equal cell bases in order to provide the most reliable estimates consistent with the economies of a modest sample' (Pymont and Welch, 1986).

Once the data have been analysed, it is necessary to validate the results by measuring if the ex-factory shipment of goods is recorded by the audit (Pymont and Welch, 1986). Validation is necessary, they continue as, 'it forms the basis of the level of confidence that can be put upon the results, indicates the adjustment necessary to account for differences and, of prime importance, the interpretation and use that can be made of the information about the market as a whole and competition, both strategically and tactically (Pymont and Welch, 1986).

This validation of results should be made at the very least in six-monthly intervals or more frequently for seasonal products. Moving annual totals of consumer sales and factory shipments should always be used to give a stable picture of the market and 'avoid freak results caused by the inevitable time lapse between shipment and delivery to the store' (Pymont and Welch, 1986). The formula is:

$$\frac{\text{Changes in stocks} + \text{Consumer sales}}{\text{Factory shipment}}$$

The lack of co-operation on the part of some large multiples or the lack of representativeness in a sample based on a shop index will affect the final figures on sales activity – allowances for this unaudited sales volume must be made in order to give as clear a view of the market as possible.

The benefits of trade audits are mainly realised in the long term since it is inherently a continuous research vehicle. Its major benefit lies in the fact that management can observe long-term trends in the market, and as a result can base future marketing decisions on relatively accurate predictions of future market activity.

Invoice analysis

In certain product classes, such as ethical pharmaceuticals it is possible for the stock counting procedure of a retail audit to be avoided, and instead, replaced by the technique of invoice analysis. Invoice analysis is the analysis of the paperwork of the distribution system, such as delivery notes and invoices. It is particularly suitable in two areas:

1. When, by the very nature of the product class, the retailer orders only what he knows will sell over a period of time.
2. When the product has a relatively short shelf life and therefore what is ordered will probably be guaranteed to sell.

Invoice analysis has the very attractive advantages of being less expensive than a trade audit, and having a faster turnround of results as the analysis will, presumably, be less complex.

Distribution checks

The main technique used for conducting distribution checks is observation, which provides a very economical means of monitoring a brand's performance. A great deal of information on 'distribution levels, pricing policies . . . (and) point-of-sale activity' can be collected (Pymont and Welch, 1986). What then, are the advantages of distribution checks over trade audits?

The answer lies in the size and composition of the sample being used, together with the analysis of the market. Whilst a trade audit provides information on distribution, the 'diagnostic detail required by a manufacturer' is not, in the main, provided in a retail audit. A distribution check will provide information not only from the broad classification of type of shops which stock the product, such as multiples or grocers, but also on *specific* chains of stores which stock the product, such as Asda or William Low's. Since the data collection method is observation, the auditors can operate without the same degree of co-operation of management needed by a retail audit.

Pymont and Welch (1986) list the range of measurements which can be offered by distribution checks, and these include average prices for particular brands and the range of prices of those brands; the degree of overlap in the stocking of various brands; the actual measurement of shelf space given to a particular brand; a count of 'facings' per brand, i.e. the number of pack fronts/pack sides visible on a shelf; the presence of promoted brands, such as special offers; and the incidence of different types of point of sale material, displays, demonstrations, taking place within the store.

A number of market research agencies offer syndicated distribution checks and these are normally carried out on a monthly or bi-monthly basis in fast moving consumer goods (fmcg) markets or quarterly in other markets. Owing to the nature of the fieldwork, clients can expect to pay a great deal less than they would in a retail audit − 'a matter of a few pence per item checked per outlet in many cases' (Pymont and Welch, 1986). The major disadvantage of the service is it is carried out on predetermined fieldwork dates, which may not suit a client if he wants to monitor a particular promotional campaign, which does not really fit in with these dates — although alternative dates can be arranged at a higher cost in most cases.

Price checks

The procedures for operating price checks are similar to those used in distribution checks, but there are some major differences between these two research services with respect to the application of the data collected.

'Most retail stores operate on two and four weekly cycles, whereby all stores or bands of stores in the chain should carry the same price "promotions"' (Pymont and Welch, 1986). In order to assess the effectiveness of these promotions, for example, in terms of an increase in sales, bonuses to intermediaries, and the extent to which intermediaries' bonuses are passed on to consumers, it is important for the manufacturer to obtain current data, which focuses on current activity in the market, rather than waiting for a few weeks before the effectiveness of the campaign can be assessed, as is the case in a distribution check. In this way, the manufacturer can renegotiate deals with the intermediary on current terms if he is not happy with the way in which the campaign is being conducted, rather than expressing his displeasure after a few weeks.

Feature checks

These checks are measures of the quality of point of sale activity carried on within stores. The effectiveness of point of sale activity can be monitored by measuring the sales of the product before the promotion begins, either by the use of retail audits or the volume of ex-factory sales and comparing it with the actual sales when the promotion is complete. It is possible for the data to be collected from only a small sample, and hence providing a fast turnround of results, as the campaigns tend to run across the board.

Panel research

There are many marketing research agencies which operate consumer panels in the UK, the most notable being the Attwood Consumer Panel, the AGB Television Consumer Audit and the AGB Index. Parfitt (1986), found:

there are two common distinguishing characteristics with regard to the type of data they are designed to obtain and the method of obtaining it:

1. Panels are based on a representative sample of individuals or households from the universe being studied . . . Each individual or household panel member records (or permits the recording of) their complete activity in some factual aspect of consumer behaviour, such as their purchases in a defined range of consumer products or their television viewing.
2. This measurement is ideally a continuous process over time, by virtue of retaining the same sample of respondents over the full period of measurement and obtaining from them a continuous and complete record of the required data. The collection of these data has, therefore, to be at regular and frequent intervals.

Panel research, therefore, is used to collect 'detailed and accurate information' about consumer behaviour and consumer characteristics. The purpose of this data is not to collect consumers' attitudes and opinions on what they would perhaps like to believe of themselves, but rather to gain factual information about what they actually purchase. Since panels monitor *actual purchasing behaviour*, they provide a higher degree of accuracy, than, for example, a one-off street interview, where consumer response may be somewhat biased. Panel research also offers the opportunity to 'understand the ways in which the consumer behaves under given stimuli' because of the depth of analysis of consumers' purchasing habits, made possible owing to the longer period of time available for data collection.

There are two main methods available for collecting the data – the home audit or the diary method.

Home audit

When a panel member agrees to participate in the panel survey, they accept two conditions of the study. First, an auditor is allowed to visit the panel member's home (usually once a week) to check what stock of a particular product (of the product category under research) they have in their home. Secondly, the panel member has to keep all the used packaging of the products she used within that week and to hand these to the auditor. The panel member also has to answer a questionnaire for the auditor at this point.

Diary method

The diary method differs from the home audit as the panel member must record all the purchases of the whole family of a given product category in a preprinted diary. This information is then sent back to the research agency, usually once a week. The panel member may or may not be visited by the researcher, although it is generally a good policy for the research company to do so. This would help answer any queries or doubts the panel member may have, and will help maintain and encourage her enthusiasm for the job.

Parfitt (1986) made a useful summary of the advantages and disadvantages of both these types of data collection, these being as follows:

1. The postal diary method is less expensive to run than home audits, as fewer personal calls by interviewers to the panel home are needed. In addition, a wider geographical spread is easier to use with the postal diary, as they are not dependent on interviewers reaching the panel home.
2. The initial panel recruitment is normally higher for the home audit than the diary method, perhaps due to the relative ease of recording purchases.
3. The continuity of panel membership is usually higher for home audit panels than for the postal diary method. A 'drop-out' rate of 25–30 per cent can be expected from a postal diary panel, compared with 10 per cent for the home audit panel. This is when establishing some form of regular contact with the respondent especially in postal diary collection helps reduce this 'drop-out' rate.
4. Home audits are dependent on getting regular access to the home for data collection, which postal diaries are not. Postal diaries, however, pose a problem when the respondent neglects to post the diary on time, and the research company needs the information quickly.
5. Both methods have different advantages and disadvantages with regards to the collection of certain types of data. For example, home audits record any types of promotions and special offers of a product with greater accuracy than a diary, as the information is recorded on the pack. However, a diary will probably pick up the purchases of other family members which is an important consideration in the collection of purchase data.
6. The diary method records a wider range of goods and services than a home audit, simply because the home audit relies on physical evidence of purchase. Therefore, services such as hairdressing and theatre visits may be missed out completely – although the researcher can ask specific questions to cover these types of purchases, or introduce a diary to monitor these purchases.

Although both these data collection methods have their limitations, they have shown 'over long periods in Great Britain to provide accurate market share and trend data over a wide range of product fields' (Parfitt, 1986).

There are a number of other panel types which can be established. Clients may specially commission one-off projects for testing specific marketing problems regarding a product and these are known as short-term consumer purchasing panels. Alternatively, a client may wish to measure product consumption, and may specially commission a consumer product consumption panel for this purpose. Both these types of panels are used for one-off projects for a specific client's use, and do not come under the syndicated sources category, which we are discussing presently.

However, a variation of the consumer purchasing panel is the *shopping panel for pre-launch predication measurements* — which again are available as short-term tailor-made panels (for example, the MPL Brandshare Service) or by a permanent syndicated panel (such as the Mini-Test Service). Both services are designed to expose the housewife to test products which have not, as yet, been launched on the national level.

The syndicated service, which is of interest to us, consists of having a 'demographically controlled sample of housewives in a town' who have agreed to buy products from a travelling shop. The travelling shop is run by the research agency and carries the normal range of goods within a product field at competitive prices, as well as those products being tested. The housewife is supplied with a brochure telling her of the range of products available and an order form which she needs to complete when she is purchasing anything. This order form is used for the same purposes as a panel diary. Although these panels 'achieve an abnormally high penetration for the new brand, compared with what would normally happen in a real test market situation', they do give a realistic impression of the likely repeat purchasing rate the brand would achieve in the market. It is on this assessment that the likelihood of success for a product is based.

Television viewing panels

This technique was first introduced by Nielsen in the States, and was copied by TAM in the UK when commercial television first began here. The service is now operated by AGB on behalf of BARB in the UK. The panel are selected from those households which own a television set. A meter is attached to the set which 'records the time when the set is turned on or off and the station it is tuned to, and aided by push-button recording, who is in the room with the set' (Parfitt, 1986). The data collected tries to 'estimate the total household viewing audiences to each channel in each ITV area, and also the demographic composition of these audiences' (Parfitt, 1986). The relatively small degree of participation of the panel ensures the recruitment rate is higher for these panels, than for a consumer panel, and there is usually a lower level of 'drop out' occurring.

Whilst panels provide a high degree of accuracy regarding the behaviour of certain sectors of the community, Parfitt (1986) cautions care in three minority areas which do not usually receive adequate coverage, and therefore, questions the representativeness of the sample used for the panel – the very prosperous, the very poor (especially the poor and old) and the 'fluctuating and transitory households composed of mainly young single men (or women) living particularly in the centres of the larger cities' (Parfitt, 1986).

Analysing panel data

Panels generate a great deal of data which has to be turned into pertinent information before it is of use to the manager. Parfitt (1986) classified the analyses of data into three groups:

1. Standard trend analyses produced at regular intervals, usually four weekly, which show the progress of the market and of its principal brands.
2. 'Simple' special analyses designed to show the anatomy of the characteristics of purchasing behaviour and of the consumers. These are not usually produced on a continuous basis but rather as and when required, usually when some significant change is thought to have occurred in the market which requires further study.
3. 'Complex' special analyses designed to examine the fundamental patterns of consumer behaviour, particularly in relation to specific bursts of major marketing activity. (Parfitt, 1986)

Panels can help analyse

1. Purchases by size of pack
2. quantity of the product bought on each purchase occasion
3. day of the week on which purchases are made
4. extent to which different individual consumers purchase products with the same 'family' brand name e.g. Colmans, Ajax, Heinz, etc.
5. the limits of duplication between brands by which consumers confine their purchases to a limited group of the total brands available.
6. the extent of purchasing 'own label' brands compared with nationally advertised brands, among consumers who shop at supermarkets.
7. loyalty to flavours rather than brands in certain food fields
8. price consciousness by demographic groups
9. the relationship of quantity of purchases to size of household. (Parfitt, 1986)

Hall tests

One alternative to panel research used to collect data regarding consumers' opinion on new products is to run a 'Hall test'. A hall test is commonly used for product testing or testing other aspects of the marketing mix, such as advertising, price, name and package testing. A representative sample of target consumers are recruited, usually in a shopping centre and brought into a conveniently located hall. Here they are exposed to the test material and asked questions about it. (Crouch, 1985)

A number of differences exist between the panel research method and hall tests, although both have the similar purpose of testing consumers' reactions to marketing mix variables.

Hall tests are used to invite respondents to express their *immediate preferences* between similar types of products which use different marketing mix variables, whereas the panel member may be allowed to form their opinions over a longer test period.

The relationship between the research company and the respondent did not exist before the respondent was invited to participate in the test, and therefore prospecting respondents in hall tests is a much less expensive process than interviewing prospective panel members. Normally, respondents in a hall test only have to fit certain requirements and have half an hour spare to discuss the product, whereas the process of collecting panel members is very much a lengthy and expensive business.

The length of time a respondent spends with an interviewer is usually only about 30 minutes, in comparison with a panel, which can take months. In this way therefore, results are analysed much more quickly in a hall test than in a panel.

The interviewer is on hand to answer any queries the respondent has immediately in a hall test, which panels cannot guarantee.

The entire procedure is conducted under a very controlled atmosphere, where respondents try the product under laboratory test conditions – by contrast, panels allow the respondent to use the product in the manner in which they normally use the product, and therefore the research company cannot fully control if the product is being used in its most desirable way.

Hall tests are used when:

an immediate reaction is more appropriate, and often more practical, than in-home trial. Examples of these include:

— the choice of perfume for a product
— choice between alternative pack designs
— taste tests between a large number of alternative formulations
— preference for different visual designs
— choice of colours/patterns for such things as paint, wallpaper, floor coverings. (Advertising Research Unit, 1987).

Omnibus hall-testing facilities are available which enable researchers to syndicate hall-testing costs. The advantage of these services is that they enable more complex stimuli to be used than in the conventional omnibus . . . . Costs are usually calculated not on a per-question basis (as in the case of normal omnibus surveys) but on a time basis, so that participating clients would buy a fixed amount of interviewing time on the survey. (Davies, 1986)

Omnibus surveys

Often a manufacturer will want to ask only one or two very simple questions, but will want to ask them of a large number of people, in order to provide very reliable results.

In the interests of time and economy, several groups of such questions about different types of products can be included in one questionnaire. This is called an omnibus. (Advertising Research Unit, 1987)

These small questionnaires are usually on completely different subject areas which are pooled together to form a large questionnaire. The time and economic benefits of participating in an omnibus mainly arise from savings in locating and securing the participation of an appropriate interviewee – the most expensive and time consuming aspect of this type of field research. Some market research agencies run omnibus services (every weekend, in the case of Audience Selection's Telephone Omnibus Service) which provide access to a large and diverse sample group who have agreed to participate in this type of research. This can give the client a choice of omnibus survey which will have the most appropriate sample composition for his needs, although the choice is limited to what the agency can offer. The cost of an omnibus depends on the type of question being asked, and the complexity of the analysis when the fieldwork is over. The client can expect to pay:

— a fixed entry fee
— a fixed cost per precoded question (usually with a restriction on the number of codes)
— a fixed cost for open-ended questions (higher than for precoded questions and again usually with a restriction on the number of codes)
— usually, extra costs for show cards. (Davies, 1986)

It is also worth noting that 'most omnibus surveys operate to a fixed time schedule and the client is provided with a deadline for receipt of the questionnaire by the research agency. Thus, if the research agency does not receive the questionnaire by the deadline date then it cannot be included on the omnibus for that period' (Davies, 1986). The deadline is normally one week before the fieldwork begins. The client should always build in some form of introduction to his questions before the interviewer asks the questions. Owing to a number of unrelated topics being queried, the client does not know where his questions are to be placed in the questionnaire. Respondents may become 'fatigued' and irritated if they are concentrating on a particular area of interest, and the interviewer is off on another tangent altogether without having the courtesy to explain the change in topic. It is for this reason, that 'complex questions and question-routing should be avoided . . . as they are generally beyond the scope of this technique' (Davies, 1986).

The coding of the questionnaire should be specified by the client before the analysis begins, and should not be left to the agency to decide. This is because many research agencies limit 'the number of coding positions available for open-ended questions' (Davies, 1986), unless the client is prepared to pay more for the service. The project is normally analysed according to a 'demographic and area breakdown as part of the standard cost' (Davies, 1986), but again, the project may be analysed according to a client's particular needs of the project at a higher cost.

Omnibus surveys are particularly useful in certain applications. Davies (1986), identifies five separate situations when this is the case:

1. *Minority samples* – this is particularly useful when seeking to question a sub-group within the population at large, such as those users of a minority brand.
2. *Sequential or cumulative sampling* – since omnibus surveys are carried out at regular intervals, it becomes possible to build up a preferred sample over time. In this way, the sample can be called upon in follow-up interviews, which would save the client a great deal of time in locating the desired members of the population. In addition, the flexibility offered by the cumulative sampling approach in generating information to a specified level of accuracy can be offered to the extent of a high degree of statistical accuracy.
3. *Split runs* – one specific application of the split run technique (i.e. exposing two halves of the sample to two different stimuli and the differences noted) is in piloting questionnaires. An omnibus survey using the split run technique can, for example be used to test two alternative forms of a question prior to the commissioning of the main fieldwork stage for a conventional *ad hoc* project.
4. *Time series* – omnibus surveys are particularly useful in measuring trends over time, although in some situations, caution has to be given if continuous interviewing is an essential requirement of the research project. A number of research agencies offer discounts for the regular use of omnibus surveys.
5. *International research* – where multinational studies are required, simultaneous research can be conducted in a number of different countries. An international research agency should be able to provide this facility which

then enables the client to obtain comparable results between countries, rather than designing a series of separate *ad hoc* studies in each country.

Benefits and limitations of omnibus surveys

Benefits

The main advantage of omnibus surveys is the cost savings involved as the costs are shared over a large number of clients. However, the client must be aware that there may come a time when the break-even point of conducting an *ad hoc* project will be reached, if the client intends to use omnibus surveys regularly. When a large study is being considered, the client should closely examine both types of service.

The cost-benefit of reaching a particular sub-group of the population was mentioned previously – this may not always be the case and the client should always look to alternative means of reaching the preferred sample.

Time savings are another benefit of omnibus surveys and Davies (1986) classified these into the following areas:

— The work of preparation before undertaking fieldwork can be considerably reduced on an omnibus survey since the sampling and fieldwork will have already been organised.
— Omnibus surveys usually have a larger number of interviewers than an equivalent *ad hoc* survey and this can reduce the fieldwork time necessary. This is particularly true when large samples are involved.
— Analysis of the results is usually quicker on an omnibus survey because the analysis routines and procedures are standardised.
— It can happen that because of crowded schedules the availability of interviewers for an *ad hoc* project may be limited and time may be lost waiting for the appropriate interviewers to be available. (Davies, 1986)

Finally, omnibus surveys may provide a greater degree of accuracy in sampling procedures.

Limitations

Davies (1986) identified a number of limitations, the more notable being:

— the length of the questionnaire may be constrained.
— Complex questions or detailed probing will be difficult.
— not all research problems will be helped by omnibus research – especially those which require a degree of experimentation.
— There are limitations on the type and number of stimuli which can be used.

— The client is constrained by the inflexible timing in the execution of the fieldwork, but some 'shopping around' for different services may overcome this problem.
— The client does not know of the other questions being included in the questionnaire, and has no influence over the positioning of his questions. This is important in two sets of circumstances:

1. When the information being collected is of an attitudinal nature rather than a factual (behavioural) nature, and
2. where time series data are being collected and the order of questions may affect the comparability of the data from a series of questionnaires.

All of these problems should be fully discussed with the client service executive in charge of the project before the research is commissioned.

Advantages of syndicated research services

The main advantages of syndicated research services may be summarised as:
1. Clients will have access to major research projects at a fraction of the total research project's costs.
2. The client, if he asks the right questions, will have a clear idea of his performance vis-à-vis competitors.
3. The research will be conducted by an independent body.
4. Syndication provides the opportunity to research difficult, expensive and time-consuming topics.
5. The research findings should be provided fairly quickly after the research proposal has been agreed upon, and certainly much more quickly than if the client were to do it himself, as the marketing research agency will have more manpower available and more expertise in the research field.
6. Because the agency has to present a report which will cater to clients with differing needs and expertise, it is likely that more effort will be expended on making the presentation full, clear and unambiguous.
7. Syndicated reports provide a sound basis for developing more focused and confidential research, specific to the users own needs.

Limitation of syndicated research services

Naturally, syndicated research services have some drawbacks and these may be summarised as:

1. There are a large number of marketing research agencies willing to provide this service. The client may have difficulty in deciding which is the best agency for its purposes.
2. Lack of knowledge regarding who initiated the research programme – the confidentiality of the client is normally maintained.
3. Lack of knowledge regarding what other clients have requested in the research programme, for example, in terms of market intelligence. It will also be unclear as to what the marketing research agency may divulge to competitors regarding information on the client.
4. Every company has access to the majority of this information, and therefore no unique piece of intelligence will be bought.
5. Will the agency's research methodology be sound? The client will have all the problems of evaluating the research that has been undertaken as you would normally do with secondary sources, but this time a much higher price will have to be paid.

Summary

From the variety of syndicated research services reviewed in this chapter, it has become clear this area is 'big business' for many marketing research agencies. The growth in this area is a result of managers' need for a fast turnround of information on areas which would prove to be too difficult, time consuming and expensive for them to undertake themselves. Syndicated research may be classified into the following areas – trade research, panel research, advertising evaluation research and omnibus surveys. The relative advantages and disadvantages of each have been covered in detail in the chapter. One final point should be made, however, on the role of the client service executive. The client should try to develop a good relationship with the executive who is in charge of the project, as very often the executive can be of assistance in giving ideas on how the data should be analysed if the client has any special problems which require special analyses to be undertaken.

References

Advertising Research Unit (1987) *Fieldwork Guide for Market Research Interviewers* (Glasgow: The University of Strathclyde).
Baker, Michael J. (ed.) (1984) *The Macmillan Dictionary of Marketing and Advertising* (London: Macmillan).

Crouch, Sunny (1985) *Marketing Research for Managers* (London: Pan Book Company).

Davies, Richard (1986) 'Omnibus Surveys', in Robert Worcester and John Downham (eds) *Consumer Market Research Handbook* (London: McGraw-Hill) pp. 231–44.

Hague, P.N. (1987) *The Industrial Market Research Handbook* 2nd edn (London: Kegan Paul).

Kinnear, Thomas C. and Taylor, James R. (1987) *Marketing Research – An Applied Approach* (New York: McGraw-Hill).

Lucey, T. (1987) *Management Information Systems* 5th edn (D.P. Publications Ltd).

Parfitt, John (1986) 'Panel Research', in Robert Worcester and John Downham (eds) *Consumer Market Research Handbook* (London: McGraw-Hill) pp. 192–230.

Pymont, Brian and Welch, Gillian (1986), in Robert Worcester and John Downham (eds) *Consumer Market Research Handbook* (London: McGraw-Hill) pp. 167–92.

CHAPTER 12

Information technology and marketing research

Introduction

The paradox of information technology is that whilst the phrase is upon everyone's lips there is surprisingly little of it to be found in practice save in a relatively uncomplicated and unsophisticated form. Thus whilst there are frequent references to the concept of the paperless office 'one per desk' (a reference to the fact that every manager and office worker would have a personal computer or terminal on their desk) electronic mail and the like all the evidence points to an explosion in the volume of paper-based information in circulation. This phenomenon is reflected in Figure 12.1 which is taken from *Industrial Market Research Handbook* (Hague, 1987) which is a representation of life-cycles in methods of copying and shows that with the advent of xerography there has been an exponential growth in the demand for copied material. Similarly the growth of information technology, which has been defined by the Department of Trade and Industry as 'the acquisition, processing, storage and dissemination of vocal, pictorial, textual and numeric information by a microelectronics based combination of computing and telecommunications', was projected to lead to mass unemployment in office based occupations. However, the job of clerk is now the single largest occupation in the United States of America and continues to grow. Just 100 years ago the single largest source of employment was farm work which is now well down in the list of major occupations. Indeed, this trend is to be observed throughout the world where employment in knowledge and service based occupations is displacing all forms of manual occupation in terms of size and importance.

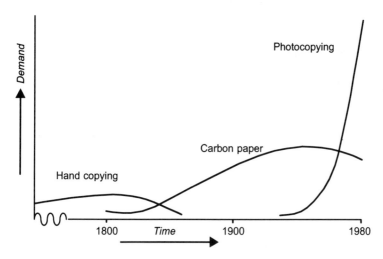

FIGURE 12.1   Life-cycles in methods of copying

Applications of information technology

Consideration of these trends would seem to suggest that information technology will have a very similar impact but as an innovation it is still at a very early stage in its life-cycle. In the great majority of instances the application of computing to business decision making has been confined to an extension of earlier data processing applications. Lucey (1987) suggests that:

> computers can be used to best advantage for processing information which has the following characteristics: a) a number of interacting variables b) speed is an important factor, c) there are reasonably accurate values, d) accuracy of output is important, e) operations are repetitive, f) large amounts of data exists.

These conditions or characteristics describe well the accounting and other records kept by commercial organisations. It is to these applications which the power of the computer has been harnessed, a development which is unsurprising on the grounds that 'innovations pursue the line of least resistance'. In other words innovations will be adopted most quickly where they can be substituted most effectively for an existing method or solution to a consumption need. It seems likely, therefore, that having established the benefits which computing can bring to business management the extension of computing and telecommunications from basic database and data handling applications into decision support systems (DSS) will soon follow.

Lucey (1987) states that:

> there is abundant evidence from numerous surveys both in the UK and USA that existing MIS, often used in advanced computer equipment, have had relatively little success in providing management with the information it needs. The typical reasons discovered for this include the following:
>
> — lack of management involvement with design of the MIS,
> — narrow and/or inappropriate emphasis of the computer system,
> — undue concentration on low level data processing applications particularly in the accounting area,
> — lack of management knowledge of computers,
> — poor appreciation by information specialists of management's true information requirements and of organisational problems,
> — lack of top management support.

Support for these findings is to be found in a recent case study describing the development of home office banking systems (HOBS) by the Bank of Scotland. Writing in the Summer 1989 edition of the *Journal of Marketing Management*, Lannon and Scarborough discovered that the application of IT in the bank was being impeded for most of the reasons cited by Lucey. Perhaps the major problem of all was that management was seeking to use IT in a tactical way and was ignoring its strategic potential. Given that the Bank of Scotland has very few outlets in England and Wales and its wish to move into this market required either that it replicated the branch network of the other major competitors or that it provided an alternative means of access to the banking services which it had to offer. HOBS offered this potential. It is interesting that Lannon and Scarborough report senior management in the Bank of Scotland as stating that this was an area where no marketing research could provide any sensible input to the strategic decision. But, once top management had perceived the opportunity IT offered it adopted it as a main plank in its competitive strategy.

Indeed it is probably true to say that the organisations with the greatest experience of the application and management of information technology are the world's major financial institutions. Consideration of their experience underlines that while return on their investment has been disappointing there is equally wide agreement that *not* to have invested would have resulted in a loss of competitive edge and a decline in market position. Much the same is likely to be true of the adoption of IT in marketing and market research – while such investment may lead to only a transient comparative advantage failure to invest could lead to a permanent loss of market share.

While banks may have come late to marketing they have responded with enthusiasm. Further, because of their experience with large scale data processing with account management they are familiar with the potential of information technology and have the resources to extend it to the marketing realm – particularly in the growing battle for 'retail' financial services. In doing so they face two major problems. The first has already been referred to in our comment on Lannon and Scarborough's case study, namely, the organisational and attitudinal barriers to extending IT from a control function to an input to decision making. The second is that early entrants to the field of information technology often face significant problems and expense in updating their software. As Alan Kane observed in a *Financial Times* survey (3 December 1987)

> the banks, trusts and building societies have a common software problem. They have an abundance of elderly software, most of it creaking at the joints and out of tune with today's competitive requirements.
>
> Their files, for example, are mainly arranged by account rather than customer. Such an arrangement makes it extremely difficult to readily extract information about customers for the purposes, for example, of special product initiatives or cross selling.

As with other realms of marketing the main challenge is the development of an integrated database. In 1987, for example, Lloyds Bank announced an initial commitment to invest £570 million to upgrade all the bank's branch technology and build a new integrated voice and data network (*Financial Times*, 3 December 1987). Among the main benefits expected from the project are speedy and integrated access to any customer file, improved marketing information, sales prompts, assistance with lending control and the ability to provide self service banking and interfaces with Lloyds' other systems. According to the *Financial Times*:

> Using a computer to assemble and analyse information such as customer age groups, income levels, occupations, savings, home ownership and so on, provides a valuable marketing tool. Successful targeting of different age and income groups for such services as pension schemes, mortgages, life assurance policies and savings plans depends on first identifying the relevant groups and having on file sufficient information to target accurately.

Clearly the same is true of marketing any other good or service and emphasises the importance of creating or gaining access to suitable databases.

From the above discussion it is clear that information technology is an enabling innovation in that it allows some tasks to be done more easily, more quickly, more efficiently and, possibly, more effectively. In his contribution to *The Marketing Handbook* (Thomas, 1989) Alan Melkman proposes four broad areas of IT application as shown in Table 12.1. These may be described as follows:

TABLE 12.1   An IT applications framework

		Marketing activities	
		existing	new
Focus of activity	Internal	1 Enhancing operating efficiency	2 Changed methods
	External	3 Enhancing customer service	4 Market innovation

1. *Enhancing operating efficiency* ' . . . those marketing activities which are already carried out in one form or another within the company. Typically, these include maintenance of customer records, budgeting, preparing and making presentations and analysing sales statistics, scheduling meetings and so on'.
2. *Changed methods* ' . . . enabling the Marketing Department to carry out internal functions which were not possible before'. This will usually start with an extension of applications in the first quadrant such as using databases for segmentation and positioning studies, more sophisticated forecasting and modelling, better and faster communication with a field sales force, etc.
3. *Enhancing customer service*   This will be made possible by better and faster communication with customers the application of CATI to obtain timely and relevant data on changing market needs, etc.
4. *Marketing innovation*   The use of video cassettes to make sales presentations and demonstrate product use, access to and use of large on-line databases such as DataScan, Information Line and Dialog; direct mail services, market identification studies such as Pinpoint, Acorn and Market Location. EPOS (Electronic Point of Sale) has already had a significant impact on retail store management and is likely to develop into EFTPOS (Electronic Funds Transfer at Point of Sale). Reference has already been made to HOBS and it can only be a matter of time before other financial service institutions follow suit. Similarly the growth of cable and satellite television is likely to increase the growth of telemarketing.

Melkman's four areas of IT application illustrate the likely sequence which organisations will follow in exploiting the potential benefits of information technology. A constant and recurring theme of this book is that increased competition has resulted in much greater awareness of the value of timely and relevant data. In parallel with other changes these have helped to accelerate the take up of IT. Amongst these changes may be numbered:

(a) The availability of much less expensive hardware.
(b) The availability of much more sophisticated software.
(c) Greater user friendliness in both.
(d) Growing familiarity with visible applications and all the output of IT based systems, e.g. detailed retail receipts generated by EPOS systems, access to and use of automatic telling machines (ATM), extensive use of word processing, etc.
(e) The availability of more skilled and trained manpower.
(f) The establishment of specialist service and software houses.

A description of the services offered by one of the leading companies in the field – Pulse Train Marketing Systems Ltd – will help illustrate the scope and contribution which IT can make to the marketing function.

The Research Machine

Pulse Train Technology Ltd (PTT) is an international company specialising in services and software for survey research and telephonic business applications. It is a leading supplier of data collection and tabulation systems to specialist computer bureaux and survey research organisations in 14 countries and is the creator of a new generation of integrated hardware and software which they have designated THE RESEARCH MACHINE.

The thinking behind The Research Machine is that early applications of IT tended to remove control from the decision maker with the result that research tended to become a stereotyped activity with canned solutions looking for the appropriate problem to solve. With The Research Machine the user has instant and personal control over all aspects of the research process. Using the system it is possible to undertake research from the users own desk. The software allows the user to design their own research instrument – the questionnaire – check out with the user or client via electronic mail or on-line access to high quality printer, select a sample and commence interviewing for a pilot study within minutes of getting the approval of the questionnaire.

Figure 12.2 provides a diagrammatic representation of the major modules contained in The Research Machine. At the centre of the system is the researcher who drives and manages the system. At the same time the software provides the capability for sophisticated data-processing tasks which may be beyond the competence and expertise of the researcher himself. However The Research Machine provides a single integrated system which is capable of serving the needs of both the researcher and the support specialists.

While The Research Machine is itself an integrated entity it is also capable of further integration to standard packages such as the SAS and SPSS statistical and graphics packages and can also provide largely automatic interfaces with

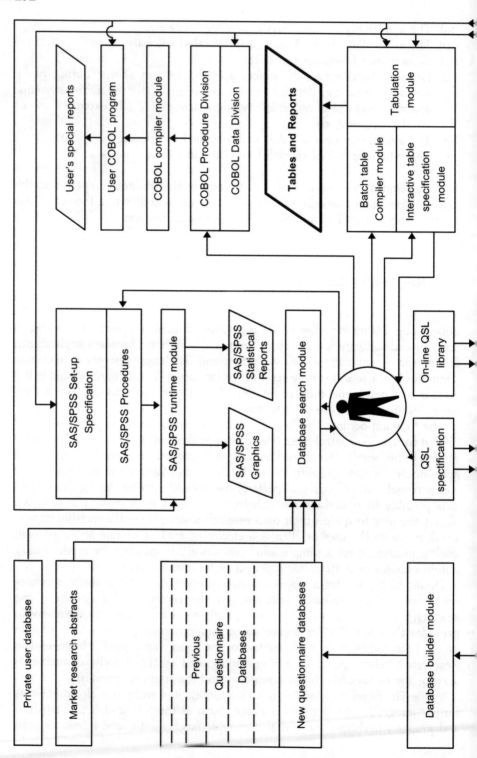

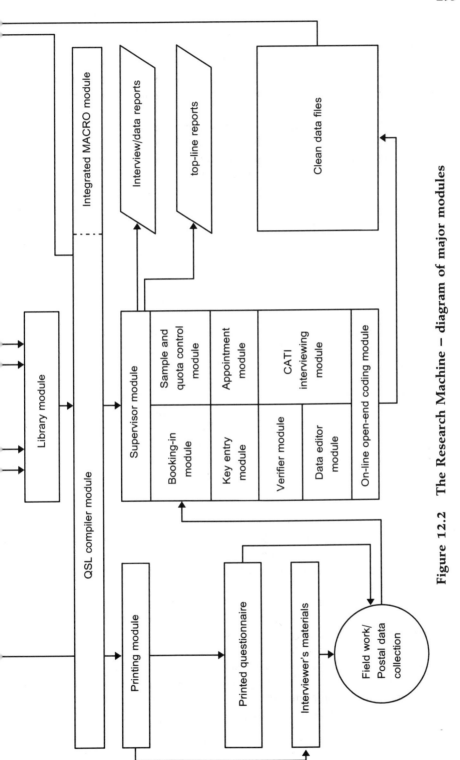

Figure 12.2 The Research Machine – diagram of major modules

the user's own software. The system also has the major benefit that while it is compatible with industry standard modern conventions it is also compatible with older standards as well. Further, if the user is currently using multipunch card formats and data in their existing installation they can still use The Research Machine software immediately and convert the more convenient character reference formats at their leisure.

The designers claim that the real corner stone of the system is a new special computer language which they have developed called the QUESTIONNAIRE SPECIFICATION LANGUAGE or QSL. QSL is a language which was designed from the ground up to be used for research applications. Its objective is to enable the user to write and design research questions and is designed to be easy to learn and use. It is a simple free format language and does not need special control forms. You can write out the QSL notation on any convenient piece of paper or type it directly into the computer via a VDU. The questions generated may be used for both printed questionnaires or for presentation on computer assisted telephone interviewing VDU screens.

Using The Research Machine it is claimed that once you have written your QSL specification then you can do all of the following things:

- Start conducting a CATI survey. You can send the completed specification from your own terminal to the interviewing room and then watch selected interviews taking place from your own terminal!
- Produce a publication quality printed questionnaire, with multicolumn formats, grids of any description whatsoever, attitude scales, etc. You can forget about boring details like question numbers, column and code assignments, pagination and layout, etc. The Research Machine will do all of these things for you, automatically.
- Produce a file of interviewer's lists and prompting materials, which are cross referenced to the printed questionnaire and lettered or numbered automatically.
- Book in your returned questionnaires as they come in from the field (or post), carrying out QSL specified quota controls automatically.
- Start key-entry and coding. No key-entry specifications have to be written by a supervisor. You do not need to specify a list of edit checks. They are all built into the QSL specification, and control the entry and coding processes automatically.
- Produce (when the data are collected) an elegant top-line report. This is the printed questionnaire with the columns and codes removed, and counts and percentages in their place.
- Produce a questionnaire database, which is added to a permanent data base of all surveys you have ever carried out. The Research Machine has a special high-speed searching module that enables you to see and review any or all questions on any topic that you have ever researched. You do not have to prepare an index. It is all automatic.

- Make additions to the question library (which you may have used in the first place), allowing your QSL specifications to be used again in future without any retyping.
- Go straight into tabulations (when the data are available) using the on-line menu driven system. You do not need to learn another language for this. Just call up the system, and select what you want from the menu. You do not have to enter labels and text as they are taken from your QSL specification. The menus themselves are tailored to your personal requirements for analysis, and can be changed or added to at any time by your own data-processing staff.
- Use packages such as SAS or SPSS if you have them installed, and produce factor analyses, regression analyses, cluster analyses, or many other kinds of statistical analyses. Your data file will automatically be compatible with those industry standard packages, and the Research Machine will have written the major part of your SAS or SPSS set up specification for you!
- Carry out simple analyses of your major research findings and use the extensive on-line graphics facilities in SAS and/or SPSS to produce presentation quality professional graphics. You can preview the results on your own VT240 or VT241 colour graphics terminal, and if you are happy with the results, produce hard copy on a plotter, or go directly to 35 mm slides and overhead projector films.
- Produce special analyses, written for you by your own data-processing department, in the widely used COBOL language. All that you have to do to use such a facility on a repeated basis is adopt conventions for naming your key questions. You can change your questionnaire as much as you want, but the COBOL program should NOT have to be changed. The Research Machine actually writes out the data-division COBOL source code, which is merely tacked on the procedure division (the report part). The two parts are recompiled, linked and run to give you your own special reports on the new data.

QSL was designed after careful analyses of the known and likely future requirements of users. This research indicated that it would not be possible to design a menu driven system for questionnaire design that had sufficient flexibility. Research questionnaires are simply too diverse and it was also apparent that the single language offered major benefits in accuracy and efficiency throughout the entire research process from conception, design and execution through to analyses and interpretation. The designers also started from the premise that the researcher was not a computer expert but that they were likely to be brighter than average and motivated to do their job as well as they could. Thus, to accommodate all the technical problems involved in question construction and questionnaire design discussed in Chapter 7 QSL provides access to an on-line library of previously written QSL constructions access to which ensures that the questionnaire conforms with the technical requirements.

It is claimed that the basic QSL language can be learned in one day and this clearly creates enormous opportunities for the organisation to undertake its own in-house research. This facility is greatly enhanced by other modules in the software package. Of particular significance is the database creation and searching module which provides the facility to build up databases and search them at very high speed. A further facility is that upon payment of a modest fee to the Market Research Society the user can have access to a magnetic tape of the market research abstracts compiled by the MRS which go back to 1965 and are the only series of abstracts published anywhere in the world which cover all fields of marketing and advertising research as well as relevant papers in statistics, psychology and sociology. Nearly 400 papers and articles are abstracted each year from some 40 different English language journals. The abstracts include as regular section headings: survey techniques; statistics; models and forecasting; attitude and behaviour research; personality and social psychology; communications; advertising and media research; specific applications of research; industrial market research; market research and general applications; and new product development.

A third major module of The Research Machine is concerned with data entry and coding. As a technical aspect of marketing research this has not been discussed in any detail in this text which is intended largely for the user. However, the beauty of The Research Machine module is that it gives the ordinary user access to all of the essential expertise which is so important in ensuring that all data is coded and entered correctly into the database for subsequent analysis.

As can be seen from Figure 12.2 other major modules available in the software are the computer-assisted telephone interviewing module, a questionnaire design and printing module an example of which is provided as Figure 12.3 and the tabulation modules which provide all the facilities for analysing the data and presenting it in a format which can be incorporated immediately into a report. Examples of the output from this program are provided as Tables 12.2, 12.3, 12.4, 12.5 and 12.6.

In addition more sophisticated analyses and output in terms of quality graphics are provided through the interface between The Research Machine and other systems such as SAS and SPSS.

The Research Machine is designed for use on the VAX family of computers. These are available in a number of different configurations the smallest of which are available at quite a modest cost. As a major computer manufacturer DEC provides extensive support and maintenance systems as well as providing access to the networking facility called Decnet which provides a worldwide information technology capability.

The foregoing description of The Research Machine has identified the benefits which may be obtained from an integrated system of this kind.

Personal details

Sex of respondent

Male 1   1

Female 2

Marital status of respondent

Married 2   1
Single 2

Divorced/Separated   3

Widowed   4

Age of respondent

18–29 3   1

30–39 2

40–49 3

50–59 . . . .

60+ 5

Age range	Total in H.H.
0–5	4 _|_|
6–12	5 _|_|
13–17	6 _|_|
18–24	7 _|_|
Grand total	8 _|_|

Accommodation classification

Local authority
Flat/house 9   1

Private flat 2

Private house
(terraced) 3

Private house
(S/Detached) . . . 4

Private house
(Detached) 5

Institutional
residential/other . 6

If head of household: What is your occupation?

If non-head of household:
What is the occupation
of the head of the
household?

If retired/widowed/unemployed:
What was the previous
occupation of the head of the
household/yourself?

Classify social group on
basis of head of household
occupation and accommodation
classification

AB 10   1

CI 2

C2 3

DE 4

Q1. Do you own a car or have the use of a car which you normally keep overnight at home?

No 11   1   CLOSE
Own a car 2   Q2.
Have use of a car . . 3

Q2. Do you personally choose the car, or have a major say in which car you have?

No 12   1   CLOSE
Yes 2   Q3.

Q3. On average, how many miles per year is the car driven?

| | | | | | | 13
Q4.

Q4. Can you tell me the age of the car, or the registration number?
Less than one year
old (D or E prefix)   14   1

One to two years
old (C prefix) 2
Q5.

Two to three years
old (B prefix) 3

More than three
years old (A prefix
or earlier) 4

Q5. When do you think the car you are now driving might be replaced?

In six months or
less 15   1   Q6.
Six months to a
year . . . . 2.
More than a year . . 3   CLOSE

IF DUE FOR REPLACEMENT IN YEAR OR LESS
Q6. Will the replacement car be a new car or a used car?

New car 16   1   Q7.
Used car 2   CLOSE
Uncertain 3

Q7. Which of the following car manufactures will you consider in your choice of a replacement? (Record in grid on next page)
READ LIST OUT TO INFORMANT

Q8. Which of the manufacturers manufactured the car you are driving now? (Record in grid on next page)

FIGURE 12.3   The Research Machine – example questionnaire

FIGURE 12.3 *continued*

OMNIDATA SURVEYS

Manufacturer	Q7. Will consider	Q8. Own it now
Audi	17 1,	18 1,
Austin-Rover	2,	2,
BMW	3,	3,
Citroen	4,	4,
Fiat	5,	5,
Ford	6,	6,
Honda	7,	7,
Jaguar	8,	8,
Mercedes-Benz	9,	9,
Peugeot	10,	10,
Porsche	11,	11,
Renault	12,	12,
Rover	13,	13,
Saab	14,	14,
Subaru	15,	15,
Talbot	16,	16,
Toyota	17,	17,
Vauxhall	18,	18,
Volkswagen	19,	19,
Volvo	20,	20,
Other	21,	21,

IF AUDI IS NOT MENTIONED IN Q7.
Q9. I notice you didn't mention Audi in your list. Can you tell me the reasons you didn't consider them?

Price too high   19 1   [CLOSE]

Not a British car   2,

Record all other reasons mentioned

3,	5,	7,	9,
4,	6,	8,	10,

IF AUDI HAS BEEN MENTIONED IN Q7.
Q10. As you mentioned Audi, can you tell me which Audi models you are considering or might consider? READ OUT LIST AND RECORD IN COLUMN 1 BELOW
Q11. For each Audi model mentioned in column 1, ask 'Are you considering the following optional extras?' ('s' means the item is standard on that model)

Audi model	Q10. Will consider	Q11. Optional extras considered/planned								
		Sun Roof	Elec. Windows	Alloy wheel	Metal paint	Leather seats	Power Steering	ABS braking	Cruise control	Air Condition
80 CL	20 1,	21 1,	22 1,	23 1,	24 1,	—	25 1,	—	—	—
80 Gl	2,	26 1,	s	27 1,	28 1,	—	29 1,	—	—	—
80 Turbo D.	3,	30 1,	31 1,	32 1,	33 1,	—	34 1,	—	—	—
80 Sport	4,	35 1,	36 1,	s	37 1,	—	—	—	—	—
80 Quattro	5,	38 1,	39 1,	s	40 1,	—	—	41 1,	—	—
90	6,	42 1,	s	43 1,	—	—	s	—	—	—
90 Quattro	7,	44 1,	s	s	—	—	s	45 1,	—	—
Coupe	8,	46 1,	47 1,	48 1,	49 1,	—	s	—	—	—
Coupe GT	9,	50 1,	s	s	s	51 1,	s	—	—	—
Coupe Quattro	10,	52 1,	s	s	s	53 1,	s	54 1,	—	—
100	11,	55 1,	56 1,	57 1,	58 1,	59 1,	s	—	—	—
100 CD	12,	60 1,	s	61 1,	s	62 1,	s	63 1,	64 1,	65 1,
100 Turb D.	13,	66 1,	67 1,	68 1,	69 1,	70 1,	s	71 1,	72 1,	—
100 Quattro	14,	s	s	s	s	73 1,	s	74 1,	s	75 1,
A.100	15,	76 1,	77 1,	78 1,	80 1,	s	—	—	—	—
A.100 CD	16,	81 1,	s	82 1,	s	83 1,	s	84 1,	85 1,	86 1,
A.100 Turb D.	17,	87 1,	88 1,	89 1,	90 1,	91 1,	s	—	92 1,	93 1,
A.100 Quattro	18,	s	s	s	s	94 1,	s	95 1,	s	96 1,
200	19,	97 1,	s	s	s	98 1,	s	99 1,	s	100 1,
200 Turbo	20,	s	s	s	s	101 1,	s	s	s	s
200 Quattro	21,	s	s	s	s	102 1,	s	s	s	s
The QUATTRO	22,	s	s	s	s	103 1,	s	s	—	s

TABLE 12.2   Consolidated brand awareness

Job 16/901   CARMELLA PROFILE TRACKING

Base: candy bar consumers

		SEX		CHILDREN	
	TOTAL	Male	Female	Yes	No
TOTAL	251	136	115	158	93
SLICKERS (Net)	247	135	112	156	91
	98.4	99.3	97.4	98.7	97.8
Any unaided (100%)	194	105	89	124	70
	77.3	77.2	77.4	78.5	75.3
Top of mind	50	28	22	32	18
	25.8	26.7	24.7	25.8	25.7
Other unaided	144	77	67	92	52
	74.2	73.3	75.3	74.2	74.3
Aided	53	30	23	32	21
	21.1	22.1	20.0	20.3	22.6
Tried	175	92	83	112	63
	69.7	67.6	72.2	70.9	67.7
CARMELLA (Net)	248	134	114	156	92
	98.8	98.5	99.1	98.7	98.9
Any unaided (100%)	132	78	54	89	43
	53.2	58.2	47.4	57.1	46.7
Top of mind	42	27	15	27	15
	31.8	34.6	27.8	30.3	34.9
Other unaided	90	51	39	62	28
	68.2	65.4	72.2	69.7	65.1
Aided	116	56	60	67	49
	46.2	41.2	52.2	42.4	52.7
Tried	125	72	53	78	47
	49.8	52.9	46.1	49.4	50.5

★ Percentage sign has been suppressed.
★ One decimal place specified for percentages.
★ Several levels of net totals with local percentages.
★ Ranking may be specified, and is sensitive to the net structure.

Source: The Research Machine

TABLE 12.3   Number of bars eaten per week

Job I6/901   CAMELLA PROFILE TRACKING

Base: candy bar consumers

		SEX		*CHILDREN*	
	TOTAL	Male	Female	Yes	No
TOTAL	251	136	115	158	93
	100%	100%	100%	100%	100%
None	70	41	29	55	15
	28%	30%	25%	35%	16%
One	42	30	12	27	15
	17%	22%	10%	17%	16%
2–5	98	46	52	53	45
	39%	34%	45%	34%	48%
6–10	35	17	18	20	15
	14%	13%	16%	13%	16%
More than ten	6	2	4	3	3
	2%	1%	3%	2%	3%

Base: excluding none

Real mean	3.97	3.65	4.31	3.55	4.51
Error variance	2.92	2.87	2.95	2.73	3.09

★ Analysis of numeric question with a distribution.
★ 'true' mean and other statistics.
★ Means and other statistics may also be tabulated in the cells of the table.
★ In a summary table you can use a different numeric question for each row/column/cell.

Source: The Research Machine

TABLE 12.4   Image rating of Carmella bar

Job I6/901   CARMELLA PROFILE TRACKING

Base: candy bar consumers

			AGE			
	TOTAL	Under 16	16–19	20–29	30–49	50+
TOTAL	177	32	30	38	44	33
A satisfying snack						
Strongly disagree	24,9%	21,9%	36,7%	21,1%	25,0%	21,2%
Slightly disagree	21,5%	6,3%	26,7%	26,3%	20,5%	27,3%
Neither	6,2%	12,5%	3,3%	5,3%	2,3%	9,1%
Slightly agree	18,1%	18,8%	13,3%	18,4%	18,2%	21,2%
Strongly agree	26,6%	34,4%	20,0%	23,7%	31,8%	21,2%
Don't know	2,8%	6,3%	–	5,3%	2,3%	–
Mean score	3.00	3.40	2.53	2.97	3.12	2.94
Std Devn	1.59	1.61	1.59	1.56	1.66	1.50
Std Err	.121	.294	.291	.260	.254	.264
Tastes too sickly						
Strongly disagree	24,9%	28,1%	30,0%	34,2%	15,9%	18,2%
Slightly disagree	11,9%	9,4%	3,3%	5,3%	22,7%	15,2%
Neither	18,1%	25,0%	20,0%	10,5%	15,9%	21,2%
Slightly agree	11,9%	12,5%	10,0%	7,9%	13,6%	15,2%
Strongly agree	26,6%	18,8%	33,3%	31,6%	22,7%	27,3%
Don't know	6,8%	6,3%	3,3%	10,5%	9,1%	3,0%
Mean score	3.04	2.83	3.14	2.97	3.05	3.19
Std Devn	1.57	1.15	1.68	1.78	1.47	1.49
Std Err	.122	.276	.313	.306	.232	.263

★ Enable percent character.
★ Use comma instead of decimal point.
★ Score statistics. Specific categories (e.g. 'Don't know') may be excluded from calculation

Source: The Research Machine.

TABLE 12.5   Summary of image ratings

Job I6/901   CARMELLA PROFILE TRACKING

Base: those aware

	Base	Strongly disagree	Slightly disagree	Neither	Slightly agree	Strongly agree	Don't know	MEAN
SLICKERS								
A satisfying snack	247	9%	14%	44%	11%	18%	5%	3.15
Tastes too sickly	247	21%	8%	34%	15%	15%	6%	2.95
An inexpensive snack	247	21%	25%	15%	25%	9%	5%	2.74
A family name	247	28%	35%	19%	4%	9%	5%	2.28
A good treat for the children	247	25%	29%	26%	4%	13%	4%	2.49
Has no nutritional value	247	18%	18%	12%	15%	34%	3%	3.30
CAMELLA								
A satisfying snack	177	25%	21%	6%	18%	27%	3%	3.00
Tastes too sickly	177	25%	12%	18%	12%	27%	7%	3.04
An inexpensive snack	177	14%	16%	23%	14%	24%	8%	3.20
A family name	177	28%	11%	13%	19%	20%	10%	2.92
A good treat for the children	177	28%	29%	14%	10%	10%	11%	2.45
Has no nutritional value	177	33%	14%	21%	13%	15%	3%	2.62

★ Row percentages.
★ Column of means.
★ Summary table: each row from a different question (column summary tables are also available).
★ When required, the width of each banner point may be explicitly controlled.
★ Height of each row is determined by the length of its label; again this may be explicitly controlled.

Source: The Research Machine.

TABLE 12.6 Image Strength and Character

Job I6/901	CARMELLA PROFILE TRACKING		
	Slickers	Carmella	Jupiter
TASTES TOO SICKLY			
Positive	22	44	29
Negative	44	47	17
Image Strength	66	91	46
Image Character	8.9%	24.9%	20.6%
	33.3%	48.4%	63.0%
AN INEXPENSIVE SNACK			
Positive	53	44	39
Negative	38	47	36
Image Strength	91	91	75
Image Character	21.5%	24.9%	27.7%
	58.2%	48.4%	52.0%
A FAMILY NAME			
Positive	52	25	20
Negative	22	43	25
Image Strength	74	68	45
Image Character	21.1%	14.1%	14.2%
	70.3%	36.8%	44.4%

★ Image strength: responses explicitly positive or explicitly negative.
★ Image character: (1) % of those aware with positive response.
                    (2) % of image strength contributed by positive responses.

Source: The Research Machine.

The value of some of these benefits such as faster service, freedom from many kinds of processing error, etc. are very real but sometimes difficult to quantify. However, other benefits can be quantified more easily but will vary according to the type of company. To assist the potential users to assess what these benefits may be Pulse Train Technology provide the following checklist which is reproduced as Table 12.7.

TABLE 12.7   The Research Machine – cost justification

This brochure has mentioned a number of the benefits an integrated system can offer you. The value of some of these benefits – such as faster service to your own clients, freedom from many kinds of processing error, etc., are very real, but are difficult to quantify. Other benefits can be quantified, but vary according to company. To better enable you to carry out this quantification, we present the checklist you see below. You should consult Pulse Train Technology directly about the cost elements.

General hardware considerations

★ Allow for up to 100% more terminals to be supported on any VAX when comparing the RESEARCH MACHINE with other CATI systems.

★ Allow for savings of up to 500% or more when comparing the cost of a VAX with computers of comparable power from other manufacturers.

Telephone interviewing

★ Telephone interviews (for individual interviews) will average about 150% less time, compared with interviewing with paper questionnaires. Allow for savings on labour AND phone charges.

★ No paper questionnaires are required with CATI. Save 100% of printing costs, comprising labour, platemaking, ink, paper, etc.

★ Save 100% of staff time associated with administration of appointments and call-backs. This applies to both interviewers and administrators. Savings of interviewer's time is in addition to interview speed-up.

★ Possible savings on supervisors: allow one supervisor for every 20 interviewers.

★ Save 100% of data-entry and verification costs compared with keying in paper questionnaires.

★ Save approximately 70% of coding time required for coding open-ended replies (if PTT recommended procedures are followed.)

★ Save 100% of costs associated with edit checking and cleaning data.

★ Save 100% of specification writing time required to set up initial specifications (labels, edit checks, etc.) for tabulation compared with non-integrated software package.

It may be possible to make substantial savings in WATS type communication costs if local interviewing centres are established, and DECnet used to co-ordinate and control via inexpensive packet switching networks. Consult with us to evaluate this.

Questionnaire design

★ Save 100% of all typing time for questionnaires, if researcher enters QSL specifications directly.

★ Save 100% of time required to assign data and column codes.

★ Save 100% of proof-reading required to check questionnaire for data column assignments, question numbers, routing, etc.

★ Save approximately 40% of printing costs, allowing for more efficient utilisation of paper areas (unless your current questionnaires are professionally typeset in multi column formats.)

★ Save 100% of any type-setting costs

★ Make substantial allowance for design time savings if some questionnaires are variants (in addition to 100% savings on typing time.)

Data-entry, cleaning, and coding of field collected data

★ Save approximately 20% of key-entry time compared with card punching.

★ Possible savings of 100% of verification costs. Edit checks are built into key-entry code, but cannot catch all possible key-entry errors. It 100% savings not possible, allow some savings as verification may be done selectively, on a question-by-question basis.

★ Allow substantial savings in labour costs for editing changes required (up to 50%) due to ease of entering required changes on random-access file.

★ Save approximately 30% of coding time (with better results) as coders enter open-ends direct into VDU. Also allow 100% savings of key-entry time for coded manual.

Tabulation and analysis

★ Save 100% of initial specification writing line time if questionnaire was written in the QSL.

★ Save up to 80% of table specification writing time (due to automatic capturing of all required texts, etc.) compared with other tabulation software.

★ Allow for possible savings on preparation of SPSS, SAS, or COBOL specifications.

★ Allow for up to 90% savings if tabulation work is now carried out by a service bureau, compared with in-house analysis.

General data-processing

Allow for up to 90% savings in programmer time if analyses of omnibus or wave studies are required, using the Extract facility.

Allow for substantial savings in data processing resources if panel analysis are carried out.

Other uses of your VAX

Because you can use your VAX computer for running software other than RESEARCH MACHINE, you should consider possible savings in other areas such as word processing, accounting, etc.

Possible extra income

Your total cost justification must take into account possible extra income as well as looking at the cost savings. Obviously, this is more difficult to quantify, but you might consider the following:-

★ If you are doing telephone interviewing now, and not using CATI, you will not be considered as a possible supplier by increasing numbers of research buyers who insist on CATI because of the time and data quality issues.

★ You may get international or consortium work through SurveyNet, the association of other RESEARCH MACHINE users.

★ Your existing clients may place more work with you when they become aware of improvements in delivery times, questionnaire quality, better coding, cleaner data, etc.

★ You may be able to obtain high-profit extra income by allowing your clients on-line access to their own data, carrying out extra analyses, etc., through the Twinkle interactive tabulation module.

Use of IT

Wilson (1989) reports that his research into the 'claimed revolutionary effect of IT on commercial competitiveness' within the marketing domain indicates no 'significant differences in the practice of strategic decision making, or even in the sort of information used in decision making, compared with more traditional industries as described in the management literature'. Citing a survey undertaken by Gill on behalf of Oasis and the Institute of Marketing into 193 UK companies it is claimed that:

> Very few UK companies are making 'good use' of marketing information, despite a widespread recognition of the potential contribution of marketing information to competitive advantage. Furthermore, according to this study, the extent of IT involvement does not seem to correlate with the extent to which information is used, and it seems to be the case that those who know what information they want and what to do with it use it best, rather than those who can generate the most information, *which emphasises the simple but often forgotten point that information is worse than useless if it is not relevant to the problem at hand.* [My emphasis].

Wilson's own depth interviews with 30 senior managers responsible for planning in marketing and strategic management led him to draw three broad conclusions:

1. that the overall level and quantity of information available on markets and competitors was adequate (i.e. most interviewees were content);
2. that *'formal' information sources* (ie. in-house, off-the-shelf and commissioned research on markets and competitors) were unsatisfactory in many significant respects;
3. that *'informal' information sources* (ie. personal contacts, favours, cooperative personnel from competitors or third parties, and even clandestine sources) were often considered very much more important than formal sources.

Despite these findings, which confirm the as yet low penetration of IT into marketing decision making, we can only reiterate our belief that the rapid growth of computer literacy and user-friendly packaged software will result in a rapid growth in its adoption in the 1990s. Certainly it will be an essential element in the development of the marketing information system and it is to this topic that we turn in the next chapter.

References

Hague, P. N. (1987) *The Industrial Market Research Handbook*, 2nd edition (London: Kegan Paul).

Lucey, T. (1987) *Management Information Systems: An Instruction Manual for Business & Accounting Systems*, 5th rev. edn (D. P. Publications)

Melkman, Alan (1989) 'Using New Information Technology', in *Marketing Handbook*, 3rd edn, ed. Michael J. Thomas (Aldershot: Gower).

Wilson, D. F. (1989) 'The Information Technology Revolution in Marketing', in *Marketing Audit of the 1980s*, Proceedings of the 22nd Annual Conference of the Marketing Education Group, ed. Louis Moutinho, Douglas Browlie and Jim Livingstone.

CHAPTER 13

Marketing information systems

Introduction

In the increasingly competitive environment which has developed in recent years there can be little doubt that marketing intelligence has become a vital factor in the organisation's ability to succeed. In the past, when change was less rapid than it is today, it was reasonable to assume that the best forecast of the immediate future was a direct extrapolation of past trends. In other words, change was seen largely as inevitable but as a continuous and predictable process. Accelerating technological change and the increase in international competition have resulted in turbulence and discontinuity and demand that we modify this assumption and recognise that to survive under these new conditions we must monitor and analyse our competitive environment continuously. To do so effectively marketing research must be seen as an ongoing process in which the organisation's database is constantly reviewed and updated. No longer will it suffice to review sales data (which records what *has happened* rather than what *might happen*) with the occasional dipstick study to confirm our prejudices and expectations. In future the firm's survival will depend fundamentally upon its ability to read and anticipate environmental and competitive change and an essential element of this ability will be the creation and maintenance of an effective marketing information system or MIS.

Of course the existence of an effective MIS cannot guarantee success as this will depend upon the ability of the firm's management to use the available information in developing and implementing an effective marketing strategy. That said, marketing information systems must be seen as a *necessary* albeit not *sufficient* condition for competitive success.

In this chapter we will examine the nature of MIS, the needs they serve and the benefits they offer. Next we look at the contribution of market research to the establishment and maintenance of an MIS and conclude with an analysis of the role of MIS in marketing decision making.

A systems approach to marketing management

In the early 1960s the need for a programmed and systematic approach to marketing research led a number of practitioners and academicians to propose the concept of *marketing intelligence* as an alternative to the traditional view of marketing research. The distinction between research and intelligence was spelled out clearly in an article in *Business Management* which asserted:

> Marketing research usually focuses on a specific problem or project. A marketing research department might seek to discover why the competition has a larger share of the market in certain regions, or it might test consumer reaction to a certain proposed product. Whatever the activity, marketing research projects tend to have a definite beginning, middle and end.
>
> A marketing intelligence system, on the other hand, does not focus on specific problems. Rather it is a thermostat that monitors the market place continuously so the company can adjust its actions from day to day or month to month. A sound marketing intelligence system should prevent real problems from arising. ('Marketing Intelligence Systems: A DEW line for Marketing Men', *Business Management*, January, 1966.)

According to the *Business Management* article the first marketing intelligence system was established at the Mead Johnson division of Edward Dalton Co. in 1961. Its creator, Dr Robert J. Williams, made the same distinction between the one-off nature of marketing research and the continuous provision of the intelligence system (MIS) in a rather more colourful way when he said:

> The difference between marketing research and marketing intelligence is like the difference between a flash bulb and a candle. Let's say you are dancing in the dark. Every 90 seconds you're allowed to set off a flash bulb. You can use those brief intervals of intense light to chart a course, but remember everybody else is moving too. Hopefully, they'll accommodate themselves roughly to your predictions. You may get bumped and you may stumble every so often, but you can dance along.
>
> On the other hand you can light a candle. It doesn't yield as much light, but it's a steady light. You are continually aware of the movements of other bodies. You can adjust your own course to the courses of the others. The intelligence system is a kind of candle. It's no great flash on the immediate state of things, but it provides continuous light as situations shift and change.

The structure of Mead Johnson's marketing intelligence system is shown in Figure 13.1 and was the subject of the first case in a new course MRIS (Marketing Research and Intelligence Systems) first offered at the Harvard Business School in 1964.

The application of the systems approach to marketing management was elaborated on in a seminal article by Lee Adler which first appeared in the Harvard Business Review (1967) and has been reprinted many times since

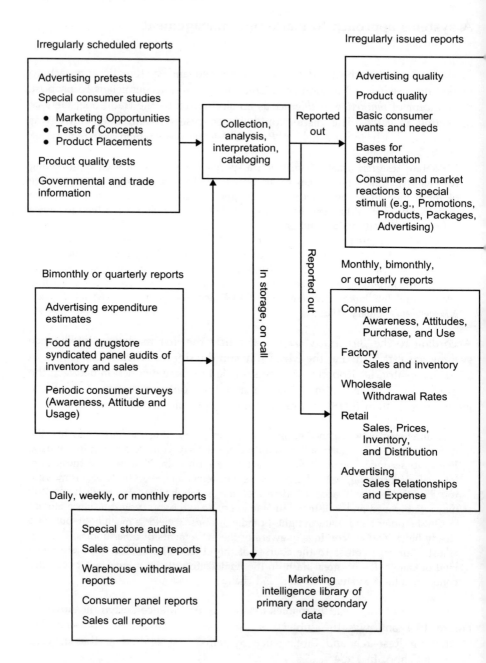

FIGURE 13.1   Mead Johnson's marketing intelligence system

Source: Lee Adler, 'Systems Approach to Marketing', *Harvard Business Review*.

('Systems Approach to Marketing', *Harvard Business Review*, vol. 45, no.3 (May–June), 1967). In this article Adler describes the systems approach as follows:

> There seems to be agreement that the systems approach sprang to life as a semantically identifiable term sometime during World War II. It was associated with the problem of how to bomb targets deep in Germany more effectively from British bases, with the Manhattan Project, and with studies of optimum search patterns for destroyers to use in locating U-boats during the Battle of the North Atlantic. Subsequently, it was utilised in the defeat of the Berlin blockade. It has reached its present culmination in the success of great military systems such as Polaris and Minuteman.
>
> Not surprisingly, the parallels between military and marketing strategies being what they are, the definition of the systems approach propounded by The Rand Corporation for the U.S. Air Force is perfectly apt for marketers:
>
> > An inquiry to aid a decision-maker choose a course of action by systematically investigating his proper objectives, comparing quantitatively where possible the costs, effectiveness, and risks associated with the alternative policies or strategies for achieving them, and *formulating additional alternatives if those examined are found wanting.*
>
> The systems approach is thus an orderly, 'architectural' discipline for dealing with complex problems of choice under uncertainty.

It follows that an MIS is a system for dealing with such problems which occur within the domain of marketing.

In promoting the development and adoption of a systems approach Adler perceived it as a substitute for the traditional approach to marketing research which he criticised for leading to:

> dreary chronicles of the past rather than focusing on the present and shedding light on the future. It is particularistic, tending to concentrate on the study of tiny fractions of a marketing problem rather than on the problem as a whole. It lends itself to assuaging the curiosity of the moment, to firefighting, to resolving internecine disputes. It is a slave to technique.

By contrast Adler believes that the systems approach will lead to the development of a system:

> tailored to the needs of each marketer. Such a system would serve as the ever-alert nerve center of the marketing operation. It would have these major characteristics:
>
> > Continuous surveillance of the market.
> > A team of research techniques used in tandem.
> > A network of data sources.
> > Integrated analysis of data from the various sources.

Effective utilisation of automatic data processing equipment to distill mountains of raw information speedily.

Strong concentration not just on reporting findings but also on practical, action oriented recommendations.

Adler's analysis and recommendations are as apposite today as they were over two decades ago for, apart from development in the application of computers to marketing, each of the characteristics he specifies is as relevant today as it was in 1967.

MIS defined

The *Macmillan Dictionary of Marketing and Advertising* offers the following definitions:

> *Marketing Information Systems.* The systematic organisation of all marketing data required by a business organisation to provide a reliable, illuminating and timely flow of information to marketing and general management.
>
> *Marketing Intelligence Systems.* A basic component of the MARKETING INFORMATION SYSTEMS, providing marketing executives with current information about developments and changing conditions in the macro and task environments (competitors, customers, suppliers, etc.). The efficiency of such systems can be augmented by improved training of sales people in their intelligence responsibilities, the development of a marketing-intelligence centre, and the purchase of information when appropriate from specialised intelligence services.

Two further definitions which have stood the test of time and which were proposed when the idea of the MIS first surfaced as a major topic are:

> An interacting structure of people, equipment, methods, and controls which is designed to create an information flow that is capable of providing an acceptable base for management decisions in marketing. (Berenson, 1967).
>
> A set of procedures and methods for the regular planned collection, analysis, and presentation of information for use in making marketing decisions.' (Cox and Good, 1967).

Smith *et al.* (1968) appear to have combined these two definitions when they propose the following in their book of readings on the subject:

> A structured, interacting complex of persons, machines and procedures designed to generate an orderly flow of pertinent information, collected from both intra- and extra-firm sources, for use as the bases for decision-making in specified responsibility areas of marketing management.

Several common elements link these definitions. Perhaps the most important is that an MIS is a means to an end and not an end in itself. The marketing information system adds value only if it informs managerial decision making and is used as the basis for future action. Thus one must be careful not to assume that the existence of an MIS will lead to competitive success – only if it is integrated into the management of the organisation will this occur for otherwise, in the terminology of Ames (1970), it is likely that it will remain a 'trapping' and add little or nothing to the 'substance' of the business. This distinction between trappings and substance is very important as has been shown by numerous investigations of critical success factors both before and since Ames' penetrating diagnosis. Briefly, Ames argues that in their efforts to improve performance managers will examine the activities of other successful firms and conclude that their success is attributable to functions or activities which are present in the other firms but absent from their own. Thus in the 1960s many industrial companies attributed the higher performance of consumer goods firms to the fact that they had a marketing function and so set up one in their own company but with no significant improvement in performance. To refute the latter's claims that 'marketing doesn't work' Ames pointed out that the mere creation of a system or function will have little or no effect unless it is supported by both attitudinal and behavioural change.

Much the same problem attended the establishment of strategic and corporate planning departments in the 1970s. Many managers who survived the recessions and shake outs of the late 1970s and early 1980s diagnosed their problems as arising from the setting up of formal planning departments with the result that they became divorced from their central responsibility for the direction of the business while suffering from the mistaken belief that a service department could discharge this activity for them. It is believed that much the same problem could accompany the setting up of formal marketing information systems in the 1990s as the evidence mounts that sound marketing information is a necessary condition for successful planning.

A second element common to the definition is the emphasis upon the systematic, planned and regular collection and analysis of data involving formal procedures and techniques. The latter procedures and techniques are very much the province of the professional marketing researcher and will be commented on in more detail below.

So much for the definition of the MIS – what needs does it serve? A recent survey by Honours Marketing Students at Strathclyde (1989) identified the following problems and pressures which have required the development of much more sophisticated data capture and analysis systems than hitherto:

— increased competition, both direct and indirect,
— accelerating technological change leading to shorter product life-cycles,
— the information explosion and the dangers of information overload,
— more regulation and legislation.

Against this background a properly designed MIS offers the opportunity to:

— handle effectively the massive amounts of data on products, channels, sales, customers and competition,
— integrate the wide variety of data encountered,
— co-ordinate the complex relationships between forecasts, plans, schedules and actuals,
— collect and deliver information tailored to the precise needs of different users and decision makers,
— speed up decision making,
— eliminate duplication and reduce confusion, complexity and uncertainty.

Thus the potential benefits to be derived from an effective MIS are considerable. Given access to the system one should be able to obtain timely and appropriate information directly relevant to the particular problem to be solved. Further, if properly designed, the MIS can give advance warning of changes or trends which call for reappraisal of the existing plan and can be used as a control device to compare actual against planned performance.

Marketing research and the MIS

The ability of an MIS to serve the needs and deliver the benefits outlined above will depend very much upon its design and the quality of the data captured and stored in it. In turn, this will depend on the principal subsystems and their effective integration. As a minimum one requires a principal subsystem for each element of the marketing mix so that the basic design would comprise the following:

1. Market research information system
2. Product planning information system
3. New product development information system
4. Pricing information system
5. Sales forecasting and planning information system
6. Distribution information system
7. Advertising and promotion information system
8. Service information system
9. Expenditure control information system.

As noted when discussing the differences between longitudinal and cross-sectional research (pp. 94–6) the normative or textbook assumption is that marketing research is undertaken on a regular and continuous basis whereas the reality is that most marketing research is *ad hoc*, intermittent and designed to address a specific problem after it has occurred. In other words, most marketing research is reactive rather than proactive. By contrast the whole idea of an MIS is that it should contain all the data required for informed decision making on marketing issues and that this data should be subject to continuous review and updating. Given the rapidly changing environment referred to earlier it is unlikely that an MIS could accommodate every possible eventuality except at an inordinate and unnecessary expense. It follows that specific, focused *ad hoc* research will always be required to complement the MIS but that the creation and maintenance of the MIS itself must be the primary concern and responsibility of the marketing research function. However, in most organisations sufficiently large and sophisticated to have an MIS of the kind implied above, the MIS will only be one element in a much larger and all embracing management information system likely to include corporate planning and research, operations research, financial planning and control, administrative and personnel systems, etc. Integration of the MIS within the larger management information system and the allocation of responsibility for areas of possible overlap are matters for corporate rather than marketing management. In assigning responsibilities the empirical evidence suggests that the marketing research function is likely to cover the following areas:

Determination of market characteristics
Measurement of market potentials
Market-share analysis
Sales analysis
Competitive-product studies
New-product acceptance and potential
Short-range forecasting
Long-range forecasting
Studies of business trends
Audit and panel data
Special projects
Customer demand schedules
Questionnaire replies
Profitability
Life cycle analysis
Inventory analysis

(List compiled from various sources by Strathclyde Honours Marketing Students (1989).)

It will be noticed from the above listing that research into advertising is not mentioned, the implication being that such research is undertaken by the advertising agents and media owners rather than by the advertisers themselves.

Organisational structure and the MIS

In order to enable organisations to deal effectively with the challenges of an increasingly dynamic and complex environment there has been a substantial shift from the traditional hierarchical structure with a centralisation of authority and control towards more flexible, organic and networked structures with considerable delegation of authority and responsibility. Given that in all complex systems, hierarchy, specialisation, and centralisation are major sources of distortion and blockage of intelligence, one would expect that the new flexible structures would improve greatly information flows within an organisation. Undoubtedly this is so with the possible exception of the complex multidivisional organisation comprising a number of discrete strategic business units. Examination of such complex organisations (which are becoming increasingly commonplace through merger and acquisition) suggests that the potential synergy which may exist between different SBUs will be lost or dissipated unless there is an effective information system shared by them all. Further, within SBUs a number of studies have indicated that inadequate communication between top and middle management is a major factor leading to poor performance with the implication that an effective information system would help reduce this problem.

As noted earlier, most MIS represent one element within a larger integrated management information system. Without wishing to exaggerate the importance of the MIS over other elements, the increased emphasis upon the marketing orientation does imply that the MIS has a particularly important role to play in enhancing managerial effectiveness. Specifically it is believed that the MIS should be the source of the key data required to inform top management in determining the organisation's overall strategy. To the extent that since the major inputs into the MIS will have originated with line management this should ensure a smooth flow of information upwards through the organisation. Similarly the clear statement of purpose and objectives contained within a formal strategy will inform line management as to what activities are to be pursued, in what manner and to what end and thereby dictate what information is to be added to or deleted from the basic MIS.

By the same token marketing research is regarded as a tool essential to the creation and maintenance of the MIS but still only a part of a much larger and comprehensive intelligence system which derives information from a variety of other sources. This distinction is important for most textbooks and courses present marketing research as a set of techniques and procedures designed to solve specific problems. Such an approach is necessary to communicate the nature of these techniques and procedures but it would be unfortunate if this gave the impression that marketing research is a discrete activity when it should be a continuous and ongoing process as indicated in the above review of the marketing information system.

Summary

Another author might well have commenced a book on *Research for Marketing* by emphasising the importance of developing a formal information system as the only sure foundation on which to build an effective marketing, planning and decision support system. Our preference has been to illustrate the wealth of information available to the marketing practitioner, both internal and external, and the means of acquiring and up-dating this information as a vital ingredient in improving the firm's competitiveness. In this chapter we have attempted to show how the MIS is the structure for storing and integrating this information in such a way as to make it readily available and useful to decision-makers. Clearly, the means of achieving this is largely a technical matter but it is to be hoped that the content of this book will enable the reader to determine what they wish to include in their MIS and how to set about commissioning the technical experts to develop a system to meet their own needs.

References

Ames, C.B. (1970) 'Trappings vs Substance in Industrial Marketing' *Harvard Business Review*, July–August.

Berenson, Conrad (1969) 'Marketing Information Systems', *Journal of Marketing*, vol. 33, October, pp. 16–23.

Cox, Donald F. and Good, Robert E. (1967) 'How to Build a Marketing Information System', *Harvard Business Review*, 45 (3) May–June, pp. 145–54.

Smith, Samuel V., Brien, Richard H. and Stafford, James E. (1968) 'Marketing Information Systems: an Introductory Overview', *Readings in Marketing Information Systems*.

Strathclyde Honours Marketing Students (1988–9) *Marketing Information Systems* (Glasgow, Department of Marketing, University of Strathclyde).

Questions for discussion

Chapter 2 Problem recognition and specification

1. Researching an unfamiliar market presents a number of problems for the researcher. What might these problems be and how would you resolve them? (The Chartered Institute of Marketing)
2. A less developed country is being considered as a possible market for a firm, but there is very little accurate information available from its government sources. How would you propose to gather the necessary information? (The Chartered Institute of Marketing)
3. Concentrated soups made by Campbell in the USA have achieved brand leadership there, but have been unsuccessful in attempting to establish a similar position in the UK market.
   Account for the possible reasons for this product failure, and suggest possible corrective action. (The Chartered Institute of Marketing)

Chapter 3 'What do we know'

1. Having either too much, or too little, information may result in poor decisions being taken. As an in-house market researcher what practical steps would you take to ensure that the correct amount of marketing information was made available? (The Chartered Institute of Marketing)
2. Secondary data may be obtained from either inside or outside the organisation. State two kinds of internal data and two kinds of external data and for each one, describe briefly their uses and limitations. (The Chartered Institute of Marketing)

Chapter 4   'What do we need to know?'

1. Write an outline Market Research Plan to identify the market for a proposed new product/service. (The Chartered Institute of Marketing)
2. What forms of research might usefully be conducted with a view to increasing the effectiveness of below-the-line activities? (The Chartered Institute of Marketing)

Chapter 5   Developing a research design

1. What marketing information should be collected by a marketing manager planning to launch a new product? How will he collect and use it? (The Chartered Institute of Marketing)
2. Why is quota sampling used in survey research extensively, in preference to the theoretically superior random sampling? (The Chartered Institute of Marketing)
3. A manufacturer of diesel engines, used in lorries and buses, wants to determine the characteristics of their domestic market. As a marketing research agency called in to advise them, produce a proposal describing how you would proceed. (The Chartered Institute of Marketing)
4. How can marketing research contribute to a better understanding of buying behaviour, so as to enhance the marketing efforts of an organisation? (The Chartered Institute of Marketing)

Chapter 6   Sampling

1. Evaluate the potential applications, advantages and disadvantages of purposive sampling. (Strathclyde University)
2. What criteria should a researcher take into account in selecting the size of sample for a quantitative survey of domestic households? (Strathclyde University)
3. 'The use of non-probability sampling methods is indicative of an ill-prepared researcher or a journalist looking for a news item.' How valid is this statement? (Strathclyde University)
4. The problems facing researchers is to identify the relevant population and then to select and contact suitable respondents. Explain the problems

involved in identifying and selecting respondents, and how sampling techniques can help. (Strathclyde University)

5. If you were to conduct a telephone survey of travel agents, what benefits would you derive from using a stratified sample compared with any other form of sampling? (Strathclyde University)

6. 'To use a probability sample where a quota sample would be suitable is to incur opportunity costs: the opportunity within the research budget to enlarge the sample or carry out further research' (Crimp). In what circumstances would you agree and when, if ever, would you disagree with this statement? (Strathclyde University)

8. 'The choice of sample size (for a survey) is a matter of subjective judgement, capable of rationalisation but not scientific justification.' Comment. (City University)

9. Kish implies that quota sampling is an art-form, highly dependent on the researcher's experience; but does it have a basis in statistical theory? Discuss the nature and the likely validity of the assumption underlying quota sampling. (City University)

10. Discuss the role of interviewers in sample surveys with particular reference to their impact on the quality of the data obtained. (City University)

11. Discuss the operational usefulness of THREE of the following outlining their possible advantages and disadvantages:

> simple random sample
> stratified random sample
> cluster sampling
> quasi-random sampling

What criteria would you find useful in evaluating the suitability of a sampling frame? (The Polytechnic, Huddersfield)

12. Random samples, for all their claimed advantages, are not often used in market research. Why is this? In what circumstances would you not recommend a random sample for a market research enquiry? What would be your alternatives? (The Hatfield Polytechnic)

13. What is sampling, how is it commonly practised, and why is it so important in survey research? (Polytechnic of North London)

14. Explain briefly the theory underlying sampling and discuss some of the sampling methods and procedures commonly used in survey research. (Plymouth Polytechnic)

Chapter 7 Data collection – questionnaire design

1. Discuss, using examples, the uses and limitations of open-ended marketing research questions. (The Chartered Institute of Marketing)
2. What are ordinal and interval scales? Illustrate how these scales may be of use to the market researcher. (Strathclyde University)
3. Discuss the advantages and disadvantages of using a Likert scale in postal questionnaires to business executives. (Strathclyde University)
4. Identify and discuss the aspects of questionnaire design with which a marketing research manager should be familiar, in order that he can evaluate a draft questionnaire put forward with a proposal by a research agency (Strathclyde University)
5. 'The major problem in constructing a battery of scales of the semantic differential type, lies in identifying the relevant dimensions, i.e. the adjectives or descriptions for each bipolar scale.' (Elliot and Christopher) Explain what is meant by 'relevant dimensions' and outline possible approaches to the task of identifying them. (The Polytechnic, Huddersfield)
6. As it is relatively easy to criticise a bad questionnaire, why is it so difficult to design a good one? (Humberside College of Higher Education)
7. 'Attitudes are complex and not completely understood. They are a composite of such things as beliefs, preferences, and readiness to respond behaviourally.' To what extent can the attitudinal scaling techniques provide an objective measurement of attitudes? (Plymouth Polytechnic)

Chapter 8 Data collection – methods

1. Researchers may collect primary data in face-to-face interviews, over the telephone or through the post. Discuss the advantages and limitations of these methods. (The Chartered Institute of Marketing)
2. Outline reasons why market researchers use focus group interviews compared with other forms of interviewing. (Strathclyde University)
3. 'Test marketing is costly and time consuming and the same information can often be obtained more efficiently through other research techniques.' Suggest some of these 'other research techniques' and give examples of when they may be used in preference to test marketing. Discuss the application and limitations of observation as a market research technique. (Strathclyde University)
4. 'Within ten years, face-to-face interviewing will by used only in qualitative research; all other research will be conducted by telephone.' To what

extent is this forecast justified by the strengths and weaknesses of telephone interviewing? (City University)

5. The group interview or discussion is a widely used technique. Explain its use and contrast it with that of the individual depth interview. (The Polytechnic, Huddersfield)

6. William Schlackman has criticised group discussions as '...Likely to give you consensus data based on the need of individuals to conform to group pressure'. What are the implications of this and how can the problems be overcome? (Ealing College of Higher Education)

Chapter 9   Data interpretation

1. In discussing the precision, reliability and relevance of quantitative research Goode and Hatt state: 'If the observations are crude, casting them in statistical form will not help the research. If other scientists cannot repeat them, mathematical manipulation is futile. If the data do not satisfy a rigorous logic of proof, the conclusions remain doubtful.' Discuss this viewpoint. (Strathclyde University)

2. 'Data dredging is the sign of a desperate researcher.' Discuss the validity of this statement. (Strathclyde University)

3. 'Wherever marketing management is interested in measuring the effects of alternative courses of action, experimentation may be a practical means of reducing the risk involved in deciding among the alternatives' (Cox and Enis). Discuss the extent to which the use of marketing experiments is a viable alternative to the questionnaire survey based approach to marketing research. (City of Birmingham Polytechnic)

Chapter 10   Report presentation

1. 'Market research reports tend to be technical and much effort is required to find the significant findings.' How may a market researcher avoid such criticisms? (Strathclyde University)

2. 'There is a standard format that all market research reports should comply to.' Critically analyse the above statement illustrating with examples where you feel differences between report formats are justified. (Strathclyde University)

Chapter 11 Syndicated market research services

1. What is a retail audit, how is it conducted and what is it used for? (The Chartered Institute of Marketing)
2. The availability of telephone omnibus surveys from a growing number of marketing research agencies in London suggests an increase in the use of these methods by client companies/organisations. Evaluate the advantages and disadvantages of this method from the viewpoints of both consumer and industrial marketing companies. (The Chartered Institute of Marketing)
3. 'The use of these data only to monitor small and usually temporary shifts in brand-shares cannot possibly justify the expenditure involved.' Discuss this comment in respect of EITHER retail audits OR consumer panels. (City University)
4. How far is it justifiable for a manufacturer of fast-moving consumer goods to buy both retail audit and consumer panel data? If you had to choose between the two, which would you choose and why? How would you seek to compensate for the loss of the other service? (City University)
5. A marketing research agency has been retained by a firm selling baby food and accessories to provide specific information regarding consumer purchases of products in this field. The agency has proposed setting up a panel of mothers who could record relevant purchases in a special diary. Discuss the advantages and disadvantages of the diary panel method in this context and the practical problems that could arise in setting up, and evaluating the results obtained in this way. (City of Birmingham Polytechnic)

Chapter 13 Marketing information systems

1. Explain the major difficulties encountered when trying to achieve a marketing information system which meets the requirements of all concerned. (The Chartered Institute of Marketing)
2. What faults can be experienced with marketing information systems? As a market planner, how would you seek to prevent their occurrence? (The Chartered Institute of Marketing)
3. Discuss the contention that marketing information systems exist in all organisations. (Strathclyde University)
4. To what extent does a market researcher need to understand the principles of successful marketing management. (Strathclyde University)
5. Starting from your own definition of a marketing information system describe the main components of such a system. Highlight the advantages

that a firm may gain from adopting a formal marketing information system. (Strathclyde University)

6. 'Information is the lifeblood of successful marketing decision-making, however, information can be expensive to obtain and process.' Discuss this statement with respect to the design and implementation of a marketing information system. What methods could be used to avoid unnecessary costs? (The Polytechnic, Huddersfield)

7. In an article on management information systems, Ackoff refers to them as management misinformation systems. In what circumstances do you think that the marketing information system might become a marketing misinformation system, and how should the marketing manager guard against this happening? (Humberside College of Higher Education)

[The author and publishers gratefully acknowledge the permission of the Chartered Institute of Marketing and the named institutions to reproduce the above examination questions.]

Index

Und   ng P   Co   cts a⁺ W